CW00718015

Customer Information Management

institute of
financial services
School of Finance

Customer Information
Management

Graham Flower
Phil Fawcett

Apart from any fair dealing for the purpose of research or private study, or criticism or review, as permitted under the Copyright, Designs and Patents Act 1988, this publication may be reproduced, stored or transmitted, in any form or by any means, only with the prior permission in writing of the publisher, or in the case of reprographic reproduction in accordance with the terms and licences issued by the Copyright Licensing Agency. Enquiries concerning reproduction outside those terms should be addressed to the publisher's agents at the undermentioned address:

Institute of Financial Services
IFS House
4-9 Burgate Lane
Canterbury
Kent
CT1 2XJ
United Kingdom

T   01227 818649
F   01227 479641
E   editorial@ifslearning.com
W   www.ifslearning.com

Published by the Institute of Financial Services (**ifs**). The **ifs** is the official brand of The Chartered Institute of Bankers, a non-profit making registered educational charity.

The Chartered Institute of Bankers believes that the sources of information upon which the book is based are reliable and has made every effort to ensure the complete accuracy of the text. However, neither CIB, the author nor any contributor can accept any legal responsibility whatsoever for consequences that may arise from errors or omissions or any opinion or advice given.

Typeset by Kevin O'Connor
Printed by Antony Rowe Ltd, Wiltshire
© The Chartered Institute of Bankers 2005
ISBN 1-84516-283-8

Contents

Acknowledgements

Professor Merlin Stone, Business Research Leader, IBM.

Bryan Foss, Global Customer Insight Solution Executive, IBM.

Alex Rodrigues, E-piphany.

Dr Laurie Miles, SAS.

One

The business and competitive environment

1.1   Introduction

Financial services organisations do not operate in a vacuum. Instead, they exist in a context defined by forces such as the government, society, their competitors and customers. These forces are usually considered under the acronym Le Pest & Co:

- **L**egal;
- **E**thical;
- **P**olitical;
- **E**conomic;
- **S**ocial;
- **T**echnological;
- **C**ompetitive.

This chapter only considers the last of these, the competitive environment. The other forces are often described as the external environment and later chapters will consider the aspects of them that are of most relevance to customer information management.

1.2   Competition and markets

A definition for competition is 'rivalry between organisations operating in a market'.

Defining a market is rather harder. One approach is to define a market in terms of a number of potential customers who have needs to satisfy and the ability to pay. However, there are alternative definitions. For example, an economist might define a market in terms of the aggregate demand for goods or services. Another definition of a market might be as a network of buyers and sellers of particular goods or services.

The scope of markets is also subject to change. Until the 1960s the banks and building societies operated in separate and distinct markets, with little or no competition between them. Porter's 'five forces' model is a useful tool for analysing competitive conditions in markets.

1.2.1   Porter's Five Forces Model

Michael Porter's five forces model is as follows:

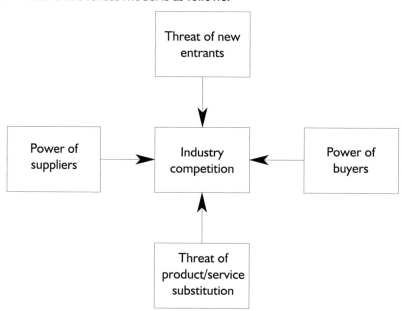

Under this model, the competitive conditions in an industry are determined by five forces:

Force	Competition is high if ...	Competition is low if ...
Power of suppliers	There are many suppliers with fragmented market power	There are few suppliers with high market power
Power of buyers	There are many customers with fragmented buying power	There are few customers with monopoly buying power
Threat of new entrants	There are low entry barriers for new competitors	There are high entry barriers for new competitors
Threat of product/ service substitution	Customers can easily switch to alternatives for the product or service	There are few alternatives to the product or service
Industry competition	There are many competitors	There are few competitors

1.2.2 Competition in financial services

Taking the UK market for retail financial services as an example:

◆ There are many suppliers of retail financial services, none of whom has high market power (ie the power to set prices).

◆ There are many customers for retail financial services, none of whom has high buying power.

◆ New delivery channels such as the Internet and the telephone have reduced barriers to entry, as organisations no longer need large branch networks to compete effectively.

◆ There is a range of substitute products such as store cards.

◆ There are many competitors.

Therefore, the level of competition in retail financial services is high. Neither customers nor suppliers control market prices. It is difficult for organisations to make high profits in highly competitive markets, but financial services organisations in the UK are very profitable. How is this achieved?

Information, including about customers and 'know how' about their own processes, is one of the most important sources of competitive advantage available to UK financial services organisations.

1.2.3 Defining the market

The financial services industry has low barriers to entry and substitute products are readily available. Therefore, the number of competitors and the number of products can change quickly, making it harder to define the market for financial services. Two important trends for the financial services industry are globalisation and convergence.

Globalisation is the tendency of financial services organisations to operate on a continental or global scale. This increases their size, which is generally seen as a source of competitive advantage as larger organisations can spread their fixed costs across more customers and transactions. Examples include the world's two largest banks, Citigroup and HSBC, both of which operate world-wide.

Convergence is important for two reasons. Convergence has taken place in financial services, and technology has also converged.

Convergence in financial services is a result of the breakdown of barriers between different types of financial services organisation. For example, banks and building societies used to be completely separate industries but are now largely indistinguishable. Convergence has also taken place with the insurance industry, and retailers also now provide a range of financial services.

Technological convergence has also had the effect of introducing new competitors into the market. Technological convergence is the tendency of technologies that were historically separate towards a single technology. Computer, television and telephone technology has converged towards a single technology based on digital computers and high-speed digital networks. This has resulted in the development of new distribution channels, allowing new competitors to enter the financial services market. Perhaps the clearest example is the PayPal payments service, a product developed by an organisation outside the financial services industry that allows low-cost international payments to be made over the Internet.

1.2.4   Characteristics of the financial services industry

The financial services industry has six characteristics. These are its fiduciary nature, fungibility, intangibility, simultaneity, heterogeneity and perishability:

- ◆ Financial services depend on trust – a fiduciary relationship – between customers and financial services organisations.
- ◆ Money is fungible – money borrowed for one purpose can be used for another.
- ◆ Financial services are intangible and do not create a physical product. Although the industry creates physical objects such as plastic cards, the product is the ability to use the card to make purchases or withdraw money rather than the card itself.
- ◆ Financial services are created and consumed simultaneously. The 'process' of creating the service and the 'product' of its consumption occur at the same time.

◆ Financial services are heterogeneous – each customer interaction is unique and there is a natural variation in the quality of the customer experience.
◆ Financial services are perishable and cannot be 'built for stock'. Staff in a branch or call centre can only produce services if customers are visiting or calling.

1.3   Competitive advantage

We have discussed customer information as a potential source of competitive advantage. What is meant by competitive advantage and how can it be achieved?

Competitive advantage is any means by which an organisation can gain an advantage over its competitors. Financial services organisations can seek to win business from competitors and/or extend the market in a number of ways.

The simplest classification is that of Xavier Gilbert and Paul Strebel:

◆ Lowest delivered cost
◆ Highest perceived quality.

Another well-known classification is that of Michael Porter:

◆ Cost leadership.
◆ Differentiation.
◆ Focus.

Other potential sources of competitive advantage are:

◆ Brand building.
◆ Creating a new market. The first entrant in a new market becomes the standard against which all later entrants are judged. This is called 'first mover advantage'.
◆ Logistics. The ability to use distribution channels as a source of competitive advantage.
◆ Mergers and acquisitions.
◆ Possession of complementary assets. These are also called network effects.
◆ Market power.

1.3.1   Lowest delivered cost/highest perceived quality

Lowest delivered cost is the ability to deliver a product or service at a lower cost than competitors. Organisations that are able to achieve this can either gain market share by reducing prices below those of competitors or can charge the market rate and earn additional profits.

Highest perceived quality occurs when customers believe that the organisation's products or services are better than those of its competitors. Such organisations are able to charge a price premium and earn additional profits or, more rarely, to price their products and services competitively to build market share.

1.3.2   Cost leadership/differentiation/focus

Although there are some similarities with Gilbert and Strebel's classification, they are not equivalent.

Cost leadership corresponds to lowest delivered cost.

Differentiation can be on perceived quality but can also be on other factors such as price. Another 'differentiation' strategy is undifferentiation – producing products and services identical to those of competitors. Undifferentiation allows the organisation to save marketing and development costs and focus on low cost production.

Because differentiation can cover so many factors, there are no simple rules as to how best to exploit differentiation once achieved. Differentiation on factors such as perceived quality, quality of support, quality of design or brand image are usually exploited by charging a premium price.

Undifferentiation usually involves using the demand for the original product created by competitors' marketing activity. Competitors may have created a niche market or may have developed a unique product position. The organisation can exploit this by charging a lower price to build market share – the supermarkets have been accused of this by marketing own label products similar in appearance to leading brands. An example from financial services might be the development of gold and platinum cards. These created niche markets which were entered by competitors and have now become standard products.

Focus allows organisations to choose to compete only in parts – or 'segments' – of the market. A financial services organisation expects to compete more effectively by concentrating on a small part of the market.

The benefits of focus are:

◆ Specialisation. By specialising in a single market segment the organisation expects to have a better understanding of the segment's needs and to be able to tailor the way it works to this segment.
◆ Possession of complementary assets. Complementary assets include anything which may add value to transactions involving customers in the market segment. Complementary assets are discussed later in this chapter.

1.3.3   Brand building

Branded goods are perceived by customers as being very different. Confectionery bars are an example – the customer will specify a Mars Bar or a Kit Kat rather than simply asking for a piece of confectionery. The demand for branded goods does not usually change much in response to price changes (in economics terminology, the price elasticity is low) and manufacturers are able to charge a premium, which represents the value of the brand.

This differentiates branded goods from commodities, which are seen by customers as virtually the same irrespective of supplier. Nails are an example – they are bought by weight and the customer does not differentiate between manufacturers. The demand for commodities is very sensitive to price changes (in economics terminology, the price elasticity is high) and the ability to produce the lowest delivered cost creates competitive advantage.

Financial services organisations largely differentiate themselves on customer service. This makes it harder for them to brand individual products, as the customer service offering covers the entire product range. Instead, financial services organisations have concentrated on building 'master brands' that define brand values for the organisation as a whole.

1.3.4   Creating a new market

These models assume that the market size is limited and organisations can only gain competitive advantage by taking market share away from competitors or by charging a premium price. An alternative way of securing competitive advantage is to create a completely new market.

Say's Law states that supply creates its own demand. Developing a new product can create a market for it. This is a high-risk strategy – most new products fail – but can be a powerful source of competitive advantage.

One reason for this is 'first mover' advantage. Organisations who are the first to enter a market can create an enduring market lead. Obvious examples – where the brand became synonymous with the product – are Hoover and Biro.

Another reason is that the creator of the market can impose standards on the market. This is harder in financial services than in some other industries, as standards are usually agreed by industry-wide bodies or by regulators, but it is possible. Perhaps the clearest example is the introduction of electronic funds transfer at point of sale (EFTPOS), where the industry-wide initiative EFTPOS UK failed to achieve a viable standard and was overtaken by Switch, introduced by Midland Bank. Switch became the standard for EFTPOS in the UK until the introduction by Visa of the Electron and Delta cards.

The characteristics of financial services discussed above allow scope for creating new markets. For example:

◆ because financial services are intangible, it is relatively simple to create a new service or to modify an existing service to meet the needs of the customer better. Manufacturing industries need to set up expensive factories to make new goods before they gain any commercial return. Financial services organisations can roll out new services relatively quickly;

◆ because financial services are simultaneous, any change to the process of creating the service directly affects the customer's experience of having the service delivered. Financial services organisations can use this to differentiate themselves on the basis of the quality of the experience offered. Some industries – notably leisure – are selling the experience as a product in its own right;

◆ because financial services are heterogeneous financial services organisations can customise the service to meet the exact needs of the customer. The ability to offer a bespoke service is itself a new product. Banking services targetted at the mass affluent sector (such as HSBC Premier and Barclays Premier) are an example. The underlying products and services are identical, but are customised by providing improved customer service (dedicated helplines) and better rates;

◆ because financial services are fungible, financial services organisations can easily introduce substitute products. Traditional overdrafts and loans have been partly substituted by credit cards and equity withdrawal products.

The role of information in the creation of new markets is ambiguous. Traditional market research and market forecasting techniques are notoriously unreliable when applied to new markets. In the early days of the computer industry, the head of IBM forecast that the worldwide demand for mainframe computers would be no more than 25 units. There were similar errors in forecasting the demand for personal and home computers.

Against this, organisations rely on information to reach potential customers. A profile can be developed based on the marketing concept and customers for 'similar' products. This is difficult for any really innovative products and test markets and focus groups are important to understand the buyers' behaviour.

Many recent innovations in the financial services industry have relied on information technology. A good example is the 'electronic wallet' smartcard Mondex. It is worth noting that although smartcards are physical objects, the services they offer are (electronic) cash and payment for goods and services. Therefore they do not break the rule about services being intangible.

It has proved very difficult for financial services organisations to protect their competitive advantage by protecting the underlying technology. There are two reasons for this:

◆ Financial services organisations usually need to develop these services in partnership with organisations who can provide the technology. For example, Mondex was developed by National Westminster and Midland banks in partnership with BT. It is in the technology partner's interests to promote and licence the use of the technology, even though the financial services organisation may prefer the technology to remain proprietary.

◆ New financial services need to achieve a general level of acceptance before they can be used. For example, Mondex only becomes useful once a significant number of retailers are prepared to accept it. However, retailers are only willing to accept Mondex if a significant number of customers are likely to use it. Therefore, National Westminster bank, who originally developed Mondex, allowed a competitor, Midland Bank, to join the consortium to ensure a sufficiently large number of potential customers to make it attractive to retailers.

1.3.5 Distribution channels

The supply chain is the link between the original supplier and the ultimate customer. For example a simple supply chain for advances is as follows.

Depositors → Financial services organisations → Borrowers

Another way of gaining competitive advantage is to gain control of the supply chain. Organisations that achieve this are able to benefit in a number of ways.

♦ They may be able to transfer costs or risks from themselves to suppliers or customers. Manufacturing techniques such as just-in-time delivery (JIT) or zero defect achieve this by transferring inventory and inspection costs to suppliers. These transfers are sometimes called upstream and downstream effects.

♦ They may achieve process efficiencies by automating part of the process. Links between the WalMart and Proctor and Gamble computer systems mean that products are automatically re-ordered when stocks reach re-order point. This saves on administration costs. Straight through processing (discussed in Chapter Seventeen), by which the customer enters an order which is processed and fulfilled automatically, produces the greatest efficiency benefits.

♦ They may benefit from greater information about the customer.

♦ They may be able to lock customers or suppliers into their systems. If customers use personal financial management products such as Money or Intuit they are unlikely to switch to a supplier of Internet financial services that does not offer that option.

♦ They may be able to increase product penetration. By making it easier for customers to buy additional products, it is more likely that they will continue with their existing supplier.

Direct banking is the main method financial services organisations are currently using to control the supply chain.

1.3.6   Mergers and acquisitions

Mergers and acquisitions deliver competitive advantage by increasing market share and by improving product penetration. As the merged organisation combines the customer bases of its components, it has more customers. This automatically increases its market share, allowing fixed costs to be spread across more customers and provides a basis for cross-selling of products to the newly-acquired customers, increasing product penetration. It also allows the merged organisation to reduce costs by eliminating duplication.

IT is often a factor in inhibiting mergers and acquisitions, and at least one UK financial sector merger is believed to have failed because of the difficulty in combining the organisations' IT systems. There are four main approaches:

- ◆ To continue to use the organisations' existing, separate systems, but to build 'bridges' between them to allow the consolidation of management information. This does not produce any cost savings and differences in the way the systems work may affect the quality of the management information – it is comparing apples and pears, to use a common analogy.
- ◆ To choose one organisation and use its systems exclusively. This usually happens where the merger is a clear take-over of a weaker organisation by a stronger. There may be significant difficulties in moving the second organisation's data onto the systems of the first and this approach badly affects morale in the second organisation.
- ◆ To choose the best individual systems from each of the organisations and combine these. For example, the first organisation's customer information system may be used with the second organisation's accounting system. This approach is called 'best of breed'. Although this is the most popular approach for mergers of equals, there are often major technical difficulties in combining the systems.
- ◆ To ignore both existing systems and build a new system for both organisations. The existing systems can be retained with bridges – the first option considered – but will be put on a 'care and maintenance' basis. The major disadvantage of this approach is the delay before the merged organisation can respond to new demand for IT systems.

1.3.7   Complementary assets

It is possible to gain competitive advantage through the possession of complementary assets. This occurs when two separate products or services complement each other in some way – an example of $2+2=5$.

An important example is the anti-trust trial of Microsoft, where the judge used the term 'network effects' to describe this. The argument is that Microsoft's ownership of both the Windows operating system and the Office suite of office products is complementary – that Microsoft can exploit its understanding of how Windows operates both to improve the performance of its own office software and to prevent its rivals from developing superior products.

An example relevant to the financial services industry in the UK is the Cruickshank report into competition in the UK Banking industry. This suggested that the major banks' ownership of the major credit card networks was a complementary asset to their main operations and had the effect of restricting competition in the credit and debit card markets.

1.3.8 Market power

Given the problems of defining the market for any particular financial services organisation, how can its market power be defined? One measure is the organisation's ability to influence pricing decisions.

At one extreme, economic theory says that monopolies can charge whatever price the market is prepared to accept and will earn excess returns – the 'monopoly rent' – as a result. It is also known that the established market leader can charge a premium price and that its pricing decisions set the general level of prices for the market.

Therefore, organisations seek to increase market share to allow them more control over pricing decisions. The ability of organisations to achieve this depends not only on market share but also on the other factors included in Porter's five forces model.

Two

Strategy

2.1   Introduction

Former Lloyds TSB Chairman Brian Pitman once said that the way for financial services organisations to gain competitive advantage was to teach their managers to think strategically.

This chapter includes an outline of the corporate strategic planning process and on the relationship between strategy, tactics and operations.

However, the main focus of this chapter is on information as a strategic resource and the factors affecting the development of an information strategy.

2.2   What is strategy?

The word strategy comes from the Greek word for 'general'. One definition of strategy is

> '...the direction and scope of an organisation over the long term: ideally, which matches its resources to its changing environment, and in particular its markets, customers or clients so as to meet shareholder expectations.'

> *Johnson and Scholes (1997)*

Strategy is the responsibility of the most senior levels of management, including the board and executive management. It defines the overall direction of the organisation over the long term, typically five–ten years. The strategic management process can be shown as a diagram:

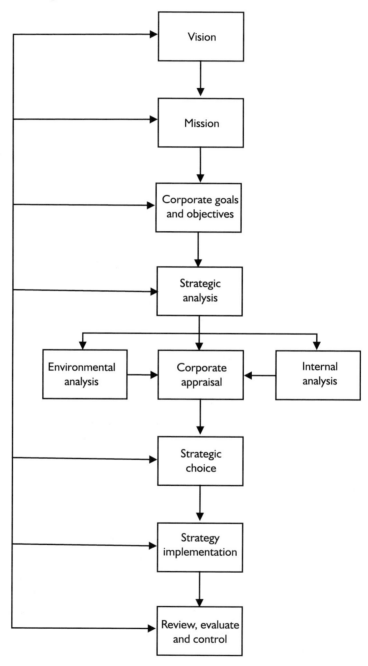

The vision is a picture of what the organisation wants to look like at the end of the strategic planning period. It is sometimes called the 'desired future state'.

The mission is a statement of the organisation's values. The organisation's business units and functions may have their own mission statements to highlight their contributions to the organisation. The idea of a mission statement is to give a clear focus to the organisation's activities.

The corporate goals and objectives are the specific and measurable targets that the strategic plan is intended to achieve.

Strategic analysis includes three activities:

- Environmental analysis considers the external business and competitive environment as discussed in Chapter One. The competitive environment is analysed using techniques such as Porter's five forces model. The external environment is analysed in terms of the legal, ethical, political, economic, social and technological factors.
- Internal analysis considers the organisation's own resources and capabilities. It uses techniques such as the Boston Consulting Group matrix to develop the organisation's understanding.
- Corporate appraisal brings together the strategy with the results of the internal and external analysis. Strengths, weaknesses, opportunities and threats analysis is an important corporate appraisal technique.

Strategic choice involves choosing between the various strategic options available. Techniques such as the Ansoff matrix can be used to help to decide between options.

Strategy implementation translates the strategy into specific plans and programmes.

The review, evaluation and control process monitors these plans and programmes.

The individual techniques are outside the scope of this course. However, students need to be aware of the overall strategy development process.

2.2.1   Strategy, tactics and operations

The implementation of strategy is dependent on tactics and operations.

Tactics are the responsibility of senior and middle managers. Most tactical management decisions are concerned with how to allocate the organisation's resources in order to achieve its strategic plans.

Operations are the responsibility of first line managers and supervisors. Operational management decisions are concerned with solving day-to-day problems.

The following diagram shows the relationship between strategy, tactics and operations and indicates the type of IT systems required to support these levels:

Each level of management needs different types of information to support the decision-making process. We can summarise some of the differences between strategic, tactical and operational management information:

	STRATEGIC INFORMATION	TACTICAL INFORMATION	OPERATIONAL INFORMATION
Used by	Senior managers	Middle managers	First line managers
Time horizon	1–10 years	3–18 months	Up to 1 month
Sources of data	External and strategic management information systems	Operational and tactical management information systems	Operational systems
Internal or external	Internal and external	Mainly internal	Entirely internal
Frequency of decision	Infrequent and at irregular intervals	Weekly, monthly, quarterly or yearly	Very frequent during the day
Basis for decisions	Facts, projections and judgements	Facts and projections	Facts
Type of decision	Unprogrammed – each decision is unique	Programmed – follows overall policies and precedents	Prescriptive – follows defined rules and procedures
Presentation	Summaries and trends	Summaries and supporting detail	Usually detailed
Examples	Market share and product profitability	Actual costs and revenues vs budgets	Customer financial histories

2.2.2   Corporate strategy and business unit strategy

Strategic planning is not solely a corporate activity. Large organisations are made up of a number of strategic business units (SBUs), each of which has its own strategic plan. The problem for strategic planners is how to ensure that the SBU strategic plans are consistent with each other and contribute to the overall corporate strategy.

In practice, strategy formulation is usually a mix of 'top down' and 'bottom up' planning. The directors set the overall direction and goals of the organisation and the SBUs help to turn these into quantified objectives.

Most financial services organisations would regard IT as a strategic resource and the IT department or division as a strategic business unit with its own strategic plan.

2.3   Corporate strategy and information strategy

The IT SBU's strategic plan will include what we are calling an 'information strategy' (different authors use other terms). This covers both the 'applications' side (the information systems or IS strategy) and the 'equipment' side (the IT or IT strategy).

2.3.1   Information systems strategy

An information systems strategy is 'a plan for the development of system towards some future vision of the role of information systems in the organisation'. In other words, the information systems strategy identifies what information systems the organisation will need to support its corporate and SBU strategic plans and defines how these systems can be developed or acquired.

Typically, the corporate strategy and the individual SBU strategic plans are analysed to identify what information or processing capabilities are required to achieve them. These are grouped together into development programmes, which are then broken down into individual projects and incorporated into the information systems strategy.

For example, most financial services organisations now recognise the importance of customer relationship management (CRM). A corporate decision to adopt CRM as a strategy must be reflected in the information systems strategy both in terms of the systems required (for example, to collect information about the customer and to deliver CRM information to staff dealing with the customer) and in terms of how these systems will be obtained (for example, whether to buy a package or build a system in-house).

2.3.2 IT strategy

The IT defines the infrastructure required to support the information systems strategy. Infrastructure includes:

◆ Hardware. This includes computers and peripheral devices such as printers.
◆ Telecommunications. This includes networks and telecommunications devices such as modems. The use of leased lines, packet switched networks or value added networks is also part of the telecommunications strategy.
◆ System software. This includes operating systems and databases. A particular issue is whether to adopt 'open' or 'proprietary' software.
◆ Development environment. This includes the methodologies and CASE tools used for developing systems.

Using the example given above (adopting CRM as a corporate strategy, collecting information from customers and delivering it to customer-facing staff), the IT strategy would need to consider:

◆ Hardware. A data warehouse may be needed to store the information collected (data warehouses are discussed in a later chapter).
◆ Telecommunications. Customer-facing staff would need fast access to customer information. The organisation may need to improve its internal telecommunications network to support this.
◆ Systems software. CRM systems are often 'packages' bought from external suppliers, rather than being developed in-house. The organisation would need to ensure that the package is compatible with its system software (package selection is discussed in Chapter Eight).
◆ Development environment. A joint application development (JAD) environment may be needed to develop the systems to allow customer-facing staff to access the information in the CRM system (JAD is discussed in Chapter Eight).

Therefore, there is a relationship between business strategy, IS strategy and IT strategy. This is illustrated in the following diagram:

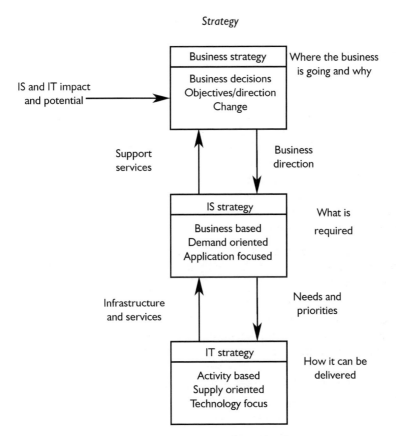

This shows that the IS strategy is driven from the business strategy, and in turn drives the IT strategy. Note, however, that the flows are not simply top-down. The IS strategy is affected by the IT strategy and affects the business strategy.

For example, time is needed to buy the hardware and software required to run a data warehouse and to load it with information about customer interactions. In the absence of a data warehouse, the organisation will not be able fully to implement the customer analytics information systems that analyse customer interactions and provide much of the information on which CRM is based. The organisation will still be able to adopt CRM as a strategy, but will not be able to implement it fully until it has put the necessary infrastructure in place.

2.3.3 Information as a strategic resource?

IT in financial services was historically associated with back office functions. It was seen as something managers were promoted away from and information was not seen as a strategic resource in its own right.

Attitudes have changed and most senior managers would now accept that information is a strategic resource. The rationale for this includes:

◆ IS and IT are major cost factors, accounting for about 15% of costs in the financial services industry. Therefore, IS and IT must be managed strategically to ensure that this investment is used in the most effective way.

◆ IS and IT are 'strategic enablers' which means that other business strategies can only be implemented if the appropriate IS and IT capabilities are available. The development of IS and IT capabilities can create a 'platform' for subsequent developments. IS and IT must be managed strategically to ensure they provide this platform.

◆ Similarly, IS and IT are 'strategic inhibitors', which means that the lack of IS and IT capabilities can prevent business strategies being implemented. One extreme example of this is that at least one planned merger in the financial services industry has been called off because of the technical incompatibility of the organisations' systems.

◆ IS and IT decisions have a long-term impact. A decision to invest in a particular technology will be accompanied by a wide range of related decisions on training and information systems that are designed to support and exploit the technology. It is very difficult simply to abandon the investment and go back to the old technology.

◆ It is now generally accepted that the financial services industry is dependent on information. Organisations must manage their business-critical resources within a strategic framework.

◆ IS and IT are scarce resources. Organisations' ability to introduce new systems is usually constrained more by a shortage of development resource than by cost and the available resource must be deployed in the most effective manner. This requires a strategic approach.

2.4   Strategic alignment and the strategic disconnect

Strategic alignment occurs when the goals and activities of the business are in harmony with the information systems that support them.

If this does not occur, this leads to a strategic disconnect. Charles Wang defines this as:

> '...a conflict ... that has misaligned the objectives of executives and impairs or prevents organisations from obtaining a cost-effective return on their investment in IT'.

Wang (1997)

2.4.1   Strategic disconnect

A strategic disconnect is often the result of a failure to treat IT strategically. There are a number of barriers that prevent top managers from taking a strategic view of IS and IT. These include:

- a lack of top management awareness of the impact of IS and IT on the business;
- a credibility gap between the promises of IT and past performance;
- information is not always viewed as a business resource;
- it can be difficult to express benefits in financial terms – financial cases are often seen as weak;
- top management may take a short-term focus. Management understanding of the long-term implications of IS and IT may be inadequate.

There may also be a 'culture gap' between the IT function and other parts of the business. One survey showed that 47% of IT managers saw the culture gap as their main problem and 56% believed that it was inhibiting their companies from achieving competitive advantage from IS and IT. The gap was seen as arising from:

- different objectives, with IT professionals seeking 'technical excellence' and driven by their own career development options whereas the business is driven to achieve 'functional excellence' and business results;
- lack of shared values, lack of agreed strategy and a history of failed projects and systems.

If IS and IT are not treated strategically, this leads to a number of problems:

- A loss of control of IS and IT investments, leading to individuals or departments striving to reach incompatible objectives.
- Problems caused by IS and IT investments can become a cause of friction within the organisation.
- Localised justification of investments can produce benefits that are counterproductive for the organisation as a whole. The investment may solve the sponsoring department's problems but create more problems elsewhere in the organisation.
- Systems, on average, have a shorter than expected business life and need to be redeveloped more frequently than should be necessary.

2.4.2   Strategic alignment

The development of an information strategy is critical to ensuring strategic alignment. The issue is whether this should be 'top down' (ie driven entirely by the corporate and SBU strategies) or whether it should be 'top down bottom up' (ie mainly driven by the corporate and SBU strategies, but with these strategies being modified as a result of the information strategy).

There are some approaches to information strategy development that are entirely driven by the corporate and SBU strategies. In the financial services industry, this approach can lead to a strategic disconnect.

For example, some organisations have completely decentralised IT, leaving information strategy decisions to their individual SBUs. This speeds up the procurement of new systems and can result in systems that are better tailored to the needs of the SBUs. The disadvantage is that these systems may be incompatible and it may be impossible to share information between them. This can make it difficult for executive management to get an overall picture of the business and can impose very considerable costs due to the need to comply with new regulations such as Basel II and Sarbanes Oxley.

If this approach is used, the contribution of the information strategy development process to business strategy becomes purely descriptive. It is limited to providing a model of the business which the executive management are free to review, but are under no obligation to take into account.

Lack of top management awareness of the impact of IS and IT has already been highlighted as a reason for the strategic disconnect. The business-driven approach does not address this, although it is possible to use techniques such as executive management workshops to influence business strategy by promoting awareness of technology trends and possibilities.

An alternative is to adopt an approach that provides an explicit link between technology and business strategy, such as enterprise-wide information management (EWIM):

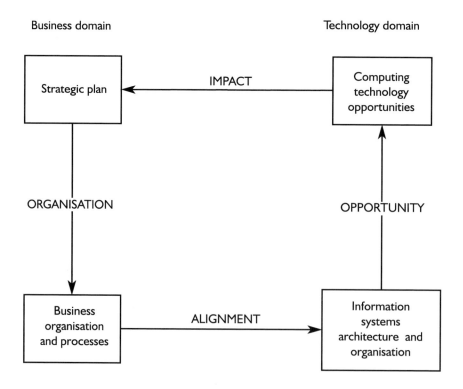

EWIM supports the traditional, top-down approach to information strategy development:

◆ *organisation*. Executive business management defines the organisational structure and business processes needed to carry out the business strategic plan;

◆ *alignment*. The technology function analyses the information systems, architecture and organisation required to support the organisation and business processes.

However, EWIM also recognises the contribution of technology to the business strategy:

◆ *opportunity*. The organisation's current information systems, architecture and organisation provide a platform that, together with technology developments within and outside the organisation, creates technology opportunities for the organisation;

◆ *impact*. Executive business management can then change the business strategic plan to exploit the technology opportunities identified.

2.5   Factors in information strategy development

Three factors that must be taken into account in the development of an information strategy are:

◆ *the vision* – where the organisation intends to go;
◆ *the architecture* – the organisation's current stock of IS and IT assets;
◆ *strategic positioning* – the extent to which the organisation is prepared to innovate.

2.5.1   Visioning

Visioning is a strategic planning technique that is used to develop a vision or 'desired future state' – a detailed statement of where the organisation would like to be at a future point.

This can be used as a basis for the development of the information strategy by identifying the business and technology implications of the vision. Visioning is a three-step process:

An important feature of this approach is the focus on the future competitive environment and the technology options for gaining competitive advantage in step 2. This allows the organisation to take future technological developments into account in developing its corporate strategy.

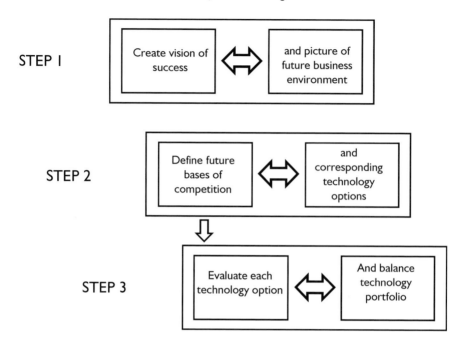

2.5.2 Information architecture

The information architecture is the organisation's stock of IS and IT assets. The IS architecture and some aspects of the IT architecture are discussed in Chapter Seventeen.

Although the IT strategy allows the organisation to change its IT architecture, the existing architecture also acts as a constraint on the IT strategy. Major changes to the architecture are expensive and, because there are inter-relationships between IT components and between the IT architecture and IS architecture, would affect other components.

It is usual to make such changes when a particular component is close to the end of its economic life, but other factors such as competition, mergers or changes in relations with a major supplier may force such changes.

2.5.3 Strategic positioning

Organisations must decide how closely they are going to follow the leading edge of technology. This is called 'strategic positioning'. There are three options.

1. *Leader*. Leaders position themselves at the leading edge of technology;
2. *Fast follower*. Fast followers position themselves just behind the leading edge;
3. *Laggard*. Laggards use only well-established and proven technology.

The advantage of adopting a leader strategy is the possibility of developing a 'killer application' – a system which gives such a large competitive advantage that it will take competitors many years to catch up. The disadvantages are the high cost and the risk that a competitor will be able to 'leapfrog' the organisation by introducing the same technology once it has been proven, without the high start up costs. The leading edge is sometimes called the 'bleeding edge', reflecting the very high costs involved and the effect on the organisation's cashflow.

Many financial organisations try to position themselves as fast followers. They try to ensure that their technology is not so far behind that they would be unable to meet the challenge posed by new developments, but they avoid the costs and risks of technological innovation.

Some financial organisations only use fully proven technology. Quite often this is by default – the result of not having an IT strategy. This can be successful if the organisation is able to exploit a market niche that does not require much use of IT.

The competitive environment is very important. Organisations cannot generally afford to fall too far behind their competitors' systems and technology. Also, an awareness that a competitor is actively looking at a particular area of technology can stimulate an organisation to investigate that area, to avoid the risk of a killer application being developed.

Consider First Direct as an example. First Direct was not the first telephone banking service, but it did stimulate those banks and building societies that did not offer telephone banking to do so. There was a similar development in Internet banking, where Royal Bank of Scotland's introduction of full service Internet banking stimulated its competitors to follow suit.

References and further reading

Johnson G and Scholes K (1997) *Exploring Corporate Strategy* 4th edition Prentice Hall.

Wang C (1997) *Techno Vision II* McGraw-Hill.

Three

The legal and regulatory environment

3.1   Introduction

The legal environment defines the rules within which financial services organisations operate. It includes a mix of case law, statute law, regulation, codes of practice and internal rules. We can consider the legal environment under the following headings:

- sources;
- privacy and data protection;
- money laundering and law enforcement;
- consumer protection and financial services;
- intellectual property;
- competition law;
- electronic commerce and the Internet.

3.2   Sources

The traditional sources of law in the UK are parliament and the courts. Financial services, in particular, have always been heavily regulated and the regulators are also part of the legal and regulatory environment.

More recent sources of the law are the European Union (EU), the European Courts of Justice and Human Rights and the UK courts interpreting European Union law.

There have been a number of very important EU directives in areas such as privacy, direct marketing and financial services.

The European Court of Human Rights and the UK courts have had a particularly important role in interpreting the European Convention on Human Rights and Fundamental Freedoms, which has been incorporated into UK law as the Human Rights Act 1998.

3.3   Privacy and data protection

Until recently, financial services organisations' legal responsibilities have been concerned mainly with data privacy. This was based on case law (*Tournier v National Provincial and Union Bank of England* (1924)) and the Consumer Credit Act 1974.

UK government legislation implementing European directives led to the strengthening of data privacy provisions and imposed on financial services organisations a legal responsibility for data security. These obligations were specified in the Data Protection Acts 1984 and 1998 and the Computer Misuse Act 1990.

3.3.1   Case law

Tournier v National Provincial and Union Bank of England defined the banker's obligation not to disclose information about customers without their consent. This applies to all information the bank may obtain provided that this arose out of the banking relationship, for example it includes records of interviews and telephone calls as well as financial records. It continues after the closure of the account or accounts, although any new information obtained after closure would not be covered.

It covers all bank records irrespective of whether they are electronic or manual – computer systems were not an issue in 1924! It has now been largely superseded by later legislation, in particular the Data Protection Acts 1984 and 1998, although it continues to form the basis of the confidentiality provisions of the Code of Banking Practice.

3.3.2   Code of Banking Practice

The Code of Banking Practice is a voluntary code of practice followed by banks and building societies and monitored by an independent review body. The code incorporates the conditions under which disclosure was permitted in *Tournier v National Provincial and Union Bank of England* and restricts the circumstances under which financial services organisations will provide information to credit reference agencies. The Mortgage Conduct of Business Rules (MCOB) replaced the Mortgage

Code in 2004. Whereas the Mortgage Code was voluntary, adherence to the MCOB is a legal requirement for mortgage lenders.

Other obligations under the Code of Banking Practice include explaining customers' right of access under the Data Protection Act and advising customers when bankers' references are given. Although the code is voluntary, it is authoritative and financial services organisations take compliance very seriously.

3.3.3   Consumer Credit Act 1974

The Consumer Credit Act 1974 (CCA 1974) was designed to control organisations involved in the granting of credit, with the particular objective of protecting borrowers from unfair lending practices.

The main relevance of the CCA 1974 to financial services is with regard to the use of Credit Reference Agencies. The Act defines a Credit Reference Agency as a business whose function is to provide information relevant to the financial standing of individuals. This includes both profit making and non-profit making organisations such as trade associations. All Credit Reference Agencies must be licensed by the Office of Fair Trading. Although financial organisations also provide financial information, this is not their main business and they are not regarded as Credit Reference Agencies under the CCA 1974.

The CCA 1974 covers printed information as well as information held in machine-readable form. The CCA 1974 gives individuals four rights.

1. It places a duty of disclosure on businesses (including financial services organisations) using the services of Credit Reference Agencies.
2. It gives the individual a right of access to the information held. The individual must request this in writing and pay a small fee.
3. It gives the individual the right to have information deleted or corrected where it is factually incorrect and likely to damage the individual (for example by making it less likely that credit will be granted).
4. If the Credit Reference Agency does not accept the removal or amendment of the information, it may serve a counter-notice of non-action. The individual has the right to add a 'notice of correction' to the information held.

3.3.4   Data Protection Act 1998

The first Data Protection Act was passed in 1984 to comply with European Union restrictions on cross-border data processing and to meet public concern about the use of data held on computer systems. This has been superseded by the Data Protection Act 1998 (DPA 1998).

The DPA 1998 protects personal data stored in a computer system or a 'structured storage system' – for example a paper filing system or on microfiche. Personal data is defined as statements of fact or opinion about living individuals. This excludes information about limited companies although information about sole traders – treated as individuals in law – is covered.

It defines a data subject as being the person about whom data is held and a data user as a person or organisation holding data. Where people access data as part of their jobs, the organisation (rather than the individual) would be the data user.

The DPA 1998 requires data users to comply with eight principles:

1. Personal data shall be processed fairly and lawfully and, in particular, shall not be processed unless:
   o at least one of the conditions in Schedule 2 is met, and
   o in the case of sensitive personal data, at least one of the conditions in Schedule 3 is also met.
   (Schedules 2 and 3 establish that either the data subject has given consent for processing or that the processing is necessary, for example to fulfil a contract or for legal reasons. Schedule 3 is concerned with sensitive data such as racial origin, religious belief or sexual preference, for which a stricter definition of necessary is applied.)
2. Personal data shall be obtained only for one or more specified and lawful purposes, and shall not be further processed in any manner incompatible with that purpose or those purposes.
3. Personal data shall be adequate, relevant and not excessive in relation to the purpose or purposes for which they are processed.
4. Personal data shall be accurate and, where necessary, kept up-to-date.
5. Personal data processed for any purpose or purposes shall not be kept for longer than is necessary for that purpose or those purposes.
6. Personal data shall be processed in accordance with the rights of data subjects under this Act.
7. Appropriate technical and organisational measures shall be taken against unauthorised or unlawful processing of personal data and against accidental loss or destruction of, or damage to, personal data.
8. Personal data shall not be transferred to a country or territory outside the European Economic Area, unless that country or territory ensures an adequate level of protection for the rights and freedoms of data subjects in relation to the processing of personal data.

The eighth principle – which was not part of the 1984 Act – has caused some difficulties. The United States does not have equivalent legislation, but has adopted a voluntary 'data safe haven' process for data protection. Where countries such as India and China are used for outsourcing, organisations must ensure that contracts providing an adequate level of data protection are in place.

All data users must register with the Information Commissioner, who ensures compliance with the DPA 1998. Information to be registered includes who the data user is, what personal data is held, the purpose for which it is held, where the data subject may apply to look at this data, to whom the data may be disclosed and any foreign countries to which the data may be transferred.

The DPA 1998 gives all data subjects a right of access to data held about them. The data subject must write to the address given in the register and, if the data user has more than one entry, the data subject must say to which entry he or she is requesting access and may be required to submit each request separately in writing. The data user may charge a fee for each request and must respond to the request within 40 days, although this period may be extended if the data user needs time to identify the individual concerned or to get agreement from other people.

If the data user does not respond to the request, the data subject can apply to the Information Commissioner or the courts. The Commissioner may serve an enforcement notice, requiring the data user to provide the information, or a de-registration notice, after which it would be illegal for the data user to continue to hold the information. The data subject may make further requests provided they are at 'reasonable' intervals.

As well as the right of access, the data subject has three other rights. These are the right to compensation for any damage caused by the data being inaccurate, the right to compensation for any damage caused by loss or unauthorised disclosure of the data and the right to have factually inaccurate data corrected or removed.

If compensation has been awarded, the courts can also order data to be removed if there has been unauthorised disclosure and the courts are satisfied that this is likely to recur. This is possible even if the data is factually correct. If a computer bureau is responsible for the disclosure, the customer on whose behalf the data is held must be notified before the data is deleted.

In addition, individuals can give notice in writing that the data user must not use their data for marketing purposes. The DPA 1998 also imposes restrictions on the use of automated decision systems. They can still be used as a condition for entering or performing a contract (therefore credit scoring a new loan application is still permitted), but, in other circumstances individuals must be informed when a decision is made on this basis and have the right to have it reassessed manually.

There are a wide range of exemptions from various provisions of the DPA 1998, covering areas such as national security, crime, taxation, health, education, social work and regulation. There are also some exemptions covering purposes such as journalism, art, literature, research, history and statistics.

There is an exemption from the non-disclosure provisions where disclosure is required by law.

3.3.5 Data safe harbours

The United States has adopted a different approach, using data 'safe harbours'. These rely on a mix of legislation, regulation and self-regulation. The safe harbour principles are:

◆ *notice*. Individuals must be informed about the purposes for which organisations collect information about them;
◆ *choice*. Individuals have the opportunity to prevent information about them being used or disclosed for purposes other than that for which it was collected;
◆ *onward transfer*. Organisations may only disclose information in a manner consistent with the principles of notice and choice;
◆ *security*. Organisations must take reasonable measures to protect data from loss, misuse, unauthorised access, disclosure, alteration and destruction;
◆ *data integrity*. Organisations should take reasonable steps to ensure that data is accurate, complete and current;
◆ *access*. Individuals must have reasonable access to data held about them and must be able to correct or amend it where it is inaccurate;
◆ *enforcement*. There must be adequate mechanisms for ensuring compliance with the safe harbour principles.

The safe harbour principles are voluntary, but are binding on organisations accepting them. At the time of writing it is thought that this will provide an acceptable level of protection to allow data transfers from the EU to the US.

3.3.6 EU model contracts

Under EU directive 95/46/EC, the European Commission has the power to decide whether standard contractual clauses offer adequate safeguards with respect to the protection of the privacy and fundamental rights and freedoms of individuals and as regards the exercise of the corresponding rights.

The effect of this is to allow organisations to transfer personal data to a country outside the European Economic Area without breaching the DPA 1998 provided that a contract incorporating these clauses is in place. These are often called 'model' contracts or standard form contracts.

3.3.7 Computer Misuse Act 1990

The Computer Misuse Act was enacted in 1990 after some highly-publicised cases of 'hacking' – unauthorised access to data held on computers. The Act introduced three new criminal offences:

- unauthorised access to computer programs and data. This is a relatively minor offence and allows the prosecution of people who simply want to look at data to which they have no right of access;
- unauthorised access with intent to commit or facilitate the commission of a further crime. This offence is far more serious and covers actions such as industrial espionage and attempted fraud;
- unauthorised modification of computer material, ie programs and data held in a computer. This is another serious offence and covers actions such as introducing computer viruses.

For a conviction under the Act, the person must be aware that he or she was not authorised to access or modify the data. This is why financial services organisation systems now display warning messages when people log on to use them. It must also be shown that the person's actions caused the computer to carry out some function – even if only to reject the access attempt.

3.3.8   EU Directives 95/46/EC and 97/66/EC

European Union directive 97/66/EC has extended the scope of the earlier directive 95/44/EC in respect of data privacy in telecommunications.

The most important part of the directive is article 12, which states 'the use of automated calling systems without human intervention or facsimile machines for the purposes of direct marketing may only be allowed in respect of subscribers who have given their prior consent'. In other words, unsolicited marketing faxes are not allowed unless the subscriber has expressly agreed to accept them.

Another important part of the directive is that it defines the subscribers' right to block caller line identification, although this can be overridden by the emergency services and for purposes such as tracing malicious calls. Caller line identification is discussed later in this book and allows someone receiving a call to identify the caller's telephone number.

This directive has been implemented in the UK through the Telephone Preference Service (TPS) and the Fax Preference Service (FPS). Telecommunications regulator Oftel has licensed the Direct Marketing Association to operate the TPS and the FPS, which complement the existing Mailing Preference Service (MPS – formerly the Mail Order Preference Service).

The TPS gives individuals the right to opt out of unsolicited direct marketing calls. This is less strict than the EU directive. The FPS complies with the directive by requiring that individuals must opt in before they can be sent unsolicited direct marketing faxes.

The European Commission is currently looking at the use of email for direct marketing and there is discussion as to whether an 'opt out' or 'opt in' system should be adopted. This is likely to be covered in a future directive.

3.3.9   Human Rights Act 1998

The European Convention on Human Rights and Fundamental Freedoms was developed under the Council of Europe and the highest court for the interpretation of the convention is the European Court of Human Rights in Strasbourg. Neither the European Union nor the European Court of Justice in Luxembourg has any responsibility for the convention. The Human Rights Act 1998 incorporates the convention into UK law.

The articles incorporated into UK law cover the following:

- the right to life;
- prohibition of torture;
- prohibition of slavery and forced labour;
- the right to liberty and security;
- the right to a fair trial;
- prohibition of the enactment of retrospective criminal offences;
- the right to respect for private and family life;
- freedom of thought, conscience and religion;
- freedom of expression;
- freedom of assembly and association;
- the right to marry;
- prohibition of discrimination;
- right to peaceful enjoyment of possessions and protection of property;
- right to education;
- right to free elections;
- right not to be subjected to the death penalty.

Article 8 – the right to respect for private and family life – also extends to a person's home and their correspondence and establishes the principle that privacy is a fundamental human right. This has had an impact in areas such as whether organisations are allowed to look at their employees' personal emails.

3.4   Money laundering and law enforcement

3.4.1   Money Laundering Regulations 1993

The Money Laundering Regulations 1993 were introduced to combat money laundering and there are equivalent European Union regulations and global conventions. These are largely outside the scope of the subject but three requirements should be noted:

- financial services organisations are required to obtain customer identification. This has an impact on providing direct financial services, where physical forms of identification may be difficult to obtain or validate. Copies of customer identification documents must be stored to prove compliance;

◆ large movements must be reported;
◆ unusual transactions must be reported.

The Joint Money Laundering Steering Group in the UK and the Financial Action Task Force worldwide monitor compliance with the regulations.

3.4.2   Proceeds of Crime Act 2002

The Proceeds of Crime Act 2002 strengthened the law on money laundering. It:

◆ introduced a new agency responsible for asset recovery;
◆ consolidated existing laws on confiscation and money laundering into a single piece of legislation;
◆ introduced new powers to recover criminal assets through civil proceedings (without the need for a criminal conviction);
◆ introduced the exchange of information between the new agency and other authorities;
◆ established that the new agency will carry out tax functions in relation to criminal gains.

3.4.3   Criminal Justice Act 1984 and the Police and Criminal Evidence Act 1984

The computer's own records (for example a list of attempts to log on to a system) can be used as evidence provided it can be shown that the recording system is proven and the computer was operating correctly. This must be certified to the court by an expert witness in order to meet the requirements of the Criminal Justice Act 1984 and the Police and Criminal Evidence Act 1984.

3.5   Consumer protection and financial services

Consumer protection and financial services regulation is largely outside the scope of this book, but there are aspects that are relevant to IT. Relevant legislation includes the Financial Services and Markets Act 2000, Basel II and bank rules.

3.5.1   Financial Services and Markets Act 2000

This Act regulates the provision of financial services in the UK. Although largely outside the scope of this text; the requirements it lays down in terms of use of information and appropriateness of advice does influence how products can be sold and the data records that have to obtained to evidence the advice given (or not) in the transaction.

The key objectives of the Act are as follows.

◆ The **public awareness objective** is promoting public understanding of the financial system.

It includes, in particular:

a) promoting awareness of the benefits and risks associated with different kinds of investment or other financial dealing; and

b) the provision of appropriate information and advice.

◆ The objective of **protection of consumers** is: securing the appropriate degree of protection for consumers.

In considering what degree of protection may be appropriate, the Authority must have regard to:

a) the differing degrees of risk involved in different kinds of investment or other transaction;

b) the differing degrees of experience and expertise that different consumers may have in relation to different kinds of regulated activity;

c) the needs that consumers may have for advice and accurate information; and

d) the general principle that consumers should take responsibility for their decisions.

◆ The **reduction of financial crime**:

a) fraud or dishonesty;

b) misconduct in, or misuse of information relating to, a financial market; or

c) handling the proceeds of crime.

3.5.2   Basel II

The Revised International Capital Framework due to be implemented by the Basel Committee on Banking Supervision, more commonly known as 'Basel II', will affect information management in financial services. Basel II is a very large subject, but two points should be noted.

◆ It will require financial services organisations to have a consolidated view of all of their dealings with a customer. This is to ensure that the organisations fully understand their risk positions with their customers and are able to produce a list of all goods and services bought by the customer in the event of default. It effectively requires them to implement a 'single customer view'.

◆ It will require financial services organisations to take account of operational risk (as well as credit risk). It extends the view of operational risk beyond fraud and into processing errors.

3.5.3 Bank rules

Bank rules were originally written to ensure that banks complied with the *Tournier v National Provincial and Union Bank of England* case. These were then modified to meet the requirements of subsequent legislation. They typically cover areas such as:

◆ who is responsible for data and what controls need to be put in place in order to ensure that data remains confidential and available and retains its integrity;

◆ measures to protect computer equipment from damage or theft, and to ensure that any equipment failure does not result in a loss of data;

◆ measures to protect telecommunications links from unauthorised access, including rules relating to accessing and receiving data from the Internet;

◆ rules governing relationships with suppliers to ensure competitive tendering, to protect the organisation against unfair contracts and to ensure that the organisation's intellectual property rights and rules of non-disclosure are respected.

3.6 Intellectual property

Intellectual property is defined as original work created by individuals and organisations. Rights to intellectual property are protected through the Copyright Act 1956, the Copyright (Computer Software) Act 1985 and the Copyright Designs and Patents Act 1988.

Contract law provides additional protection for software purchased from external vendors.

3.6.1 Copyright and patent law

Computer programs are the 'intellectual property' of the author and copyright law exists to protect the author's rights. Under the Copyright Act 1956 and the Copyright (Computer Software) Act 1985, original works such as computer programs cannot be copied without the permission of the author for 50 years after publication.

As far as computer software is concerned, the author is usually the organisation that produced or commissioned it. The individual or software house who wrote the computer programs usually waives any rights in favour of the organisation.

Copyright law also prevents the production of programs that do the same thing as the originals. These design rights are protected under the Copyright Designs and Patents Act 1988. This is important in IT where the identification of requirements and design of the system accounts for much of the cost of systems development.

Patent law protects inventions. It can be used to protect business processes and the Halifax has applied for patent protection for some of the techniques used in its IF electronic banking system. Software is not normally covered by patent law in the UK, but it is covered in the US and the European Union has proposed adopting a similar approach in the EU.

3.6.2 Law of contract

Software purchased from external vendors is also covered by contract law. This takes the form of a licence agreement, which the purchaser accepts as part of the purchase of the software, limiting the purchaser's rights to copy or to sell the software.

As an example, consider the purchase of 'shrink wrapped' package software for a personal computer. The media (usually CD-ROMs) that contain the software are in a sealed plastic wrapper. By breaking the seal, the purchaser agrees to the terms of the licence. This restricts the number of copies that can be made and if the purchaser makes more than the licence allows, he or she can be sued for breach of contract.

In the UK, an organisation called the Federation Against Software Theft (FAST) represents the interests of the software producers and has prosecuted some very large companies for breaches of copyright and contract law. The Business Software Alliance (BSA) is the US equivalent.

Financial services organisations also protect their intellectual property by requiring employees and suppliers to sign non-disclosure agreements, preventing them from revealing confidential information. These may appear as clauses in other contracts, for example employment contracts, rather than being separate agreements.

3.7 Competition law

Competition law in the UK is governed by the Competition Act 1998. This implements the provisions of articles 81 and 82 of the European Community treaty, by prohibiting agreements between firms which distort competition and by limiting the behaviour of dominant firms. The Competition Commission oversees the structure with the Office of Fair Trading (OFT) responsible on a day-to-day basis.

The Financial Services and Markets Act 2000 disapplies some aspects of the Competition Act 1998 from the financial services industry, but includes additional provisions relating to market abuse.

OFT regulation sometimes affects the financial services sector. For example, an OFT ruling has inhibited financial services organisations from using information from standing orders for marketing purposes. Although this ruling only covered one specific circumstance, the financial services sector has been reluctant to test it.

Corporate governance was the subject of a series of enquiries, of which the first was the Cadbury Committee in 1992. The Turnbull Committee reported in 1999 on the implementation of the 'supercode'. This placed two relevant obligations on directors.

◆ It extended the responsibility of directors for risk. This now includes non-financial risk in areas such as the environment, markets and technology.

◆ It placed a focus on ongoing internal control. Companies are now required to satisfy their auditors that these controls are embedded in their operations and that they can respond rapidly to change.

The United States has historically lagged behind the UK in corporate governance. It used to be said that the US authorities could obtain information about the activities of companies in the British Virgin Islands (a traditional offshore centre), but not those in Delaware. This changed after the collapse on Enron with the passage of the Sarbanes Oxley Act (usually known as 'Sarbox' in the UK or 'Sox' in the US) in 2002. Sarbox applies to all companies with a US listing, which includes UK financial services organisations that have listed in the US to gain access to the American capital markets.

The element of Sarbox that presents the most problems is section 404, which requires a review of a company's internal controls. This is similar to the supercode provisions on embedding internal controls, but is much stricter and requires organisations to document their processes and procedures to a very detailed level in accordance with standards set by the US regulator (the Securities and Exchange Commission or SEC). Outsourced business processes may also be subject to Section 404 controls.

3.8   Electronic commerce and the Internet

The main legal issues associated with electronic commerce are:

◆ how to establish identity and legal capacity;
◆ legal jurisdiction;
◆ content ownership and legal responsibility for content;
◆ taxation;
◆ contractual status.

The issues with identity and legal capacity arise because of the difficulty of unambiguously establishing the identity of the parties to an electronic commerce transaction. Physical proofs of identity such as a passport or driving licence cannot be presented over the Internet and the parties are not physically present, which makes it difficult to establish age.

This can lead to problems such as fraud and to individuals entering into contracts which are illegal or which cannot be enforced against them, for example, minors entering into loan contracts.

39

The issue with legal jurisdiction is: which set of laws should apply if the parties to an e-commerce transaction are in different countries? At the time of writing, there are three possibilities.

1. For business-to-business e-commerce, the contract will specify which legal code applies. Unlike business-to-consumer e-commerce, consumer protection legislation is not applicable.
2. The provision of information to consumers. The general view appears to be that the laws of the country of the information provider apply – if a business is allowed to provide information in its country of domicile then it is allowed to provide the same information over the Internet.
3. The provision of a service to consumers. The general view appears to be that the laws of the country of the consumer apply. Therefore a business may be breaking the law because its service offering does not comply with local consumer protection legislation.

The situation on business-to-consumer electronic commerce is clearly inconsistent.

The issues with content ownership and legal responsibility for content include:

◆ *responsibility for illegal material*. This category can include material governments regard as seditious and material which is banned under national laws or international conventions;
◆ *responsibility for libel*. This includes the publication of libellous statements on the Internet;
◆ *responsibility for copyright breaches*. This is further complicated by differences in copyright law between different countries, and as copyright may be held by different people or organisations in different countries;
◆ *intellectual property rights in domain names or 'assigned names'*. 'Cybersquatting' is the practice of registering as a domain name the name of a famous individual or a well known organistion, with the intention of selling the name to the individual or organisation at a high price;
◆ *deep linking*. The Internet allows links to be built to any web page. Deep linking occurs when a link is built to a page that would normally only be accessible through an entry screen, as in the diagram below:

The problem with the first three issues is, who has legal responsibility for ensuring that the content of the Internet complies with local legislation? In particular, if an Internet service provider (ISP) 'hosts' material that breaches local legislation, is this the ISP's responsibility?

The current view appears to be that the ISP is not a 'publisher' in the legal sense, but does have a duty of care and is required to remove illegal or libellous material if this is brought to the ISP's attention. In the US, ISPs are regarded as 'carriers' similar to the Post Office or courier companies rather than as a publisher. However, there has been a case in Germany in which the ISP was held liable for publishing illegal material.

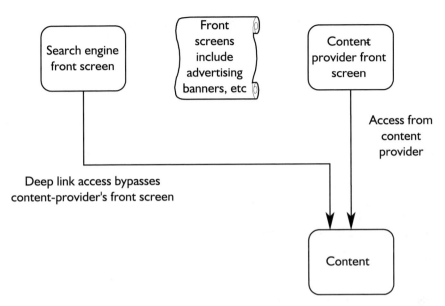

The World Intellectual Property Organisation has set up an arbitration service to address the issue of cybersquatting. Arbitration is binding, which prevents the more flagrant abuses of the domain names registration system.

The issue with deep linking is that this allows Internet users access to material without going through warnings screens or seeing advertising banners. Therefore, the site providing the content may be in breach of local legislation by failing to provide warnings about unsuitable material and may lose advertising income as there is a lower 'click through' rate.

The position on deep linking is currently unclear, although there has been at least one successful lawsuit to prevent this.

The issues on taxation include whether electronic commerce transactions should be liable to tax and where and how tax should be collected.

There is currently an international agreement that these transactions should not be taxed. However there are exceptions – the US state of Michigan requires that purchases made over the Internet should be listed on individuals' income tax returns and the state sales tax should be paid. Courts in France have ruled that online auctions should be subject to French law for French residents – which includes tax liability and a requirement that they should be conducted by an auctioneer licensed to conduct auctions in France. The European Union favours taxation of electronic commerce transactions.

The issue on contractual status is whether advertising goods and services on the Internet is legally an offer or an invitation to treat. This became an issue in a case in which televisions were advertised for sale at a very low price, due to an error in setting up the web page.

The position on this is not entirely clear. The current view seems to be that this is an invitation to treat (and therefore legally similar to displaying goods in a supermarket). Therefore, the customer will make an offer for the goods, which the seller must accept to make the contract legally binding.

There is some uncertainty whether an acknowledgement of the order is legally an acceptance. Many Internet retailers (or e-tailers) have systems which automatically produce an acknowledgement of the order. As this is a purely automatic process, its legal validity as an acceptance is uncertain.

3.8.1   Electronic Communications Act 2000

The Electronic Communications Act 2000 was introduced to provide a legal framework for electronic commerce in the UK. The original bill contained provisions on encryption which proved controversial and have now been put forward as separate legislation, the Regulation of Investigatory Powers Bill, and is discussed below.

The Act contains two main provisions.

1. *A register of suppliers.* All suppliers of cryptography must be registered and licenced.
2. *Recognition of digital signatures and digital certificates as legally admissible evidence of identity.* The Act also gives the Secretary of State the power to amend existing legislation to allow the use of digital signatures and digital certificates where these are not currently allowed.

3.8.2   Regulation of Investigatory Powers Act 2000

Governments around the world are concerned about the potential use of the Internet by criminals, terrorists or those opposed to the government. This resulted in the US government restricting the export of encryption technology by classing it as a munition.

The UK government attempted to restrict the use of encryption in the Electronic Communications Bill. Some of these provisions proved controversial and were taken out of the Electronic Communications Bill and included separately in the Regulation of Investigatory Powers Act 2000.

The main requirements of the Act are:

◆ *a requirement to provide the key or the information.* Internet Service Providers (ISPs) carrying email or electronic data are required to supply 'black box' technology to intercept and copy it, and to provide either a decryption key or the information in decrypted form. This does not require a court order; and

◆ *a provision against 'tipping off'*. This prevents ISPs receiving a request for the key or the information from making this known. Such a request will form part of an investigation and this provision is intended to prevent the person under investigation becoming aware of the fact.

3.8.3 Civil Evidence Act 1995

The Civil Evidence Act 1995 extended the acceptability of computer records as evidence into civil law. The Act was particularly concerned with the acceptability of images of documents stored on microfiche or optical disk to a court of law.

The Act requires that the recording system is proven and the computer was operating correctly. It also requires that a complete audit trail is kept and that the recording medium is of a form which cannot be altered undetectably. For example, write once read many optical disk (WORM) and compact disk recordable (CD-R) are acceptable, whereas compact disk rewritable (CD-RW) is not. Provided that the requirements laid down in the British Standards Institute's code of practice are met, images are acceptable, although they are not considered to be as good as the original documents.

Four

The social environment

4.1   Introduction

Technology has had a considerable impact on society as a whole, as well as the individual customers, employees and managers of the financial services industry. This chapter considers these impacts.

4.2   Impact on society

The impact of technology on society is a consequence of two developments: the use of computers to capture and store information and recent developments that allow computers to identify and track individuals.

4.2.1   Information storage

Automated processes collect information as a by-product of processing. In the first generation of computer processing, storing this information was difficult and expensive and it was held for as little time as possible. As the cost of storage has fallen, the information collected has become more important and is increasingly seen as a valuable resource.

This raises privacy issues, which are magnified as more information from different sources is brought together and cross-referenced. Supermarkets and governments, as well as financial services organisations, have made use of this.

Supermarkets combine information from automated tills and loyalty cards to improve their understanding of customer behaviour. This allows them to target special offers at selected groups of customers.

More comprehensive was the US government's proposed Total Information Awareness programme. This was overseen by the Information Awareness Office and aimed to gather as much information as possible about everyone. This included Internet activity, credit card purchase histories, airline ticket purchases, car rentals, medical records, educational transcripts, driving licences, utility bills, tax returns, etc.

The US Congress halted funding in 2003, even though the US government re-named it the 'Terrorist Information Awareness' programme, because of concerns about privacy and civil liberties issues.

In the UK, the proposed ID card database also raises privacy issues. Although it does not have the same scope as the Total Information Awareness programme, it could be used as a basis for cross-matching information held on other government databases and may pose a greater threat to privacy than the introduction of ID cards does.

4.2.2 Identification

In the film Minority Report, advertising hoardings identify Tom Cruise from an eye scan and broadcast personalised advertising messages to him, but, of course, this is only possible in films. Or is it? How realistic is this and is it desirable? Technology offers a number of methods for identifying people, either as individuals or through their property.

Methods for identifying individuals are called 'biometrics'. They include facial geometry, iris recognition, retinal scans, fingerprints, signature recognition and voice recognition.

If advertisers are going to start sending targeted messages to individuals, facial geometry is the most likely biometric in the short term. A digital camera is used to acquire an image of the face and the system analyses its geometry in terms of factors such as the distance between the eyes and the nose. Face recognition systems are designed to compensate for glasses, hats and beards.

Facial geometry systems are most often used to identify individuals in libraries of photographs, for example, to match criminals in the records of different police forces. However, there are examples of using facial geometry systems to track individuals.

- ◆ In Malaysia, an airport security system takes a picture of each traveller and converts it to a digital template that is stored on a smart card containing a computer chip. A similar card is also placed on the passenger's luggage and these are cross-matched when the traveller arrives at the departure gate.

♦ Newham Borough Council in East London uses closed circuit television to scan the faces of people passing cameras located around the Borough. The system searches for matches in a video library of known criminals stored in a local police database. When the system gets a match, it alerts a security officer who can then contact the police.

Eye scans, as in the film, can use either iris recognition or retinal scanning.

♦ Iris recognition matches the pattern of the iris. Nationwide Building Society has used iris recognition in an automated branch pilot in Swindon since mid-1998.

♦ Retinal scanning, which used a laser to scan the pattern of blood vessels on the back of the retina, has largely been replaced by iris recognition.

Fingerprints, palmprints and hand and finger geometry can also be used as biometrics.

♦ Fingerprint and palmprint recognition relies on the pattern of lines on a fingerprint, thumbprint or palmprint. Some personal computer manufacturers include fingerprint readers, either as optional attachments or built into laptops. ING bank has experimented with using a modified mouse that can read fingerprints. This is perhaps the most likely approach to using biometrics for identifying individuals in an office environment.

♦ Hand and finger geometry systems, like facial geometry systems, identify the shape of the hand and fingers. Characteristics such as the three-dimensional shape of the hand, the length and width of fingers and the shape of knuckles can be examined. The US Immigration and Naturalisation Service uses a system that measures the three-dimensional configuration of an individual's hand to speed entry for qualified low-risk travellers at airports in Newark, New Jersey, New York and Toronto.

Such biometrics are being tested for the proposed UK ID cards.

Signature recognition systems can use two systems.

♦ Signature dynamics such as speed, stroke order and pressure can be analysed. This compares how the signature is made as well as what the signature looks like.

♦ Signatures can be recognised based only on what they look like. This is less accurate than the recognition of signature dynamics. It is most useful in checking signatures on cheques, credit card slips, etc.

Voice recognition can be used in telephone banking and recognises the pattern of the voice. Do not confuse voice recognition with speech recognition (which interprets speech) or voice response (which recognises the tones from a touch tone telephone). Voice recognition systems achieve an accuracy of about 95% and are less reliable than fingerprint or iris recognition. The Nationwide Building Society is the first UK financial services organisation to trial the use of voice recognition software.

Technology can also be used to identify property and, by extension, the people using that property. Examples include car number plate recognition, mobile telephones location by cell, location-aware mobile telephones, Radio-Frequency Identification Tags (RFIDs) and tags and badges.

Car number plate recognition uses optical character recognition technology to read car number plates, which are matched against the Driver Vehicle Licensing Centre database to identify the owner. This technology is used in speed cameras, in London to enforce the congestion charge and to identify stolen vehicles.

Mobile telephones are also easy to trace. Calls can be traced to the small geographic area covered by the 'cell'. Some mobile telephones use the Global Positioning System so that they are aware of their location and this information can be monitored. Mobile telephones equipped with short-range technologies such as Bluetooth can also be traced through other Bluetooth-equipped devices.

RFID tags can receive and respond to a radio signal over a short distance, typically up to about five metres. They are commonly used as security tags to prevent shoplifting. However, unless the tag is deactivated, it remains active and can be detected at a later time. Similar tags can also be included in badges, allowing the movement of individuals within a building to be monitored.

Perhaps the problem with the film Minority Report is that it does not go far enough. Would it be possible for a fugitive to avoid capture in the world of the future? Would this only apply to suspected criminals – and Tom Cruise was an innocent man who had been framed by his boss – or would the authorities track the activities of a whole range of people who happened to disagree with them?

4.3 Customers

4.3.1 Relationship banking and transaction banking

Financial services organisations traditionally operated according to the 'relationship banking' model. This was based on the assumption that 'the banker knew his customer' and this is the legal basis of the banker–customer relationship. The term 'relationship banking' implies this level of knowledge as well as a relationship of trust – a fiduciary relationship – between banker and customer.

Financial services organisations found it difficult to sustain the relationship banking model for mass market customers. Competitors with lower cost bases prevented them from charging high enough margins to support relationship banking. The financial services organisations found staff costs growing faster than their income and were forced to introduce automation to allow them to service larger numbers of customers in order to remain competitive.

The automation resulting from the first two generations of information technology allowed financial services organisations to handle increased number of customers without increasing staff numbers. However, this increase in numbers and other changes in banking practice, such as the more frequent rotation of managers between branches, made it impossible for banks to have the personal knowledge of their customers implied by relationship banking.

This resulted in a switch to 'transaction banking'. The fiduciary relationship was replaced by a simple buyer–seller relationship and the principle of caveat emptor ('let the buyer beware').

Transaction banking had its disadvantages.

◆ Courts were not always willing to accept that financial services organisations had no fiduciary duty towards their customers.
◆ Transaction banking undermined traditional customer loyalty. This allowed new entrants to the financial services market to cherry pick the most profitable customers and products, reducing financial services organisations' ability to subsidise less profitable operations.

4.3.2 Re-personalising the relationship

Has the traditional banker–customer relationship gone forever? Although we may not know our customer in the traditional sense, we can use information to behave as if we do. We can describe this as 're-personalising' the relationship. Instead of relying on staff knowledge, financial services organisations are increasingly relying on capturing this knowledge in computer systems.

One of the earliest examples of this is the 'customer view'. Early computer systems often viewed the banker–customer relationship as based on the account. There was no attempt to connect different accounts held by the same customer. This led to absurd situations such as customers with thousands of pounds in their deposit accounts having cheques referred if they exceeded agreed limits by a few pounds. The customer view gives us the ability to take an overall view of the relationship with the customer.

Other examples will be discussed later in this book.

4.3.3 Know Your Customer (KYC)

Know Your Customer (KYC) is an important issue for governments, who are concerned to prevent money laundering, and financial services organisations, who are concerned to prevent fraud and money laundering. The Financial Services Authority fines UK financial services organisations that fail to comply with KYC regulations.

KYC requires that financial services organisations obtain and record evidence of customers' identities.

4.3.4   Technophobia

There is a general perception that customers suffer from 'technophobia' – a fear and dislike of technology. It is not clear that there is any real evidence for this (some surveys have suggested that many customers prefer using ATMs for balance enquiries and withdrawals), but financial organisations need to take care when they introduce new methods of service delivery.

Customers are cautious about innovations. There is a relatively small number of 'early adopters' and a significant minority of 'laggards'. This applies to any form of innovation and does not necessarily imply any fear of technology as such.

It is also clear that some customers prefer traditional branch delivery. Some 20% of customers have never used an ATM and 70% of customers in the US express a preference for using branches as their main delivery channel.

Technophobia may be a result of bad experiences with technology. We need to be aware of the problems that can arise and to treat customer concerns sympathetically.

The main sources of concern include:

◆ ATMs not being available;
◆ fraudulent EFTPOS transactions;
◆ phishing and pharming;
◆ spyware;
◆ identity theft;
◆ fraudulent Internet transactions.

ATM failure

Customers rely on ATMs for cash and can find ATM non-availability very irritating. There are three possible reasons for ATM failure:

◆ the failure of the ATM itself. This is quite rare. ATMs are very robust devices and it is unusual for them to fail;
◆ the failure of the telecommunications links to the main computer or of the main computer itself. This is rather more common; or
◆ running out of money. This is the most common reason for ATM unavailability.

Financial services organisations manage these risks by providing customers with information about alternative ATMs. Stickers can be used to remind customers of those other organisations whose ATMs they can use through reciprocity arrangements or to direct customers to the location of alternative ATMs.

The amount of money loaded into an ATM depends on the anticipated demand, but financial services organisations also need to consider the cost of using money in this way. Money held as notes in an ATM cannot earn interest. Financial services organisations can reduce the risk of ATMs running out of money in two ways.

◆ Developing models to predict the expected pattern of demand for ATM withdrawals. The systems that control the ATM maintain statistics about the actual pattern of demand, which can be used to refine the models. This allows ATMs to be loaded with the minimum amount needed to ensure that the ATM will not run out of money provided there is no major departure from normal patterns of demand.

◆ Using the controlling software to check that the ATM still has money and is still functioning. If the ATM runs out of money a local branch can be notified and instructed to fill it. This can also be carried out by a central group. Other sources of failure can also be notified and an engineer sent.

Fraudulent EFTPOS transactions

Fraudulent EFTPOS transactions may be due to fake, lost or stolen cards. There is also the possibility of collusion between the retailer and the fraudster.

Card issuers have tried to make cards more difficult to counterfeit and to make stolen cards more difficult to use. The main card-based precautions are:

◆ tamper-proof signature strips, which prevent a signature being erased;
◆ holograms on the card, which make it more difficult to counterfeit;
◆ Card Verification Value (CVV – Visa) or Card Validation Code (CVC – Mastercard), which is additional information making the card difficult to counterfeit;
◆ photographs on the card, which make stolen cards more difficult to use.

The first three of these are already widely used. CVV/CVC is particularly useful for preventing fraud when 'card not present' purchases are made, for example over the telephone or the Internet. Although photocards have been effective in cutting fraud, this may be because they are uncommon so retailers are more likely to check them.

Issuers have also introduced system precautions, designed to detect lost and stolen cards. The main system precautions are:

◆ hot card files, held either locally or centrally, which record lost or stolen cards and prevent their being used;
◆ floor limits, which can be used to force authorisation of all transactions in retailers particularly likely to be targeted by fraudsters;
◆ online authorisation, preventing cards being used beyond the funds and credit available;
◆ expert systems, which detect patterns of use that may indicate fraudulent behaviour.

All of these are widely used. Expert systems used in the UK include Fraudwatch (Barclaycard) and Falcon (MasterCard).

Procedures are designed to prevent cards from being intercepted. The main procedures include:

- advising customers that they will shortly be receiving a new card and to contact the issuer if it does not arrive by the validity date;
- requiring customers to validate cards before use;
- card collection from branches, which prevents cards being intercepted in the post.

Requiring customers to collect cards from branches has service implications and financial services organisations generally prefer to use secure alternatives such as courier delivery.

The UK financial services organisations are in the final stages of rolling out 'Chip and PIN'. This replaces magnetic strip cards and signature verification with cards carrying a computer chip and verification by entering a four-digit Personal Identification Number (PIN). This technology has been used in countries such as France and Japan for many years.

The security advantages of Chip and PIN include:

- the computer chip makes the card much harder to copy or 'clone';
- PIN is a better method of verification than signature-checking and customers can change the PIN to a number that they can easily remember (this is called 'self-select PIN'), making it less likely that they will compromise the card's security by writing the PIN down.

There are some disadvantages of Chip and PIN.

- The cost of Chip and PIN is higher that the cost of magnetic strip cards. The financial services organisations and retailers expect to recover this through lower fraud costs.
- Retailers will still need to accept some cards on the basis of signature verification. This will include cards from countries where Chip and PIN is not used and cards where the Chip has been damaged.
- Chip and PIN cannot currently be used to verify transactions over the telephone or the Internet.

The chip could carry much more information, including, for example, additional security information, in future.

Phishing and pharming

Fraudsters use phishing and pharming to mislead customers into revealing their security details, for example, user IDs and passwords for Internet financial services.

Phishing involves sending an email asking customers to confirm their security details. They are usually directed to a website that resembles that of a financial services organisation and asked to enter their user ID, password and any secondary identification information such as memorable dates. The fraudster then uses this information to log on to the real financial services organisation website and transfer money out of the customer's account.

Pharming also uses a spurious website. When the customer attempts to log in, he or she is redirected to the fraudster's website and asked to enter security details. Again, the fraudster can use this to transfer money out of the customer's account. Pharming exploits a weakness in the software of the Domain Name Servers that run the Internet.

Spyware

Spyware is any technology that aids in gathering information about a person or organisation without their knowledge. On the Internet (where it is sometimes called a 'spybot' or 'tracking software'), spyware is programming that is put in someone's computer secretly to gather information about the user and relay it to advertisers or other interested parties. Spyware can get in a computer as a software virus or as the result of installing a new program.

Data collecting programs that are installed with the user's knowledge are not, properly speaking, spyware if the user fully understands what data is being collected and with whom it is being shared. However, spyware is often installed without the user's consent as a drive-by download or as the result of clicking some option in a deceptive pop-up window. Software designed to serve advertising, known as 'adware', can usually be thought of as spyware as well because it almost invariably includes components for tracking and reporting user information. However, marketing firms object to having their products called 'spyware'. As a result, McAfee (the Internet security company) and others now refer to such applications as 'potentially unwanted programs'.

The cookie is a well-known mechanism for storing information about an Internet user on their own computer. If a website stores information about you in a cookie that you don't know about, the cookie can be considered a form of spyware. Spyware is part of an overall public concern about privacy on the Internet.

Identity theft

Identity theft is a crime in which an imposter obtains key pieces of personal information, such as Social Security, driving licence or bank account details, in order to impersonate someone else. The information can be used to obtain credit, merchandise and services in the name of the victim or to provide the thief with false credentials. In addition to running up debt, an imposter might provide false identification to the police, creating a criminal record or leaving outstanding arrest warrants for the person whose identity has been stolen.

Identity theft is categorised in two ways: true name and account takeover. True name identity theft means that the thief uses personal information to open new accounts. The thief might open a new credit card account, establish cellular phone service or open a new bank account in order to obtain blank cheques. Account takeover identity theft means the imposter uses personal information to gain access to the person's existing accounts. Typically, the thief will change the mailing address on an account and run up a huge bill before the person whose identity has been stolen realises there is a problem. The Internet has made it easier for an identity thief to use the information they have stolen because transactions can be made without any personal interaction.

Although an identity thief might break into a database to obtain personal information, experts say it's more likely the thief would obtain information by using old-fashioned methods. Retrieving personal paperwork and discarded post from waste bins is one of the easiest ways for an identity thief to get information. Another popular method to get information is shoulder surfing – the identity thief simply stands next to someone in a public office and watches as the person fills out personal information on a form.

To prevent identity theft, experts recommend that you regularly check your credit report major credit bureaus, follow up with creditors if your bills do not arrive on time, destroy unsolicited credit applications and protect yourself by not giving out any personal information in response to unsolicited emails.

Fraudulent Internet transactions

The Internet is a new medium and stories about fraud and breaches of security seem to be a daily occurrence. Although there are many similarities between Internet and EFTPOS fraud, there are three significant differences.

◆ *The Internet is an open network.* Therefore, it is exposed to the additional dangers of hacking and virus infection. There have been cases of credit or debit card numbers being stolen, with their secondary verification details, and posted on the Internet.

◆ *The Internet is global.* Internet fraud may be perpetrated by people in different countries, which may make it difficult and time-consuming to recover any losses and which limits the legal protection available under the connected lender liability provisions of the Consumer Credit Act 1974.

◆ *Internet fraud can affect banking transactions as well as electronic commerce.* Internet banks have, in some cases, refused to limit customers' responsibility for losses due to fraud, on the grounds that these services are offered over a secure link and any fraud is presumed to be a result of the customer's carelessness.

Internet security is discussed at greater length later in this book.

Overcoming technophobia

How do we overcome technophobia?

We need to ensure that our systems are easy to use. This applies to all computer systems, of course, but is particularly important for systems that customers are expected to use without assistance.

Systems designed to be used by customers must be very easy to use. They should include the following points.

- Screen designs must be clear. Too many colours should be avoided and colours should contrast well. The screen should be legible even if sited in sunlight or where there are reflections from internal lights.
- The screen should give clear instructions to the customer. Courtesy words such as 'please' and 'thank you' may be used at the start and end of a transaction where appropriate.
- It should be clear when the customer is expected to enter something. If there is likely to be a delay while the system carries out some processing a message such as 'busy – please wait' should be displayed.
- Navigation – the way the customer moves from one screen to another – should always be clear. The customer should always be able to cancel a transaction if he or she wishes.
- Transactions should not take too long. Not only is there a risk of the customer forgetting what he or she wants to do, the effect on other customers who may be queuing to use the system also needs to be considered.

New technology, such as touch-sensitive screens and multimedia, have made it easier to design systems which are customer-friendly.

Staff should be willing and able to help customers – if staff do not understand how to use the equipment, how can customers be expected to? If equipment is located in branches, staff should be trained to deal with enquiries and problems. If possible, staff should be available to assist customers who are not happy to use the equipment unaided.

4.4   Employees

Many of the changes that have affected employees have been IT-enabled rather than IT-led. For example, the move from 'teller to seller' was a result of business changes – the move away from relationship banking and the bancassurance model – rather than IT changes, but IT systems such as sales prompts enabled and supported this change.

The effects of IT and IT-enabled change on employees includes:

- increased workload;

- career development;
- industrialisation;
- teleworking.

4.4.1   Increased workload

IT has allowed work to be done much faster, hence increasing the amount of work individuals are expected to do. The introduction of IT has also had an impact on the nature of jobs staff are being asked to undertake. This is often called 'teller to seller' and describes how the job of branch staff increasingly involves selling products to the customer, rather than simply waiting for the customer to ask what is available. The emphasis now is on selling skills rather than the traditional skills of the teller.

Staff have also been required to take on many more IT-related responsibilities, varying from an awareness of the main data protection and intellectual property legislation, through taking system back-ups to quite technical responsibilities such as system upgrades.

It is possible for staff to take on too much work and karoshi, or death from overwork is a well-documented phenomenon in Japan and elsewhere. As a reaction to this, there is an increasing emphasis on a better balance between work and family responsibilities and initiatives such as work–life balance in the UK and quality of working life in the US have received a high level of support from governments and major companies.

One good effect of IT is to make information much more freely available to first line managers and supervisors. They now have the information to take decisions which would have had to be referred to middle management. This is often called 'empowerment'.

Another benefit is that IT may prompt employee development, by requiring a wider range of skills and more use of intellectual skills such as abstraction. This, in turn, leads to a requirement for continuous learning and for skill sharing.

4.4.2   Career development

Banks and building societies used to offer a 'job for life' – a career with a steady progression through the organisation until the employee reached the limit of his or her abilities or ambitions. There were many reasons for this including the organisational culture of banks and building societies – large bureaucracies which placed a high value on staff loyalty.

Another reason was the type of skills required to work in a bank or building society. These did not change – lending assessment now is practically the same as it was one hundred years ago. An employee would become more valuable over time because he or she would still be using the same skills but would also be improving them through experience.

The large scale introduction of IT has completely changed this. Tasks such as lending assessment are now largely carried out through credit scoring. Employees are finding that the skills for which they were recruited and trained are increasingly unimportant to their employers.

The most obvious effect of this is on job security. Staff no longer feel that their jobs are secure. Managers need to consider the effect on staff motivation and to find ways to motivate people who are worried by the future.

One response to this has been a stress on lifetime employability rather than lifetime employment. As financial services organisations are no longer able to offer the latter, they try to offer the former by keeping employees' skills up to date and by offering transferable qualifications such as national vocational qualifications. The emphasis on continuous professional development by the Institute of Financial Services is part of the same overall trend.

4.4.3   Industrialisation

Call centres and processing centres are a recent feature of the financial services industry. These have introduced a factory or industrial way of working into the industry.

Some important features of the industrial model include the following.

- *Narrower skill requirements*. Staff working in traditional branches may well use a large number of different skills during the day, as they carry out a variety of tasks. Staff working in centres will typically be trained in a maximum of six different work types.
- *Machine measurement and pacing*. The amount of work carried out is measured, either manually or through the use of IT. IT may also be used to control the pace of work, by setting up personal work queues of outstanding items.

4.4.4   Teleworking

Teleworking involve employees working away from the office. 'Telecommuting' is an alternative term for teleworking. We can identify three main forms:

- homeworking;
- knowledge working;
- mobile working.

We need to look at these together with the related topics of telecottaging and hot desking.

By 'homeworking' we mean relatively simple processing tasks carried out by employees at home. Data entry tasks such as entering details from application forms provide a common example. Another example is a 'virtual call centre' by which calls into a call centre can be routed to agents working at home. BT ran a virtual call centre pilot for their directory enquiries service in Scotland.

The technology required is relatively simple. A workstation with a built in modem will be connected to a server in the financial services organisation's data centre, usually through a digital line. Security is very important and there will be passwords to get into the workstation, to use the application software and to access the data centre. Messages will usually be encrypted to prevent their being intercepted and there may be a firewall between the workstation and the server to prevent attempts at 'hacking'. These security measures are discussed in Chapter Nine.

We can show the technology as follows:

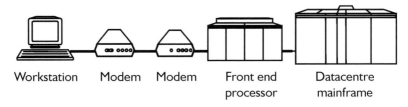

| Workstation | Modem | Modem | Front end processor | Datacentre mainframe |

By knowledge working we mean more complex roles such as consultancy and research. Management – especially project management – is possible on a teleworking basis. The requirement is usually to use a range of software tools such as word processors, spreadsheets, databases, presentation tools and Internet browsers.

The technology required is very similar. The workstation will be a powerful PC with a wide range of software. Knowledge workers may require access to customer or commercially sensitive data, in which event there may be additional security devices attached to the PC.

We can show the technology as follows:

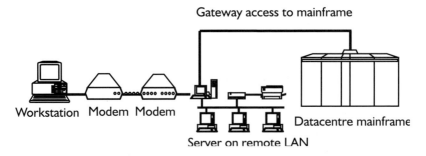

Gateway access to mainframe

Workstation   Modem   Modem

Server on remote LAN

Datacentre mainframe

Mobile working refers to employees who travel for a large part of their working day and need to process information while on the move. This is becoming increasingly important as financial services organisations deliver services to their customers rather than expecting customers to visit them.

A number of technologies can be used including the following.

◆ The simplest option is to use a stand alone laptop or notebook computer. The employee will return to a central office from time to time to transfer the data into the organisation's systems. The main disadvantage of this approach is that the data may be lost or damaged before it is transferred.

◆ An alternative is to transfer information from the portable computer to the organisation's systems using a dial up connection over the public telephone network. Messages will need to be encrypted because of the risk of interception. A variation on this is to use a mobile phone link to transfer the information. These are probably the most common forms of mobile working.

◆ Another alternative is to transfer information over the Internet. The security issues associated with the Internet are discussed later in the book, but messages will need to be encrypted and a virtual private network can be used to provide a higher level of security. The increasing availability of wireless Internet connection through WiFi allows mobile teleworkers to transfer information more frequently and easily, although there are potential security issues with WiFi networks that must be addressed.

Teleworking has both advantages and disadvantages. If we consider the advantages and disadvantages for the organisation first:

Advantages	Disadvantages
Savings on premises costs	More difficult to control
Employees do not have to travel	Higher equipment costs
Access for employees who cannot travel	Higher telecommunications costs
Security issues	
Health and safety issues	
Perceived as 'skiving'	

There are savings on premises costs as employees are providing their own place of work.

Employees do not have to travel to work. This reduces the risks of lateness or disruption due to travel problems. Some organisations expect employees who are teleworking to work longer hours to reflect the saving in travelling time.

Access for employees who would not find it easy to travel to work. These included carers and the disabled.

It may be more difficult to control the work being done. Control must be in terms of what is produced rather than the way the employee works and this is not suitable for all jobs. Employees may suffer from distractions, affecting the quality or quantity of their work.

There are higher equipment costs. If employees are sick or on holiday, the equipment is idle and cannot be used by others. The equipment may be more likely to suffer damage either accidentally (for example, from children or pets) or through environmental factors (dust and humidity levels may be higher in domestic premises). The cost of supporting and repairing equipment will be higher as the equipment will need to be brought into a centre or an engineer will need to be sent to the employee's home.

There are higher telecommunications costs as employees must connect to the office over public telephone lines.

There are security issues. Data confidentiality may be difficult to guarantee as family members, visitors and others may have access to the equipment. There is a risk of viruses being introduced. It is difficult to ensure that backups are taken. There may also be data security issues associated with documents and forms sent to or produced by the employee.

The are health and safety issues. It is difficult to ensure that employees use appropriate office furniture providing adequate support. Problems may be more difficult to detect as employees may change their pattern of work to hide problems.

Other employees and managers may perceive working at home as 'skiving', which can damage morale.

The advantages and disadvantages for employees who telework are outlined below.

Advantages	Disadvantages
Control over working hours	Isolation
Reduced travel time	Overwork
Control over working environment	Access to support services

- ◆ *Better control over their working hours.* Employees are not restricted to 9–5 working and can choose to work predominantly early in the morning or late at night. They can also split their work – this can be useful for parents with school age children, who may choose to work, for example, 10–3, together with a two hour period either early morning or late evening. This is also useful for staff who work predominantly 9–5, but have the option to stretch their day by doing additional work in the evening or at weekends.
- ◆ *Reduced travel time.* As we have discussed, this benefit may need to be shared with the organisation. Teleworking is also useful for employees who spend a lot of time travelling as part of their job, as it provides them with a base for administrative tasks without additional travelling.
- ◆ *Better control over their working environment.* Employees can organise their working environment in the way which best suits them, without the constraints provided by the office. This freedom must be used with care to minimise distractions and avoid health and safety risks.

◆ *Isolation*. Employees can feel very isolated. This is partly physical – they are no longer part of a team – but it is also partly an isolation from information. Employees do not know what is going on in the office, they have no access to the grapevine or to their network of colleagues and mentors. Employees who telework can find it difficult to secure promotion simply because they are never in the office – their achievements are less noticeable than those of their peers. It may also be more difficult to secure access to training as training needs may be less apparent.

◆ *Overwork*. Because employees can work extended hours, they may be under pressure so to do. This pressure may come from the organisation, although it is more usually self-imposed.

◆ *Access to support services*. Employees do not have access to support services such as photocopying.

Telecottaging is a variant on teleworking. Instead of employees working at home, they work in office premises close to their homes. Financial services organisations can use spare space in branches for this purpose or local business centres can be used.

Telecottaging overcomes many of the disadvantages of teleworking. Although the organisation still incurs premises costs, these are often cheaper than the premises released (for example, out-of-town sites rather than city centre) and may be in buildings that are underutilised. They have disadvantages of their own, of which the most important is probably the need for the telecottager to conform to the culture of the premises in which he or she is located.

Hot desking allows employees to work away from the office much of the time but to book a desk (and sometimes an office) for when they need to come in. Again this overcomes many of the disadvantages of teleworking.

In practice, hot desking is often done badly. Successful hot desking requires:

◆ An effective system for booking desks, offices, meeting rooms and equipment.

◆ Storage space for employee's possessions which can be moved into position quickly and easily.

◆ Equipment must be set up in a standard way so that it does not need to be individually reconfigured for each employee.

4.5 Managers

Another effect is to take away layers of middle management. One of the main functions of middle management used to be processing information – deciding what information was sufficiently important to be passed on to higher management. IT can now do this. This has produced a flatter organisation, with fewer opportunities for promotion. Employees looking for promotion now need to be willing to move 'sideways' – broadening their experience in other areas of the organisation – as they can no longer rely on a regular series of promotions within the same branch or department.

Five

The technology environment

5.1   Introduction

The technology environment defines the technology potentially available to financial services organisations. The main focus of this chapter is on information technology (IT).

IIT is a term that encompasses all forms of technology used to create, exchange and use information in its various forms (business data, voice conversations, still images, motion pictures, multimedia presentations and other forms).

It is perhaps worth noting that IT is not the only relevant technology. Devices such as cheque reader/sorters and automated teller machines (ATMs) also use mechanical technology for the physical paper handling. Communications technologies are also very important for financial services organisations and the convergence between IT and communications technology (among others) is discussed later in this chapter.

5.1.1   Moore's Law

A unique feature of information technology is the speed of technological innovation. This is reflected in Moore's Law.

Gordon Moore was one of the founders of computer chip maker Intel. Moore's Law predicts that the processing power of computer chips will double every 18 months. This rule has held true since the mid-1960s and is predicted to continue until at least 2010.

As well as this increase in processing power, there has also been an increase in the amount of storage available and the amount of information that can be transmitted over data communications networks. This itself has increased the use of information within organisations. Fourth generation systems, the Internet and broadband networks now provide individuals with access to a quantity of information that is, for all practical purposes, unlimited.

Businesses have exploited this opportunity and collect an increasing amount of information, which is now critical to their operations. Computer Associates' Chief Executive Officer Charles Wang says:

> 'Your core business is information. I don't care if your operation makes door knobs or services fire alarms, your core business is information.'
>
> *Wang (1997)*

In this view, information is not only the business's most important asset, but is also a tradable asset. This has been described as the 'information economy'.

5.1.2 Meredith's Law

The Internet is undoubtedly the most significant recent development in IT. Why is there so much interest in the Internet?

Bob Meredith was one of the founders of the Internet. Meredith's Law states that the value of a network is proportional to the square of the number of nodes or users. Therefore, as the size of a network increases, its value increase exponentially.

This is the point about the Internet. It is already very large and it is still growing very fast. The value of the Internet as a method of contacting customers and suppliers is only exceeded by the value of the telephone network. Comparing this to the (very low) cost of connecting to the Internet shows why the Internet has become the most important current technology.

5.1.3 Evolution of IT

Many authors classify the evolution of IT into a number of eras or generations. We will use a classification based on that of Robin Bloor, a leading UK authority on IT:

- ◆ early developments;
- ◆ first generation – batch;
- ◆ second generation – online;
- ◆ third generation – client/server;
- ◆ fourth generation – web/Internet.

5.2 Early developments

We will say very little about early developments. World War II stimulated developments in electronics and work on codebreaking at Bletchley Park led to the development of Colossus, the first stored program computer. Early commercial computers were developed after the war, for example Leo (Lyons Electronic Office) developed by J Lyons and Manchester University.

The development by John Von Neumann of the Von Neumann architecture also followed the war. The Von Neumann architecture represented a different approach from that used in Colossus and other early computers such as ENIAC and is still used today.

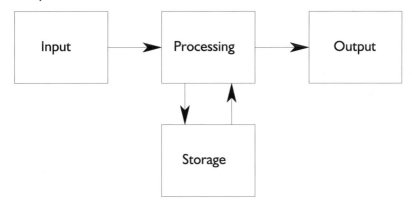

5.3 Subsequent generations

Each of the subsequent generations has been characterised by the development of new enabling technologies to meet changing business needs. We can summarise these as a table:

	First generation	*Second generation*	*Third generation*	*Fourth generation*
Generation	Batch	Online	Client/server	Web/Internet
Duration	1965–1975	1975–1985	1985–1995	1995–????
Business driver	Automation	Online/real time	Re-engineering	E-business
User interface	Paper	Terminal	Workstation	Browser/Java
Enabling technology	Mainframe	Communications database	Workstation Local area network	Internet

(Continued)	First generation	Second generation	Third generation	Fourth generation
Topology	Stand alone	Centralised	Distributed	Network
Transaction processing	Batch	Remote batch Online Real time	Client/server	Internet
Data storage	Files	Hierarchical and network database	Relational database	Relational and object database
Data structure	Rigid	Fixed	Structured	Unstructured

5.3.1   Duration

The durations are approximate and show the period when the technology was at its most dominant. These technologies continue to co-exist with their successors and there are still first generation systems in existence.

The durations also suggest that a fifth generation is emerging or is shortly due to emerge. The obvious driver for this would be mobility, through the development of 'third generation' mobile telephones and Wi-Fi wireless networks.

5.3.2   Enabling technology

The enabling technologies shown are the technologies that most clearly distinguish the generation from its predecessors. However, each of these generations has been made possible by a large number of technological developments.

5.3.3   Transaction processing

A transaction is a logical piece of work such as an account opening or a cheque encashment. Transactions are applied against a master file, for example, in a cheque encashment, the amount is applied against an accounts file. Systems that process transactions are often called applications.

There are a number of different approaches to transaction processing, which are discussed in Chapter Seventeen.

5.3.4 Data storage and structure

Data storage considers how data is organised and accessed.

Data structure is concerned with how 'structured' the data is. Early in the evolutionary process data was highly structured – only characters (such as letters and numbers) could be stored and data had to be presented to the computer according to very rigid rules. As IT has evolved, it has become possible to process other types of data, including multimedia data such as pictures, voice recordings, video and music.

We will not discuss the physical storage media used to hold data in this chapter. These have remained relatively constant over the generations and most data is still held using magnetic storage media such as magnetic tape and magnetic disk.

5.4 First generation

The first generation was concerned with data processing and was the dominant model from the mid-1960s until the mid-1970s.

5.4.1 Business driver

The main business driver was the need for automation to support existing manual processes. These were almost entirely back office processes and many financial services organisations developed their cheque clearing and main accounting systems during this period.

Users interacted with the systems through paper. Data was entered into the computer using punched paper tape, punched cards or Magnetic Ink Character Recognition (MICR). Computers read punched cards and punched paper tape by shining lights through the holes, which were detected using sensors. MICR was magnetised and the computer was able to read the numbers or letters – special shapes were used to make the magnetic ink easier to read.

Printed reports were produced which contained the same information as the manually produced reports they replaced.

5.4.2 Enabling technology

The advance in technology which made this possible was the availability of reliable, affordable mainframe computers. The mainframe computers were stand alone – there were no connections between them and the rest of the business. They were located in special purpose buildings called 'data centres'.

We can show how these operated as follows:

5.4.3 Transaction processing

Transactions were processed in batches. Information was sorted into batches of the same type of form and sent to a data entry section, which would type the information onto punched cards for input into the computer.

5.4.4 Data storage and structure

First generation systems usually stored data as files.

The word 'file' sometimes causes a bit of confusion. Manual filing systems have files which hold all the information we have about a customer and 'Mr Smith's file' will hold a record of all our dealings with Mr Smith over the years.

IT does *not* use the word in this way. A file in IT is more like a card index file, possibly holding customer addresses for a mailing campaign. Within this file, there will be a record card for Mr Smith.

This is how IT uses the words 'file' and 'record'. A file holds similar data – such as all customer addresses or all customer accounts. A record within the file refers to a particular customer or a particular account. So 'Mr Smith's file' in our manual filing system could be a *record* (or a series of records – one for each letter sent or received) in our customer correspondence file on the computer.

Records are made up of pieces of data called 'fields'. A customer record will usually contain fields called Customer Name, Date of Birth, Sex, etc, which are pieces of information about the individual customer.

Each record may have a 'key' field, which allows it to be identified. We usually use numbers such as a customer number or account number. We could use names instead, but these might change (by deed poll or marriage) and it could be difficult to find the record afterwards. There are three types of key.

1. The primary key uniquely identifies a record. For example, the primary key for an Account file will generally be the account number.
2. There may be one or more secondary keys. These can be used to identify a record but are not necessarily unique. For example, a secondary key for an Account file might well be the account holder's surname.
3. There may be one or more foreign keys. A foreign key is a piece of data on one record that is the same as the primary key of another record (which may be in the same file or in a different file). For example, a foreign key on an Account record may well be a currency code. This will be the primary key for the Currency file.

We use foreign keys to define relationships between files. The ability to define such relationships is an important feature of file-based systems and is of critical importance to databases.

5.5   Second generation

The second generation provided the bridge from data processing to IT and was the dominant model from the mid-1970s until the mid-1980s.

5.5.1   Business driver

The main business driver was the need to access information online or in real-time. At the start of the period, online enquiry systems were developed to allow financial services organisations' staff to access the information held in their mainframe systems.

Another business driver was the desire to allow data to be entered into the system locally, rather than being sent to a separate data entry section. This reduced the time before the computer records were updated and made it easier to resolve any errors. The first generation approach to batch processing was increasingly replaced by remote batch, online transaction processing and real-time processing.

This generation saw the use of IT being extended into the front office. This occurred mainly in wholesale applications such as foreign exchange dealing rooms where the benefit of up-to-date information was sufficient to outweigh the costs of the system.

Users interacted with the system using a computer terminal. This is a screen and keyboard with no processing or data storage capability of its own. Unlike the paper interface of the first generation, the terminal is both an input and an output device

69

allowing users to interact directly with the computer for the first time. However, reports continued (and continue to this day) to be one of the most important forms of output.

5.5.2 Enabling technology

The main advance in technology which made this possible was the availability of affordable data communications networks. The network was arranged on a centralised basis with terminals connected to the central mainframe computer, still located in a data centre. Later in the second generation, smaller computers were introduced between the terminals and the mainframe computer either as front end processors to reduce the workload on the mainframe or as data concentrators to allow the telecommunications links to be used more efficiently. Front end processors carried out tasks such as validation, preventing transactions with errors from reaching the mainframe. Data concentrators collected the information from a number of terminals, allowing it to be sent over a single telephone line. A telecommunications device called a 'multiplexor' could be used instead of a data concentrator.

Another important technology was the development of the database, which had a critical role in transforming data into information.

5.5.3 Transaction processing

With batch processing, the master files are not updated until the overnight processing run. This leads to two possible problems.

◆ There is a limited 'processing window' between the point at which the online systems are closed to allow batch processing and the point at which they re-open. As financial services organisations have moved closer to '24x7' (24 hours a day, seven days a week) processing this window has grown shorter.
◆ The information on the master file is out-of-date during the day, as the transactions are not processed until the evening. This creates a significant risk for financial services organisations because of the possibility of fraud or customers going over-limit.

Remote batch processing was an approach to overcoming the processing window limitations. Remote batch allowed data entry to take place during the day and, as the technology evolved, it also allowed the master file updates to take place during the day. However, remote batch does not generally support 24x7 processing.

A number of technologies were used to address the problem of out-of-date information. 'Shadow files' were used in conjunction with remote batch processing, and online and real-time processing were introduced.

A shadow file holds information that needs to be kept up-to-date – for example account balances. The transactions were stored and used as remote batch files to update the mainframe systems overnight.

Online and real-time processing both update the master file when the transaction is entered (this is also called 'demand processing').

The processing of transactions using online transaction processing (OLTP) increased during this period, although batch processing was still important. Hybrid approaches were also common, for example, using OLTP only for a small amount of processing.

One example – an approach that is still used – is to process house cheque encashments online while other cheques are processed in batch or remote batch. The additional cost of online processing could be justified for house cheque encashments as these carry more risk, because they involve paying out money immediately and the bank does not have the normal paying banker protection.

5.5.4   Data storage and structure

Second generation systems needed online access, perhaps to more than one file at a time. Therefore they needed to be able to link a record in one file to the corresponding record in another file, without the need to sort the files. Second generation systems used databases to achieve this.

Hierarchical databases

The hierarchical database was the earliest type of database. We can think of an hierarchical database as storing data as a 'tree' structure:

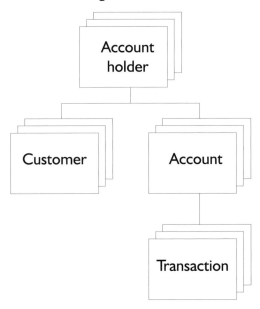

Data stored in hierarchical databases can only be accessed by going up and down the tree. In the example given, we can only find out which accounts the customer holds by going through the account holder. It is very inefficient to access data that is not held on the same 'branch' of the tree.

Hierarchical databases are very efficient provided that the way the data is needed conforms to the tree structure and they are still used for applications that need to process large amounts of data rapidly. Their great disadvantage is that they are inflexible – they have to be designed specifically for the application for which they will be used.

5.6   Third generation

The third generation completed the transition to IT and was the dominant model from the mid-1980s until the mid-1990s.

5.6.1   Business driver

The main business driver was the requirement to allow staff to work on more than one task at a time. The processes automated in the first and second generations were labour intensive, with different people required for each different task. Third generation technology allowed processes to be 're-engineered' so they could be carried out by a single individual.

Users interacted with the system using a workstation capable of displaying multiple windows.

5.6.2   Enabling technology

The advance in technology which made this possible was the availability of workstations capable of storing data and carrying out processing without reference to the central mainframe computer. The network was distributed – data and processing was shared between the workstations, the server and the central mainframe computer. Workstations could also be used independently of the mainframe computer, as a local area network or as stand alone personal computers.

This resulted in networks as follows:

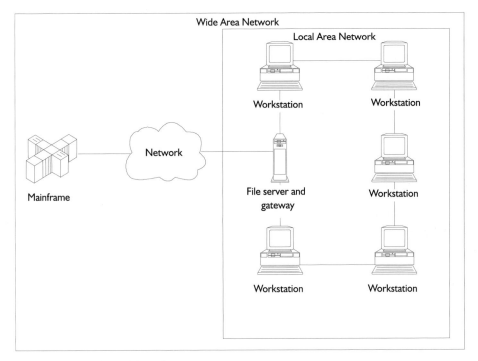

Windows and multitasking

A computer with a single processor, for example a PC, can only carry out one task at a time. PCs are able to use 'multitasking' to carry out several tasks apparently simultaneously.

The operating system schedules work such that only one task is using the processor at any one time. Other tasks in the computer may be suspended or they may be using an input, output or storage device. As the processor can only carry out one process at a time it needs to switch between these tasks to achieve this.

The terms 'multiprogramming' and 'multiprocessing' are also often used. Multiprogramming means that the computer can run more than one program apparently at the same time. It is very similar to multitasking. Multiprocessing means that the computer has more than one processor and can run more than one task at the same time – it can run one task for each processor. Minicomputers and mainframes usually have a number of processors, each of which is capable of multitasking. Most microcomputers now have a second processor for mathematical calculations known as a 'maths co-processor'.

Windows were developed by Xerox at their Palo Alto Research Centre and were first commercially used by Apple in their Lisa and Macintosh computers. Windows are one of the four main components of a Graphical User Interface (GUI).

◆ *Windows*. A window is an area of the computer screen. A GUI can have several windows on the screen at the same time, each of which may contain information about a different computer program. We can copy information between windows – for example, copying a table from a spreadsheet into a word processor.

Windows were particularly important to the third generation as they allowed one person to use a workstation to carry out a number of tasks simultaneously. This was not practical with terminals, where the operator would have needed to log off from one system and log on to a different one, which would greatly increase the time needed to carry out the transaction.

◆ *Icons*. An icon is a picture that represents a computer program or some data. We can use the mouse to start the computer program from the icon (by moving the cursor to point at the program icon and clicking twice), or to move or copy the data (by moving the cursor to point at the icon, holding the mouse button down and 'dragging' the icon to where we want it).

◆ *Mouse*. We can move the mouse until the cursor is pointing to the right place on the screen. We can then press (or 'click') one of the buttons on the mouse to tell the computer to carry out an action. We have discussed the use of the mouse to start programs and to move or copy data, but it can be used for a number of other reasons including:

– to press a button on the screen instructing the computer to carry out an action;
– to choose items from a list offered by the computer; and
– to position the cursor on an input form so the user can enter data.

◆ *Pull-down menus*. GUIs have a 'menu bar' – a list of options – which is usually across the top of the computer screen. If we use the mouse to point at one of the options and click the left mouse button, a more detailed list of options will appear below the option chosen. This is a pull-down menu. We can use the mouse to select the option required.

GUIs are also sometimes called WIMPs after the initial letters of these four components.

5.6.3 Transaction processing

The technology introduced during the third generation did not greatly change the approach to transaction processing. Intelligent workstations allowed processing to be shared between the central computer and the workstation, an approach called 'client/server'.

This allowed an updated form of remote batch processing, with transactions entered and validated at the workstation before being sent to the mainframe for final validation and updating. However, a mix of online and real-time transaction processing remained the dominant approach.

5.6.4   Data storage and structure

Second generation databases were very limited. The introduction of network and relational databases during the third generation was an attempt to overcome the problems associated with hierarchical databases.

Network databases

Network databases stored data as files. Relationships could be created between any two files, without the need for a hierarchy. In a network database, the relationship is defined by adding to the records on one file a pointer to the related records on the other file. The pointer is, in effect, the address of the related records. Pointers could be one-way or two-way.

Relational databases

A relational database holds data in tables, rather like a spreadsheet. To set up a relationship between two tables, we put a common item of data in both tables. Let us consider an example.

Customer Table

Customer No.	Customer Name	Date of Birth	Sex	Occupation
111111	Ann Barrow	12-Mar-45	Female	Manager
222222	Colin Davies	03-Apr-56	Male	Accountant

Account Table

Account No.	Customer No.	Account Type	Currency	Balance
12345678	222222	Current	Sterling	376-00
23456789	111111	Deposit	US Dollar	5,000-00
34567890	222222	Deposit	Sterling	528-00

Here we have two tables. There is a common item of data (Customer No) in both tables and this defines the relationship between them. Ann Barrow has Customer No 111111 and this can be used to find her record on the Customer Table and the record of all her accounts on the Account Table.

In a relational database, holding this common item of data creates the relationship. This makes it much easier to create relationships between rows in different tables (in relational databases, records are called 'rows' and files are called 'tables').

Customer No. is the *primary* key for the Customer Table and is unique – only one record in the table can have a particular value of Customer No.

Customer No. is the *foreign* key for the Account Table. It is not unique but provides a way of getting from the account details to the customer details. Account No. is the primary key for the Account Table.

Relational databases are much more flexible than network databases. In a network database, a relationship needs to be specifically defined through the creation of a pointer. The pointer is an address which must be changed as the database changes. In a relational database, the relationship exists because there is common data. There is no need to define it explicitly or to keep the address up-to-date.

The data in a relational database must be normalised. This is a process that ensures that all data (except for keys) is held in only one place. Problems that may be encountered if data is not normalised include the following.

◆ *Poor data integrity*. For example, if the customer address is held more than once, there is a risk that an update may not be applied to all of them. The data will be inconsistent and confidential information may be sent to an old address.
◆ *Loss of data*. For example, if information about currencies is held with the accounts, rather than as a separate currency table, this information may be lost when the last account denominated in that currency is deleted.
◆ *Items must be stored and updated in more than one place*, which requires more storage and leads to higher processing costs.

Relational databases allowed much more information to be held and, for the first time, it became feasible to store data other than text and numbers. An early example was the Model 204 database, which was used by the US Navy to store naval charts. Relational databases increasingly became capable of holding multimedia data such as pictures and drawings.

5.7   Fourth generation

The fourth generation is the bridge from IT to knowledge management and is the dominant model from the mid-1990s.

5.7.1   Business driver

The main business driver is the growth in electronic commerce or 'e-commerce'. This is the use of electronic channels (such as the Internet) for ordering and delivering services. Another factor is the continuing fall in telecommunications costs which has undermined the cost justification for the client server approach.

5.7.2   Enabling technology

The most important enabling technology was the development of the Internet. This is of sufficient importance to be discussed below as a separate section. Another enabling technology was object orientation.

Object orientation

Most approaches to IT kept data and processes separate. For example, the data was held in files or as a database and the processes were incorporated in computer programs which used the data.

Object orientation is a different approach, in which data is associated with the processes that can use it. These are called 'methods' and a method must be defined for every process that is allowed for the data. Programs cannot access the data directly, but must call the appropriate methods using a 'message'. This has the advantage of protecting the integrity of the data – programs can only use the methods for which they are authorised.

Associating data with processes in this way is called 'encapsulation' or 'wrapping'.

The biggest impact of object orientation has been on PCs through Object Linking and Embedding (OLE). OLE provides a way of linking a document created in one PC application with a document created in a completely different application, in such a way that the first document can be read and changed through the second document.

For example, if we regard a word processor document as the 'data', then the word processing capabilities are the 'methods'. The encapsulated document can be linked to or embedded in another type of document – for example, a spreadsheet. This allows us to read and change the word processor document through the spreadsheet.

OLE embeds a *copy* of the document, so changes would be applied to the copy and not to the original. Another approach, called 'dynamic data exchange', allows a link to be established to the original document so any changes would affect that as well.

Object orientation has also been seen as a way of improving the development of computer systems by 'reusing' proved components. Because objects link data and processes, they are seen as easier to reuse than either data or processes on their own.

This allows financial services organisations to build up 'libraries' of objects that they can combine when they want to develop a new computer system. A technical architecture called the 'Common Object Request Broker Architecture' (CORBA) allows the objects to be linked together. Objects can be developed by other organisations and, provided they comply with the CORBA architecture, linked to objects in the organisation's own library or objects developed by other organisations. This is called 'componentware'.

Although CORBA, object libraries and componentware offer very large potential savings to financial services organisations, their use has been somewhat limited. The financial services organisations have very large investments in their existing systems, which do not comply with CORBA, and this limits their ability to use componentware.

5.7.3   Transaction processing

Fourth generation technology has not fundamentally changed the approach to transaction processing, where online transaction processing continues to dominate.

The major change has been the growth in 'customer self-service' or 'outsourcing to the customer', with customers entering information into the computer themselves over the Internet. Customers are not trained to use the system and this has placed an emphasis on designing simple and easily understood transactions.

This has encouraged financial services organisations to develop straight through processing. This allows the processing of information with no requirement for manual intervention by staff, unless a problem is detected.

5.7.4   Data storage and structure

The relational database continues to be the dominant form of data storage.

Object databases are also found. These are hierarchical in structure. Important characteristics of object databases are:

◆ *classification*. Objects are categorised into classes and super-classes to create the hierarchy;
◆ *inheritance*. Objects inherit the methods of the objects above them in the hierarchy – objects inherit the methods of their class and classes inherit the methods of their super-classes;
◆ *polymorphism*. Although objects inherit the same methods, they are able to interpret incoming messages in different ways.

Fourth generation data storage systems are able to hold a wide range of different types of unstructured data. The fourth generation draws on the technology of the Internet and the web, which is designed to hold multimedia data. In addition to pictures and drawings, other forms of multimedia such as video, animation and sound can be held.

Another difference between the third and fourth generations is the ability of the latter to understand multimedia data. Relational databases typically held this data as objects – binary large objects or 'blobs'. The relational database management system could store multimedia data, but it would have to be interpreted by a different computer program. Fourth generation technology such as Internet browsers can use 'plug ins' to both access and interpret multimedia data.

5.8   The Internet

The Internet is characteristic of the fourth generation as well as being the most important development in IT of the last decade. What is the Internet and why is it so important?

The Internet is the name given to a world-wide network of computer networks. The term 'Internet' refers to the physical computers – the hardware – and the telecommunications links. In order to use the Internet, we need to access the software, of which the best known is the 'World Wide Web' ('www' or the 'web'), which allows the Internet to carry text, pictures, audio and video.

The term 'Information Super Highway' is often used and refers to the process of integrating computer networks into a world-wide network which makes best use of technology such as fibre optic data-communications links. The German term 'Infobahn' is sometimes also used. The Internet is the position which has currently been reached in this process.

5.8.1   History and evolution

The Internet's history is closely tied up with the USA's military requirements. In 1969, the US Department of Defence's Advanced Research Projects Agency (ARPA) constructed a research network called 'ARPAnet', which linked together military and university staff to facilitate the quick and easy exchange of government information via electronic means. One important feature of ARPAnet was that it was designed to withstand possible destruction, for example, from a fire, bomb or nuclear attack, and could easily send information from A to B, bypassing the damaged or destroyed section of the network. That is, it was a distributed, non-centralised and robust communication medium. ARPAnet was also designed to be as flexible as possible to cater for the wide variety of computers and equipment that would be plugged into the network.

The following were the main features of both ARPANET and the Internet.

   ◆ It did not need a central controlling computer. The Internet is an example of a peer-to-peer network in which computers send messages addressed directly to each other without going through a central computer. One reason for this was to allow the network to function even in the event of a nuclear attack – the network did not contain a 'single point of failure' the destruction of which would close down the entire network.

◆ It sent information over the telecommunications network using packet switching, developed in the UK. Packet switching allows much more information to be sent over a telecommunications network than other methods.

◆ It allowed computers to instruct other computers in the network to carry out actions. This is called 'interoperability' and was developed at Bell Laboratories in the US. This was the ancestor of client/server and computers attached to the Internet are able to request services that they would be unable to carry out themselves.

ARPAnet grew in size over the years to accommodate the ever-increasing number of institutions that had adopted the technology. One key player here was the US government's National Science Foundation (NSF) that had built several supercomputers for use within selected US universities.

The military decided to pull out of the project because the network had become too popular and created its own network (Milnet) for its exclusive use. NSF then maintained and developed the non-military or citizen's side of ARPAnet, now referred to as NSFnet. Other partners and companies were soon involved in developing NSFnet. It was eventually decided that the NSFnet should be available to any university, company or organisation wishing to use it and should not just be available to the elite.

This de-centralised the NSFnet forever and, by the late 1980s, the NSFnet had become the Internet (an abbreviation for 'Internetworking'). It took the introduction and development of the World Wide Web in the early 1990s for more companies, individuals, countries, institutions and organisations to get themselves connected to the Internet. The web provided a distributed network of information and resources, accessible via mouse clickable 'hyperlinks' contained in web documents. This easy way of linking together associated information resources proved to be a major breakthrough in raising the profile, facilities and benefits of the Internet.

The involvement of research organisations such as NASA greatly expanded the amount of information available through the Internet. The US government, in particular, played an important role in encouraging the use of the Internet by subsidising telecommunications costs.

The World Wide Web was developed in 1990 by Tim Berners-Lee at the European nuclear research agency CERN in Switzerland. Scientists had the problem of cross-referencing large amounts of information, which could include diagrams and photographs, as well as text. He created a browser that would enable his colleagues to access up-to-date academic information on his research held on his own computer – eliminating the need to constantly distribute printed material. From these early beginnings, the WWW has probably been the main service that has generated today's huge interest in the Internet.

The WWW allows individuals, organisations, and companies to publish all manner of information on the Internet in the form of a website. The contents of this website are linked together by a serious of so-called 'hyperlinks', which can be text or graphics. Clicking on such a hyperlink displays new information, which again can be text, graphics, sound, video, etc. The effect of these links is to create a web of information and resources on a site – hence the name. These links do not have to point to information within the same website – the WWW is a distributed information resource, so these links can point to other web sites located anywhere in the world, thus forming the web structure of this Internet service.

More and more companies and organisations are getting a web presence. Early websites merely included the company's product brochure, background information, a contact address and generally little else. However, with the accelerated adoption of this Internet service, websites are becoming increasingly more sophisticated and offer access to complex information sources such as online databases, multimedia information, Internet telephony facilities, etc.

In recent years, commercial information providers have become increasingly involved in offering services on the Internet. This may result in a greater proportion of Internet services being charged for – a move away from the principle of free access – but perhaps the most important aspect of website adoption and development is that companies are realising the potential of their website as a central means of conducting business (e-commerce). The Internet can provide a powerful method for presenting products, services and company profile to a global audience.

5.8.2   Accessing the Internet

Internet service providers

Although it is possible to access the WWW directly, most subscribers register with an Internet service provider (ISP). ISPs can offer dial-up or broadband access.

Dial-up access is through the normal, analogue telephone system and can be metered or unmetered. Subscribers install a dialler on their PCs, which includes the telephone number (also known as a 'point of presence') for the ISP. If access is metered, the subscriber will incur telephone call charges and ISPs usually offer at least one local number and are increasingly offering connection through a single 0345 (local rate) number. If access is unmetered, a free (0800) number is used. Unmetered access usually has restrictions, for example, a limit on the number of hours or restrictions limiting the subscriber to unmetered access at evenings or weekends.

Broadband access is increasingly common and is rapidly catching up with dial-up access. Ofcom figures show that the percentage of UK adults connecting to the Internet using dial-up fell from 79% to 67% between February 2003 and February 2004, whereas the percentage connecting using broadband rose from 16% to 25% over the same period.

The most common form of broadband access in the UK uses asynchronous digital subscriber line (ADSL) technology, which offers very high connection speeds. Next in importance is cable, which uses optical fibre cables and offers television, telephone and Internet access over the same connection. Wireless access is of increasing importance. Older broadband technologies such as Integrated Services Digital Network (ISDN) are still found, mainly among business users. Many broadband technologies have the advantage that the subscriber is permanently connected to the Internet. Broadband access may have usage restrictions, which are usually based on the amount of information that is downloaded from the Internet each month.

Subscribers need a modem to connect to the Internet. A modem, or modulator/demodulator, converts the analogue signals used by the telephone system to the digital signals used by computers and vice versa. A modem is needed for all Internet connections, including those to digital telephone technologies such as ADSL or ISDN.

Home networks, almost unknown a few years ago, are increasingly common. These can be wireless, wired (which are scaled down versions of the local area networks used by organisations) or can use power line networking. Whichever technology is used, there is a single, central connection to the Internet and this is shared between Internet devices (PCs, games consoles, etc) distributed around the home.

Wireless

Wireless is a term used to describe telecommunications in which electromagnetic waves (rather than some form of wire) carry the signal over part or all of the communication path. Some monitoring devices, such as intrusion alarms, employ acoustic waves at frequencies above the range of human hearing; these are also sometimes classified as wireless.

The first wireless transmitters went on the air in the early 20th century using radiotelegraphy (Morse code). Later, as modulation made it possible to transmit voices and music via wireless, the medium came to be called 'radio'. With the advent of television, fax, data communication and the effective use of a larger portion of the spectrum, the term 'wireless' has been resurrected.

Common examples of wireless equipment in use today include the following.

- *Cellular phones and pagers* – provide connectivity for portable and mobile applications, both personal and business.
- *Global Positioning System (GPS)* – allows drivers of cars and lorries, captains of boats and ships and pilots of aircraft to ascertain their location anywhere on earth.
- *Cordless computer peripherals* – the cordless mouse is a common example; keyboards and printers can also be linked to a computer via wireless.
- *Cordless telephone sets* – these are limited-range devices, not to be confused with mobile phones.
- *Wireless LANs or local area networks* – provide flexibility and reliability for business computer users

Wireless technology is rapidly evolving, and is playing an increasing role in the lives of people throughout the world. In addition, ever-larger numbers of people are relying on the technology directly or indirectly. (It has been suggested that wireless is overused in some situations, creating a social nuisance.) More specialised wireless communications and control include the following.

◆ *Global System for Mobile Communication (GSM)* – a digital mobile telephone system used in Europe and other parts of the world; the de facto wireless telephone standard in Europe.

◆ *General Packet Radio Service (GPRS)* – a packet-based wireless communication service that provides continuous connection to the Internet for mobile phone and computer users.

◆ *Enhanced Data GSM Environment (EDGE)* – a faster version of the Global System for Mobile (GSM) wireless service.

◆ *Universal Mobile Telecommunications System (UMTS)* – a broadband, packet-based system offering a consistent set of services to mobile computer and phone users no matter where they are located in the world.

◆ *Wireless Application Protocol (WAP)* – a set of communication protocols to standardise the way that wireless devices, such as mobile telephones and radio transceivers, can be used for Internet access.

◆ *i-Mode* – the world's first 'smart phone' for Web browsing, first introduced in Japan; provides color and video over telephone sets.

Wireless can be divided into the following.

◆ *Fixed wireless* – the operation of wireless devices or systems in homes and offices and, in particular, equipment connected to the Internet via specialised modems (see Wi-Fi).

◆ *Mobile wireless* – the use of wireless devices or systems aboard motorised, moving vehicles; examples include the car phone and PCS (personal communications services).

◆ *Portable wireless* – the operation of autonomous, battery-powered wireless devices or systems outside the office, home or vehicle; examples include handheld phones and PCS units.

◆ *IR wireless* – the use of devices that convey data via IR (infrared) radiation; employed in certain limited-range communications and control systems.

Wi-Fi

Wi-Fi (short for 'wireless fidelity') is a term for certain types of wireless local area network (WLAN) that use specifications in the 802.11 family. The term 'Wi-Fi' was created by an organisation called the Wi-Fi Alliance, which oversees tests that certify product interoperability. A product that passes the alliance tests is given the label 'Wi-Fi certified' (a registered trademark).

Originally, Wi-Fi certification was applicable only to products using the 802.11b standard. Today, Wi-Fi can apply to products that use any 802.11 standard. The

802.11 specifications are part of an evolving set of wireless network standards known as the '802.11 family'. The particular specification under which a Wi-Fi network operates is called the 'flavour' of the network. Wi-Fi has gained acceptance in many businesses, agencies, schools and homes as an alternative to a wired LAN. Many airports, hotels and fast-food facilities offer public access to Wi-Fi networks. These locations are known as 'hot spots'. Many charge a daily or hourly rate for access, but some are free. An interconnected area of hot spots and network access points is known as a 'hot zone'.

Unless adequately protected, a Wi-Fi network can be susceptible to access by unauthorised users who use the access as a free Internet connection. The activity of locating and exploiting security-exposed wireless LANs is called 'war driving'. An identifying iconography, called 'war chalking', has evolved. Any entity that has a wireless LAN should use security safeguards such as the Wired Equivalent Privacy (WEP) encryption standard, the more recent Wi-Fi Protected Access (WPA), Internet Protocol Security (IPsec) or a virtual private network (VPN).

Wireless networks are showing the fastest rate of growth. A wireless access point router must be connected to the modem (some routers include a built-in modem). Each Internet device will need a wireless adaptor, which may be built in to the device, plugged into a Universal Serial Bus (USB) port or may be a PC card that fits into a slot on the side of a laptop computer. The main problem with wireless networks is security – anyone setting up a wireless network needs to take security precautions or anyone in the vicinity will be able to use it.

Wired networks also use a router. Computer cables must be run from the router to every location where network access is needed. This is more secure than a wireless network, but it is usually more expensive and it is difficult to move the cables once they have been installed.

Power line technology uses the electrical sockets in the house. This has the advantage that no new wiring is required as every room in the house is likely to have an electricity supply. This technology offers very fast connection speeds. It is not a particularly common approach, however, perhaps because much equipment is designed for the US where a 110-volt electricity supply is used (the UK uses a 220-volt supply).

Internet devices

Most people access the Internet through a PC with a modem. The PC's hard disk stores the web browser and the other software (word processor, spreadsheet, database, etc) that we might want to use. We also copy information from the Internet onto the PC's hard disk.

This has a number of disadvantages. There are a lot of things that can go wrong with a PC. The PC is a complicated and expensive piece of equipment. The software loaded on the PC soon gets out of date and it is expensive and time consuming to upgrade to the latest version. Research by consultants Forrester Research shows the annual support cost of a typical PC is $2,680 on top of the original purchase price in the range $2,000–$3,000.

The alternative is to access the Internet using simpler - and cheaper - devices. These are called 'thin clients' because most of the work is carried out on the Internet servers. So instead of having a word processor installed on a PC, we might access a word processor located on a server through the Internet. We would not have to buy the word processor and we would always be using the latest version. The PC is called a 'thick client' by comparison.

The first serious attempt at a commercial thin client device was the network computer (NC). This had a powerful processor, but no hard disk storage. Annual support costs for the NC would be about $800 on top of the initial purchase price in the range $700–$1,000. A commercial response to this was the Net PC, a low power, low cost PC designed to access the Internet but with a lower total cost of ownership than a fully functional PC. Annual support costs would be $1,480 on top of an initial purchase price in the range $1,200–$2,000.

Neither the NC nor the Net PC were particularly successful, although the NC was used by organisations such as insurer General Accident (now part of CGU) and the Association of British Insurers (ABI) to replace terminal computers.

A new generation of thin client devices has emerged as a result of the convergence of computing with telephony and consumer electronics. Important thin client devices are:

- TV set top boxes. These allow a television set to be used as an Internet access device;
- 'third generation' mobile telephones can be used to access the Internet;
- smart phones. These can work in a number of ways, including using a touch-sensitive screen as a keyboard or having a fold out keyboard;
- games consoles. Internet adaptors can be attached to games consoles to support online gaming and the next generation of games consoles is expected to have Internet connectivity built in;
- Windows-based terminals. These are successors to the Net PC. They include the Java virtual machine, but run under Microsoft's Windows operating system.

The relative advantages and disadvantages of the approaches depend on cost and convenience. For example, the advantages of thick clients include:

- telecommunications costs are lower as the device can be used on a stand alone basis, being connected to the Internet as required;
- similarly, the device can be used if the telephone network is not available or Internet performance is unacceptably slow;
- the user has more control over data which can be stored locally.

The advantages of thin clients include:

♦ the total cost of ownership is lower as a less complicated device with less software is needed;
♦ the latest versions of programs and data are always available.

To date, thin clients have made little progress in the market place. There are a number of reasons for this, including the large number of PCs already in use, customer concerns about the performance of the Internet and the additional facilities available to PC users such as CD-ROMs and DVDs.

It might be expected that thin clients would be successful in the corporate market. The lower cost of ownership is obviously attractive and the inability to store data or programs long term has security benefits – there is no possibility of out-of-date information being stored and there is less likelihood of virus infection. So far, this has not happened with organisations continuing to use fully functional PCs.

Web browsers

Most software is designed to use data of one specific type. For example, a word processor will read and change files either created using that word processor or exported into that word processor format. Browsers can understand a range of different types of data and can be used to look at files of different types. Browsers are becoming increasingly important and much recent software is able to view files in a number of different formats.

Browsers are a very effective way to access data stored on the web. Web browsers use the links provided by HTML both to move between different places on the web (navigation) and to access files of different types (for example, pictures, video and audio) which are then interpreted using the browser technology.

Most people access the Internet through a web browser.

The most important web browser is Microsoft's Internet Explorer, although Netscape Navigator (the first browser marketed) still has a market presence and Firefox is gaining market share. Web browsers also have standard buttons allowing access to common functions such as email and locations such as the ISP's home page and the main search engines.

Push technology

We use browsers to request information, but we can also ask for information to be sent to us. This is called 'push technology' and was originally developed by Pointcast, although it is now a standard feature in browsers.

Push technology allows us to say what information we want and when we want it – usually when telephone charges are low and the Internet relatively quiet. This will be sent to our computer at the specified time.

The effectiveness of push technology depends on its ability to customise the information it delivers to meet the needs of the user. This requires it to categorise and filter.

◆ Categorisation is the ability to look for types of information which may be of interest.
◆ Filtering is the ability to exclude items from the category if they are not of interest.

These features are also found in search engines. They are discussed later under knowledge management.

One problem with push technology is that it can use telecommunications resources – bandwidth – very heavily. Because it requires no effort to get the information, users are less selective about what they ask for. There are technical solutions to this problem ('caching' – moving the data through additional servers to distribute the workload), but these incur additional costs. This may be a factor which explains the limited take up of push technology within organisations despite its obvious potential for distributing information.

Do not confuse push technology with mail enabling, although there are some similarities. Mail enabling allows an email message to be sent in response to an event. Push technologies send data rather than messages and this is sent at a specified time rather than being in response to an event. Email messages are delivered to a server while push technology delivers the data directly to the PC.

Search engines

One of the main problems with the Internet is that it contains so much information. Links between sites provide one way of getting around the Internet, but are of little use for finding anything new.

One approach, which was taken by Yahoo!, is to build an index. Information is classified into about twenty main categories and each category is further broken down into a number of sub-categories. These may be further broken down. Therefore, we should be able to find any piece of information by following it through its categories and sub-categories.

This works well for most routine enquiries, but sometimes there is not a category which matches what we are looking for. Alternatively, it may fall into two or three categories. Although we could use the index to find what we are looking for, we may have to try several different categories, which is time consuming and can be frustrating. Search engines allow a search for a word or words within an item of information. Google is the most popular search engine.

Even using a search engine, there may still be a very large number of items found. Some search engines can group similar items together – they will show one of the items with the option to look at the similar items.

The most popular index and search engine sites now offer additional services such as email. These are called 'portals' to show that they offer a wider range of services. For example, Yahoo! offers services such as a currency calculator and a global weather service.

Intelligent agents

Intelligent agents are a development of search engines. A search engine is passive – we have to ask it a question before it will provide the information we need. It does not tell us when the information changes and we may need to access the search engine again in order to identify any new sites relating to our topic of interest.

Intelligent agents are dynamic. They know the topics in which we are interested they can carry out periodic searches to identify more up-to-date information and even new sites. Intelligent agent technology is still quite new, but it has immense potential to ensure that users of the Internet have access to the latest information.

They can also understand the information. For example, an intelligent agent can be used to identify the lowest price from suppliers of a product. This is used in shopping sites and it is this ability that distinguishes intelligent agents from push technology.

5.9   Open and proprietary systems

We can distinguish between the following systems.

- *Open systems.* These are systems about which sufficient information is published to allow others to use them and to develop complementary products. A licence fee may be payable. Note that a system can be open without everything about it being published. Mondex and VisaCash do not publish information about how their security systems work as this would increase the risk of fraud.
  Open systems allow others to enter the market with complementary products, which increases the acceptance of the system.
- *Proprietary systems.* These are systems about which no information is published and which only the vendor is allowed to develop. Most early IT systems were proprietary.
  Proprietary systems lock customers into the vendor. This protects the vendor's competitive advantage provided that customers are prepared to accept being restricted to a single supplier.
- *Public domain systems.* Public domain systems are a form of open system in which the specification is freely published and can be used with no restrictions and no licence fee. The Internet is an example of a public domain system.
- *Open source software.* This is software for which the source code is publicly and freely available. The Linux operating system, the Firefox browser, the Thunderbird email system and the Open Office office suite are examples of

open source software. These products are available without charge under a General Public Licence, which also allows users to change the software without asking permission.

Open source software is currently gaining market share. It is available without charge and organisations have access to the source code, which allows them to identify any possible security flaws. The main disadvantage is that the level of support may not be the same as that available from commercial vendors selling proprietary or open systems.

Most first and second generation systems were proprietary. IT suppliers provided a 'bundle' including the hardware and the system software. Organisations would develop applications software themselves or buy packages from their IT supplier or one of the supplier's business partners.

This had the effect of restricting customers' choice of supplier. This became increasingly unacceptable to both customers and the authorities, and the US Department of Justice brought anti-trust proceedings against IBM – then the world's largest computer company – to prevent them from bundling computer hardware and software.

Even open systems can be seen as restricting customers' choice. Companies that sell open systems but do not release their source code, are also subject to anti-trust proceedings, as happened to Microsoft.

Most systems are now open and public domain and open source systems are becoming increasingly important.

References

Wang C (1997) *Techno Vision II* McGraw-Hill.

Ofcom www.ofcom.org.uk

Six

Business analysis and change management

6.1   Introduction

Financial services organisations use IT to improve business performance. The approach taken during the first and second generations of IT was the automation of existing business processes. As IT has become more powerful, it has become possible to improve performance further by re-engineering business processes.

An important component of business process re-engineering is the management of change. This is a major topic in its own right and this chapter outlines some of the most important aspects of this.

6.2   Business process automation

During the first and second generations, organisations exploited IT through the automation of existing processes or Business Process Automation (BPA). BPA produces only limited cost savings. Bill Gates makes the point in his book *The Road Ahead* that 'automation entrenches inefficiency'. If a process is inherently inefficient, automation will have the effect of making it more difficult to change. The real savings come when IT is combined with re-engineering the business processes.

6.3   Business process re-engineering

Business process re-engineering (BPR) was the business driver for the third generation and attempts to overcome the limitations of business process automation.

In July 1990, management consultant Michael Hammer wrote an article in the *Harvard Business Review* entitled 'Re-engineering Work: Don't Automate, Obliterate'. This article launched a management philosophy called BPR, which is often portrayed as a panacea to financial organisations' long-standing IT problems of systems taking too long to develop and then being too inflexible to change. The term 're-engineering' is now used widely as a magic solution to business problems promising:

◆ reduced costs;
◆ increased quality;
◆ improved customer satisfaction;
◆ increased profitability.

The original definition of BPR from Hammer and Champy's 1993 book was

'... the fundamental thinking, rethinking and radical redesign of business processes to achieve dramatic improvements in critical contemporary measures of performance, such as cost, quality, service and speed'.

Other definitions extend this to include a focus on customers and the marketplace.

Another feature of BPR is that it looks to make the most effective use of IT. Instead of adapting the existing processes, as in business process automation, BPR ignores the existing processes and considers how the results can be achieved while making the best use of IT.

Some consultancies and texts describe BPR using other terms, for example, Business Process Redesign, Business Process Engineering and Business Process Transformation.

One approach to BPR breaks it down into seven stages.

1. Identify the core business processes.
2. Map and cost these core processes.
3. Conduct detailed analysis of customer requirements to identify what the customer wants.
4. Prioritise the core processes for BPR.
5. Radically redesign the processes by simplifying and rationalising.
6. Manage the change to ensure benefits are achieved.
7. Establish ongoing measurement systems to ensure continuous improvement.

6.3.1 Identify core processes

BPR focuses on the core business processes. These are the processes that are central to the business, as opposed to support or peripheral activities that should perhaps be outsourced.

6.3.2 Process mapping

Process mapping is a technique for describing business processes. A business process describes an entire (also called 'end-to-end' or 'E2E') interaction with a customer or supplier. Mapping this results in a process map, which provides a basis for examining and questioning the process.

The methods we use to describe processes have their origins in the second half of the 19th century. The theorists of the Scientific School of Management identified techniques for describing business processes, which later developed into 'work study' or 'Organisation and Methods' (O&M).

These techniques are mainly concerned with describing flows of information between processes. O&M considers physical flows – for example, the movement of documents in an office or parts on a factory floor. Process mapping is concerned with the physical and logical flows of data within a business process.

The first stage in process mapping is process decomposition – breaking the process down into a logical sequence of sub-processes. Each sub-process will involve some form of value-adding activity and if the sub-processes are taken together they form a 'value chain' showing how the inputs to the process are transformed into the corresponding outputs.

Identifying the processes and their inputs and ouputs, together with the timescales, can be a difficult task. A technique that is often used to map the value chain and understand the whole process is tagging.

In tagging, a form (the tag) is attached to each unit of work entering the process. For example if we wished to process map the account opening process in a branch then a tag form would be attached to the application form. Every person receiving that input form must complete the relevant details on the tag. The time taken in each stage of the process will be logged on the tagging form.

The tag must be simple, to ensure it is accurately completed without significantly impacting the workflow. There may be many products or processes involved in producing the final product – for example, a cheque book and cheque card would have to be ordered for a new account. It is essential to identify and define each of these as products within the process map.

Each tag form should be sequentially numbered to ensure that all are returned, and missing tag forms should be investigated as these may reveal other parts of the process map.

An example of a tagging form is:

Date attached   _____   Serial No   _____

Time attached   _____

Department

Product

Processes   Actions

1. Pre Advice   1. Receive

2. Open Debit   2. File

3. Amend
Debit   3. Print

4. Blank Doc   4. Check

                                        5. Despatch

                                        6. Open

                                        7. Amend

                                        8. Pay

                                        9. Other

Desk Code	Time In	Action Taken	Time Out

Date Detagged   _____

Time
Detagged

For processes where volumes are fairly constant, tagging a process for one day may be all that is needed to produce an accurate process map. If there are large daily, weekly or seasonal variations in the volume of work handled, there may be corresponding wide fluctuations in the time taken or even the steps in the process. For example, during quiet periods, counter staff may answer customers' balance or other account enquiries, but during busy periods such as lunch times, refer customers to a specific enquiries desk. Tagging would need to cover an extended period and the process map would need to cover all of the variations.

Tagging will help identify:

- the steps in the process;
- average overall processing time taken;
- delay between steps in the process;
- process times at each stage;
- incidence of holdover (work processed following day or period);
- the workflow through the process;
- sources of bottlenecks and under-utilised resources.

The result of this analysis is a process map that can then help identify whether the whole process needs radical re-engineering to achieve the customers' requirements or if only parts of the process need to be changed.

These type of questions should be asked at the process mapping stage.

- The purpose of the process. What is being done? Why is it being done? What else could be done? What should be done?
- The place. Where is it being done? Why there? Where else could it be done? Where should it be done?
- The process timing. When is it done? Why then? When else could it be done? When should it be done?
- The person. Who does it? Why that person? Who else might do it? Who should do it?
- The procedures. How is it done? Why that way? How else can it be done? How should it be done?

6.3.3 Customer requirements analysis

The customer is central to BPR. If a process does not add value for the customer, we need to question why it is being carried out at all. The purpose of customer requirements analysis is to establish what the customer needs from the process.

6.3.4 Prioritisation

We need to apply some form of prioritisation to ensure that we concentrate our re-engineering effort where we will get the greatest benefit.

One method is Pareto analysis, also known as the '80:20' rule. Organisations will typically find that about 20% of their processes account for 80% of their costs. Prioritisation will focus effort on the processes which account for the highest proportion of costs.

Another approach would be to focus on processes that are known to be unsatisfactory, perhaps from customer satisfaction measures or work measurement. An alternative is to use gap analysis and focus on the processes where there is the greatest gap between customer requirements and the actual outcomes of the process.

6.3.5   Redesign

Redesign involves simplifying and standardising the processes, together with the creative use of IT.

Most processes have become more complicated than they need to. There are a number of reasons for this – the complications may be a result of the physical layout of the office or the process may have needed to provide reporting information that is no longer required. Any step in the process that does not directly contribute to meeting customer requirements should be challenged.

Processes also often have a range of exceptions. This makes them excessively complicated. The choice is usually between removing the exceptions and splitting the complex process into two or more simple processes – one for the main process, with the others dealing with the exceptions.

Most processes were originally developed as manual processes, with automation being introduced at a later stage. Therefore, they contain steps relating to the physical movement of documents and restrictions such as two people being unable to work on a document at the same time. IT can be used to avoid these steps and restrictions and to produce a faster and simpler process.

6.3.6   Management of change

Management of change is considered later in this chapter.

6.3.7   Work measurement and continuous improvement

There is a general axiom to the effect 'we cannot improve what we cannot measure' and the measurement of results is essential to provide a basis for process improvement.

We discuss continuous improvement later in this chapter under Total Quality Management.

6.3.8   Examples

TSB Mortgage Process

One example of the benefits of BPR is the mortgage process formerly used by the TSB (now Lloyds TSB).

The process mapping within TSB revealed that the average turnaround time from mortgage application to formal offer was 30 days, with less than one third achieved within 20 days. It took an average of four to five interviews with the customer to achieve completion, and there were five forms covering 167 questions, of which only 24 were unique. For example, the customer's account number was required no fewer than seven times! There were two different processes with loans that were managed centrally and some that were managed within the branch. Four different computer systems were involved and five different functional areas.

Customer research identified the customer needs as:

◆ fast decision;
◆ to be kept informed as the application proceeds;
◆ simple application;
◆ good advice on appropriate repayments and insurance.

Clearly, the existing process was not only very inefficient, but it failed to meet the customers' basic requirements.

Having built the process map, TSB then looked at how their mortgage system could be radically changed using BPR. The redesigned process reduced the cost of processing by 25% and cut the time from application to formal offer to less than seven days. The customer was only required to complete one simplified form and was given a single contact point within the branch. This also enabled the computer systems to be rationalised.

District service centres

Another example is the re-engineering of the branch back office. Traditionally branches processed most of the work generated by their customers within the branch. This required the bulk of the space in the branch to be dedicated to this processing work leaving limited space for the customer and branch sales staff.

BPR was used to think radically about how back office processing could either be undertaken outside of the branch at regional processing centres or automated completely.

In 1988, all cheque processing for Midland Bank (now HSBC) was undertaken within the branches with each branch submitting its cheques to the bank's clearing house each day. This involved the sorting of cheques, their encoding and daily balancing of the work. Because the work was being undertaken in almost 2,000 different branches, the quality varied enormously and each branch had to have sophisticated machines to read, sort and encode the cheques with magnetic ink. The volumes of cheques varied dramatically from branch to branch and there were many different ways that branches organised their staff to achieve the work.

Customers required that their cheques were accurately processed and at a low cost. The existing process met neither of these requirements and so Midland used BPR radically to re-engineer the process. The result was to establish eight district processing centres to which all of the cheques and credits were delivered unprocessed. These centres would then use the latest very high-speed encoders and reader sorters to process the work using production line techniques taken from industry. The result was dramatically to reduce the cost of processing whilst reducing error levels from over 100 in a million to single figures. Space and time was freed up in branches and Midland achieved a competitive advantage in both processing costs and quality that it could use to obtain bulk cheque processing work from major retailers.

6.4   Quality and total quality management

The concept of 'quality' is poorly understood. It may help to start with four definitions.

- ◆ Quality is 'fitness for purpose' – how good something is at doing the job for which it is intended. If you want a family runabout, you buy a Ford Mondeo in preference to a Rolls Royce. For this particular purpose, the Ford Mondeo is the 'quality' car.
- ◆ Quality assurance (QA) is concerned with ensuring that all the checks in a defined process have been completed. The Systems Development Lifecycle, for example, usually has checks at the end of each stage and QA ensures that these have been carried out.
- ◆ Quality control (QC) is concerned that the tasks in the process are carried out to standard. This is measured by the checks built into the process.
- ◆ Total Quality Management (TQM) brings together QA and QC into an approach for managing quality throughout a process or an organisation.

QA can be validated externally and quality standards such as BS5750 and ISO9000 are QA standards.

6.4.1   Total quality management

We defined quality as 'fitness for purpose'. Alternative definitions include.

- ◆ Conformance to the customer's requirements through setting and monitoring standards and ensuring value for money by avoiding extra checking, reworking and servicing.

◆ Giving the customer what they want, when and where they want it, at the right price, without mistakes.

Many companies measure service levels and define acceptable levels of service. A company may, for example, consider that an error rate of 1% is acceptable. On the face of it a 99% success rate may be considered reasonable, but would you fly with an airline that considered this failure rate acceptable?

TQM is a philosophy where the objective is to conform fully, without error, to the customer's requirements. It is focused on the requirements of the customer. A satisfied customer will return, an unhappy or dissatisfied customer will not.

TQM originated in Japan after the Second World War. American Dr W Edwards Deming, working with the US Army in Japan, convinced Japanese industrialists that the production of reliable goods at lower prices was the way to take on, and to beat, the Western manufacturers. Deming was a statistician and his approach to quality control was based on his experience of consumer research and analysis. Instead of designing a product and then trying to stimulate a demand for that product, his approach was based first of all on the identification of the needs of the consumer and then developing and manufacturing products to meet those needs, to the required standards, at the lowest prices.

Financial services is about long-term customer value. Customers are encouraged to stay with a bank for their entire life and therefore repeat business is critical to the success of a financial services organisation.

Research has shown that financial services organisations are not always very good at maintaining customers in the long-term, for example, an analysis of why customers close their accounts shows:

◆ 40% because of poor service;
◆ 13% because of unhelpful staff;
◆ 11% consider banks impersonal.

It costs six times as much to acquire a new account as to retain an existing account.

Another influential thinker on TQM, Dr Joseph Juran, regarded the commitment of management to quality as the first and most important factor in successfully achieving a TQM programme. In his book, *Planning for Quality* (Free Press 1988) Juran defines an approach in three stages:

◆ quality planning;
◆ quality control;
◆ quality improvement.

Juran explained this approach in his 'quality planning roadmap' with its key elements.

◆ Who are the customers?
◆ What are their needs?

99

◆ How are those needs best described?
◆ Develop a product that meets those needs.
◆ Design the product to meet our needs as well as the needs of our customers.
◆ Develop the means to make the product.
◆ Design the most favourable method of making the product.
◆ Prove that the method can produce the product successfully under actual operating conditions.
◆ Transfer the process to operations.

6.5 Management of change

Managing change is a complex subject deserving of a book of its own. In addition to the disciplines of change management, there are a number of related disciplines relating to the management of expectations, benefits, issues, problems and changes.

6.5.1 Managing change

Managing change is concerned with organisational change. When people are subjected to change they go through a transition curve.

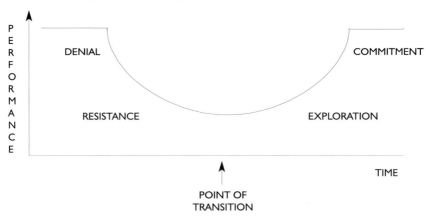

The stages are as follows.
◆ *Denial*. The first stage is a denial that the change will happen or that the change will affect the individual.
◆ *Resistance*. The second stage is resistance to the change which often takes the form of non-co-operation with those implementing the change.
◆ *Exploration*. The third stage is an acceptance that the change is going to happen and exploration of its possible consequences for the individual.
◆ *Commitment*. The fourth stage is the individual's commitment to the change.

The objective of managing change is to ensure that fastest possible progression through the stages to commitment.

Two important models of change are:

◆ *The force field model*. This looks at change as a balance of driving forces and restraining forces. Change will only occur if the driving forces are stronger than the restraining forces. This can be achieved by strengthening the driving forces or weakening the restraining forces.

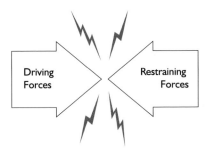

◆ *The unfreeze–change–refreeze model*. This looks at the process of change. The first stage is to 'unfreeze' the current situation. This includes making people aware that change is inevitable. The second stage is to make the change. The third stage is to 'refreeze' the situation into the new pattern. This includes reinforcing the change and making sure that people do not revert to their old pattern of behaviour.

In the context of information management, the key processes are as follows.

◆ *Communication*. The project team should communicate with all stakeholders throughout the process.
  Communication is essential to manage expectations. If this does not take place, stakeholders will be influenced by the grapevine and 'fear, uncertainty and doubt'. Communication helps to weaken the restraining forces and is important both in unfreezing the current situation and refreezing the changed situation.
◆ *Consultation*. As far as is possible, all affected stakeholders should be consulted and involved in the process. Some groups, such as the unions, may need a formal communication structure.
  Consultation gives a sense of ownership of the change. Those consulted may also be able to identify possible problems with the change and suggest improvements. Consultation helps to weaken the restraining forces and can improve the quality of the change.
◆ *Training*. Those expected to work with the system will need to be trained in its use.
  We discuss the benefits of training in Chapter Seventeen. Training is critical to the refreezing process.

◆ *Support.* Those affected by the change need both technical and personal support. Technical support usually takes the form of helplines. Personal support may be provided through counselling and assistance, especially to those whose jobs will be adversely affected by the change. Even where people are not directly affected, they may still need support – 'survivor syndrome' is a bereavement reaction found in organisations where large numbers of staff have been made redundant. Support is important to the refreezing process.

◆ *Continuous improvement.* Major changes are rarely perfect when they are first implemented and a programme of continuous improvement is of benefit in eliminating any problems. It has the further benefit of transferring ownership of the new system to those who are using it.

Continuous improvement is part of the refreezing process. It is likely to produce further changes to the system to support or implement the changes made and weakens the restraining forces for these subsequent changes. The idea of continuous improvement is strongly associated with the TQM ideas of W Edwards Deming.

6.5.2   Managing expectations and benefits

Managing expectations

One reason why project sponsors are often disappointed by the results of systems development is a failure to manage expectations. Business cases may present an optimistic assessment that may not be realised in practice.

Stakeholders may also develop unrealistic expectations. The development process involves finding out what the business wants. This may create the expectation that all the requirements identified will be satisfied.

Those involved in systems development must set realistic expectations and manage these actively. This includes:

◆ a clear distinction between the 'vision' of what is expected in the long term and what will be delivered initially;

◆ a focus on the 'must have' requirements rather than those that are less important;

◆ open acknowledgement that not everything that is requested will be delivered;

◆ a means of 'parking' requirements that are identified as important but which fall outside the scope of the development.

Managing benefits

Managing benefits is an increasingly important part of systems development. Benefits management involves:

- identify anticipated benefits as part of the initial business case;
- identify how to measure whether the benefits have been achieved and allocate responsibility for realising each benefit to the relevant senior manager in the business;
- ensure that the information required to assess the achievement of the benefits is collected and monitor progress towards it;
- assess whether the benefits have been achieved as part of the post implementation review.

Many organisations still make little systematic attempt to assess whether the benefits anticipated are realised in practice. Note that measures such as number of staff employed are not good for benefits measurement as they are affected by other factors such as changes in business volumes.

6.5.3 Managing issues, problems and changes

Issue, problem and change management are of particular importance during development projects.

Issue management

An issue is anything that arises during the project that needs to be resolved before project completion. Issues may include items such as:

- possible new legislation which could have an impact on the project;
- changes to the organisation's strategy which could change the project's priority;
- competitor activity to which the project may need to respond.

The distinctive feature of issues is that they cannot be resolved by the project team or the sponsor alone. They will usually require a decision from the executive management and may require outside opinion, for example, from the Inland Revenue, regulatory bodies or legal opinion from counsel.

The issue management process is as follows.

- Record the issue on an issues log.
- Identify the impact of the issue and the date by which it must be resolved.
- Identify the appropriate escalation route and allocate responsibility for resolution.
- If necessary, seek the sponsor's approval for any budget required (for exampe, for external legal opinion).
- Escalate the issue.
- Monitor the issue resolution process and, if necessary, follow the issue up to ensure that it is resolved in time.

Problem management

Problem management starts with a problem report (also known as 'fault report') being raised and allows users to report perceived problems for resolution. The user will also indicate the priority allocated to its correction. The stages in the problem management process are as follows.

- ◆ Record the problem and allocate responsibility for dealing with it.
- ◆ Check that it is a problem. Problem reports are sometimes raised because the user is not fully trained in the use of the system or has not consulted the system documentation.
- ◆ Analyse the causes of the problem and identify what changes need to be made to rectify it.
- ◆ Progress the changes through the relevant stages of the change control process.
- ◆ When the problem has been rectified, mark the problem report as closed.

Change management

Changes can arise as a result of the following.

- ◆ *Changing business requirements.* Major changes to market activity will affect the system and competitive activity or customer pressure may well change the functional requirements.
- ◆ *The issue management process.* Resolution of issues may change the scope of the project.
- ◆ *Problems encountered during the development process.* A common example of this is where a system component from an external vendor does not work in the way expected. The system may need to be changed to use a different component or to perform additional tasks to remedy deficiencies in the component. More rarely, the component may have capabilities beyond those anticipated allowing it to perform tasks that the system would otherwise have to perform.
- ◆ *Changing technology.* Changing technology during a project is not usually recommended, but it may be necessary. One example is where the intended technology is becoming obsolete. The project team may have to choose between changing technology and proceeding in the knowledge that competitors will be able to leapfrog them by using the new technology.

Change can also arise after the system has been implemented as a result of either changes in business requirements or problems with the system.

The change management process starts when a change request is raised. These are the stages.

- ◆ Record the change request.
- ◆ Link the change request to any corresponding issue or problem record.
- ◆ Analyse the impact of the requested change.

- Review the change. This is usually carried out by a Change Control Board of senior managers who will decide whether the change will go ahead and allocate a priority to it. Small changes can sometimes be approved under a small changes budget without approval by the Change Control Board.
- Schedule the change.
- Small changes will often be bundled together into a software 'release' to avoid staff being subject to constant minor system changes. Large changes, such as the implementation of a new system, will usually form a release on their own.

References

Hammer M and Champy J (1993) *Re-engineering the Corporation* Nicholas Brealey.

Juran J (1988) *Planning for Quality* Free Press.

Seven

Projects and project management

7.1 Introduction

We usually talk of activities such as developing a computer system as a 'project'. Definitions of a project include:

- a group of connected activities with a defined starting point, a defined finish and a need for a central intelligence to direct it, carried out in order to achieve a business objective; and
- a discrete undertaking with defined objectives often including time, cost and quality (performance) goals. All projects evolve through a similar 'lifecycle' sequence during which there should be recognised start and finish points. The project objectives may be defined in a number of ways, the important point being that the goals are defined and the project is finite [Association for Project Management Body of Knowledge].

Features of projects include the following.

- They have defined start and finish points.
- Each project is unique.
- There is a 'contract' between the project manager and the business sponsor.
- The project organisation is temporary and may change during the project.
- There is an element of risk and uncertainty.
- The project team may need to interact with other groups within and outside the organisation.

It is worth noting that this is different from the way in which most of us work. Most work in financial services organisations is driven by the customer – we do not start the day with the specific objective of serving exactly 500 customers before the branch closes! Nor is there any obvious relationship between tasks such as cashing a cheque, looking up an account balance and amending a standing order.

However, there is a recent trend for 'business as usual' to be run on a project basis. This has always been true for activities such as marketing campaigns, new branch openings and product launches. Events of this type are becoming more common and project management techniques are being applied to new activities requiring organisational change. Therefore, it is likely that there will be a greater transfer of project management responsibility into the business over time.

7.2 Programme management

A programme has been defined as 'a specific undertaking to achieve a number of objectives. The most common examples of programmes are development programmes or large single purpose undertakings consisting of a series of interdependent projects'. The second of these definitions – a series of interdependent projects to achieve a single business objective – is the most significant for this course.

So how does this differ from a project? Differences include:

◆ a programme does not necessarily have a defined end point;
◆ programmes usually have more complex objectives than projects;
◆ programmes are usually larger than projects.

These may seem to be differences of degree rather than substance, but in practice programme management is very different from project management. Programmes are usually organised as a number of projects and the programme manager's role is to manage the *relationships* between these projects. The programme manager is not responsible for the individual projects.

7.3 Project management

Project management is

'...the planning, organisation, monitoring and control of all aspects of a project and the motivation of all involved to achieve the project objectives safely and within agreed time, cost and performance criteria'.

Association for Project Management Body of Knowledge

Project management includes the following stages:

◆ agree the project objectives and define the project manager's role;
◆ plan the project;
◆ monitor and control the project;
◆ close the project.

7.3.1 Objectives and role

We have said that one difference between projects and other types of work is the 'contractual' nature of projects. Because each project is unique, the project objectives and project manager's role will vary and must be specified in some form of contractual document. The most important documents are:

◆ the project terms of reference;
◆ the business case.

Terms of reference

Terms of reference are the contract between the project sponsor and the project manager. They are essential because:

◆ they set the sponsor's expectations for the project;
◆ they define the project manager's mandate and authority;
◆ they provide a framework for the development process.

The acronym BOSCARDI is sometimes used for the contents of the terms of reference. This stands for:

◆ **B**ackground;
◆ **O**bjectives;
◆ **S**cope;
◆ **C**onstraints;
◆ **A**ssumptions;
◆ **R**eporting;
◆ **D**eliverables;
◆ **I**ssues.

Background is the background to the project.

Objectives say what the project is trying to achieve. The objectives section of the terms of reference will be used to assess the overall success of the project and they need to be SMART (specific, measurable, achievable, relevant and timebound).

Scope says what the project will and will not consider. The scope may relate to a business process or a functional area. One approach that is sometimes used is to draw up a table of what is and is not included in the scope.

Constraints are any restrictions within which the project team must operate. The most common constraints are project cost and time taken.

Assumptions document any assumptions made by the project team. Common assumptions include access to senior management within the organisation.

Reporting defines to whom the project team reports. This is discussed later in this chapter under project organisation and accountability.

Deliverables define what the project team is expected to produce. The terms of reference will only specify the key deliverables that are subject to sign off. This is discussed later in this chapter under project control.

Issues include anything that still needs to be resolved. All issues should be resolved before the terms of reference are finally signed off.

Terms of reference for IT projects will usually cover the entire project up to implementation. They may need to be revised during the development as conditions change. Alternatively, separate terms of reference may be produced for individual stages within the development.

Business case (cost benefit analysis)

The business case is the financial justification for the project. It considers the costs and benefits of the project and uses accounting techniques to determine whether the project should go ahead.

We can classify costs as one off or recurring. One off costs can be classified as capital or development costs. Recurring costs can be classified as maintenance or operating costs.

- *Capital costs.* These include the cost of new hardware (processing power, storage and peripherals) and telecommunications links such as installing new lines. They may also include the costs of additional office equipment. Additional space might be needed (for example to house a new computer) and the associated property costs would be included.
- *Development costs.* These include the costs of the staff involved in building the new system. They may also include overhead costs for managing the project and for non-IT staff (for example, the user department or internal audit staff). They include one off costs associated with any new software licences which may be needed.
- *Maintenance costs.* Where new software or hardware is purchased these will be specified in the contract. There will be an allowance (typically 10% of the development costs) for changes and improvements to the system.
- *Operating costs.* These include the cost of additional resources required to run the system – for example, the annual cost of any additional processing or storage requirements. They will also include any annual licensing costs for new software or hardware. They will include the predicted costs for 'consumables' such as additional telecommunications line charges, paper, floppy disks, etc.

We can classify benefits as tangible or intangible. Tangible benefits result in a direct financial return, for example, in reduced costs or increased income. Intangible benefits are less easy to quantify. Common sources of tangible benefits include:

◆ *benefits due to cost savings*. These include any projected savings due to being able to use fewer staff or lower graded staff, together with any associated premises cost savings. They may include one off cost savings through not renewing equipment leases or contracts with suppliers;
◆ *benefits due to cost avoidance*. Organisations may carry out projects to avoid costs that they would otherwise incur – for example, to replace equipment which is expensive to operate with equipment with lower operating costs;
◆ *benefits due to increased earnings*. These usually arise when the new system provides an additional business opportunity. For example, EFTPOS not only saves financial organisations the high cost of processing cheques, it also provides opportunities to earn fees from the retailers for processing EFTPOS transactions;
◆ *benefits due to income protection*. These may arise when organisations have to respond to the actions of competitors to avoid the loss of market share.

Common sources of intangible benefits include:

◆ *benefits due to better quality*. In principle, better quality can improve customer loyalty and market share, reduce the costs associated with correcting mistakes and lead to better decisions. In practice, it can be difficult to quantify these in money terms;
◆ *benefits due to reduced risks*. Reduced risks can reduce the costs needed to manage those risks. These are usually intangible, but calculations such as the annualised loss expectancy (discussed in Chapter Nine) can be used to get an indicative saving;
◆ *benefits due to improved information*. These can improve management decision making or the ability to identify business opportunities. In practice, these are very difficult to quantify.

In assessing the business case for a project, we need to apply two tests. First, is it a good investment? We need to estimate all the costs and all the benefits from the solution in money terms and use an investment appraisal technique in order to decide whether spending money on this particular solution is a good investment. Secondly, is it within the overall projects budget? Many organisations limit their overall budget for projects to prevent costs growing faster than the overall growth in earnings. If the cost of an investment is greater than the available budget, it will only be approved under exceptional circumstances – for example, if it is necessary to meet a legal obligation or if the return on the investment is exceptionally high.

Cost benefit analysis uses standard accounting techniques to decide whether the investment in the project will be justified. These are the most important.

◆ *Net present value*. This looks at the amounts which will be spent (costs) or earned (benefits) over the expected life of the project. These are discounted by a notional 'interest rate' to allow for the fact that interest needs to be paid on money spent now, so future earnings need to be at least as great as the lost interest if the project is to be financially justified. The value of all the discounted costs and benefits is added up to find out what the total would be now – the 'net present value'. If this is greater than zero, the amount the project will earn is more than the amount of lost interest and the project is financially justified.

◆ *Internal rate of return*. This works on the same principle as the net present value calculation (this principle is called 'discounted cashflow' or 'DCF'). However, instead of setting a rate for discounting cashflows, it calculates the actual rate required to produce a net present value of zero – the 'internal rate of return'. If this is greater than the organisation's target rate for return on investments the project is financially justified.

◆ *Payback*. This works by comparing the project's initial costs (capital costs plus development costs, less any one off savings due to sale of surplus equipment or premises) with the future earnings (benefits less maintenance and operating costs). The amount of time that will be needed before the benefits pay back the initial investment is calculated and compared with a target. If the investment will be paid back in less than the target the project is justified.

◆ *Economic value added*. This works by estimating the operating revenue after tax due to the investment and subtracting a funding charge for the capital employed (the amount of capital multiplied by the organisation's cost of capital). One benefit of economic value added is that it relates directly to market value added – the net impact of the investment on market value and therefore on the share price. According to financial theory, the market value added is the net present value of the economic value added.

◆ *Total cost of ownership*. This is usually used to compare hardware investments. Total cost of ownership calculations take account of a wide range of costs including management costs and the costs of keeping software up-to-date.

◆ *Option pricing*. The techniques of option pricing are outside the scope of this book. The principle is that an investment in technology gives the organisation the right, but not the obligation, to make further investments to exploit the technology. In effect, the organisation has purchased a call option on the exploitation of that technology and it has the option of allowing this to lapse or investing further.

Let us consider an example. Project A requires an investment of £4.5m and has a negative net present value of £460,000. Project B can only take place if we go ahead with project A. It requires an investment of £9m and has a net present value of £4.5m. There is a high level of uncertainty associated with project B and the decision whether to go ahead with project B will take place in three years.

Under option pricing, project B is a three-year call option on an asset with a value of £4.5m and an exercise price of £9m. The value of such an option may be £500,000. If we adjust the net present value for project A to take account of the option value, we end up with a positive net present value of £40,000 and the investment is cost justified.

DCF calculations rely on a notional interest rate, which in theory is the cost of capital for the organisation. In practice, financial services organisations often use 'hurdle rates' which compare the investment with the opportunity cost of using the capital elsewhere. International comparisons show a higher rate of return is expected in the UK than in countries such as Germany and Japan and this has been suggested as a reason for the relatively low level of technology investment in the UK.

Net present value is generally accepted as the best of the established techniques, but internal rate of return and payback are widely used. Internal rate of return is often used to compare projects but this can be slightly misleading (for reasons of interest to those studying accountancy, which we will not go into here). Payback is a very crude technique which has the benefit of providing a simple way of assessing risk – the longer the payback period the more likely it is that changes in the nature of the business or in technology will make the system obsolete.

Economic value added, total cost of ownership and option pricing are newer techniques. Economic value added is the most common of these, reflecting the financial services industry's adoption of the ideas of shareholder value theory, but is open to the objection that it is too complex. Total cost of ownership is a simpler measure usually used to compare the cost of computer equipment. Option pricing is particularly useful for strategic, long-term investment decisions.

7.3.2 Project planning

Project managers try to balance what is to be delivered, when it is to be delivered and how much is will cost – function, time and cost. The project terms of reference will define what is to be delivered and may set some limits on time and cost, but the project manager must produce a plan identifying the likely time and cost.

The project planning process involves the following:
- work breakdown structure;
- milestone plan;
- logic network;
- estimating;
- critical path analysis;
- Gantt chart;
- resource histogram.

Another technique is the Programme Evaluation and Review Technique (PERT).

Work breakdown structure

Project planning starts by breaking the project down into its component tasks and activities. Project management specialists draw a distinction between tasks and activities, but we will use the word 'activities' to cover both. We can simply show the result of the breakdown as a hierarchy of activities. This is called a 'work breakdown structure' and is a useful way of showing what needs to be done.

There are various ways in which we can break projects down. An engineering project might be broken down into the main sub-assemblies. Projects might be broken down by time – the systems development cycle (discussed in Chapter Eight) is an example of this – or by the department responsible.

Another approach is to break the project down into different types of work or 'workstreams'. As an example, let us consider the activities associated with opening a new branch:

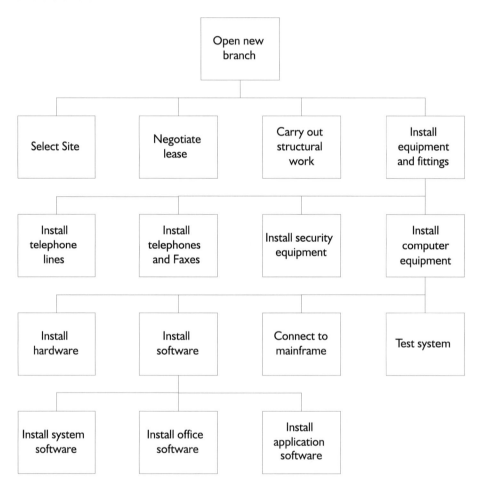

Each workstream represents a different type of work. Site selection is a marketing activity, lease negotiation is a procurement activity, structural work and installation of equipment and fittings are both project management activities, but are likely to use different people and to require different skills.

The work breakdown structure is the starting point for the next stage of the planning process.

Milestone plan

The next stage is to produce a milestone plan. A milestone is a significant event associated with the project or one of its workstreams. For example, signing the lease will be a milestone for the lease negotiation workstream.

Milestones are physical outcomes or results that the project sponsor can see. By defining the milestones for a project, we are able to manage the sponsor's expectations and provide a basis for the sponsor to monitor the progress of the project.

We have already discussed how we break projects down into activities. Milestones result from the completion of activities. We also need to take account of the relationships (or 'dependencies') between activities – for example, where one activity must precede another. By considering these dependencies, we are able to show the project milestones in a clearly-defined order:

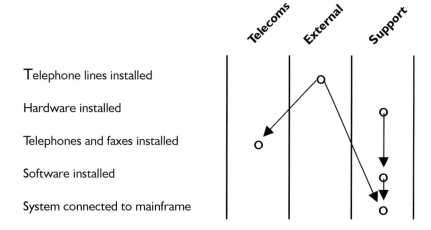

This diagram demonstrates two dependencies which cross workstreams – from the installation of the telephone lines to the installation of the telephones and faxes and to the mainframe connection.

Logic network

We can also show the activities and the dependencies between them as a logic network. This will have a start point (which shows when the first activity can start) and an end point (which is after the last activity has been completed). This is the basis for identifying how long the project is expected to take.

It might help to illustrate this with an example. Consider our computer equipment installation. The computer must be ordered and delivered before we can do anything. We then need to install the system software. After that, we can connect the computer to the mainframe, install the office software and install the application software at the same time. When all of these have been completed we can test the computer.

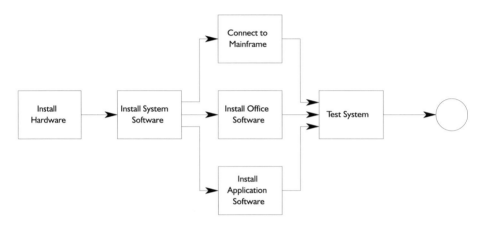

Estimating

From the work breakdown structure, the next stage is to estimate how long each activity will take. Various methods can be used for estimating. Three of the most common are outlined below.

- *Factor analysis*. We can analyse each task into various components and use this as a basis for estimating. An example of an estimating method based on factor analysis is Function Point Analysis (FPA). FPA takes account of factors such as the number of transactions and the amount of data to produce an estimate for the size of an activity in terms of 'function points'. We can then use productivity information about how long it takes to complete one function point to produce an estimate for the activity.
- *Extrapolation*. We can extrapolate how long the task will take, either from how long similar tasks have taken in the past or how long earlier phases of the development have taken.
- *Delphi technique*. We can ask experienced staff how long they think the task will take. If we ask a number of people and get broadly similar answers, they are likely to be reasonably accurate.

Assume we have the following estimates for the activities identified above:

- ordering and delivery   7 days;
- system software installation 5 days;
- mainframe connection   9 days;
- office software installation   5 days;

- ◆ Application software installation   7 days;
- ◆ Testing   20 days.

We can show these estimates on the logic network:

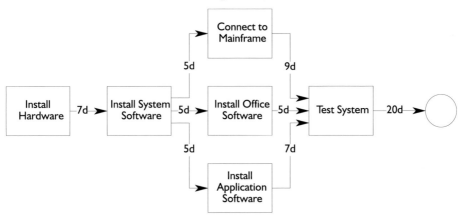

Estimates are shown in terms of effort – man-days or person-days. To convert this to elapsed time, we must take account of weekends and holidays.

Critical path analysis

The next stage is to estimate how long the project as a whole will take. The project manager works out the longest way through the logic network. This is called the 'critical path' and is the shortest time in which the project can be finished.

The longest path through this is 41 days (7 days + 5 days + 9 days + 20 days). Therefore, the shortest time in which we can install the computer equipment is 41 days.

We cannot start testing until we have completed mainframe connection – 21 days after the start. However, if we start office software installation at the same time as mainframe connection, we will have completed this 17 days after the start – four days before we can start testing. This four days is called the 'float'. This means we can delay the start of office software installation by up to four days without delaying the start of testing. Application software installation also has float, this time of two days.

This method of project planning is also called critical path analysis because the manager needs to find the project's critical path in order to estimate how long the project will take. The critical path activities are shown as shadowed on the diagram overleaf, and these activities have zero float.

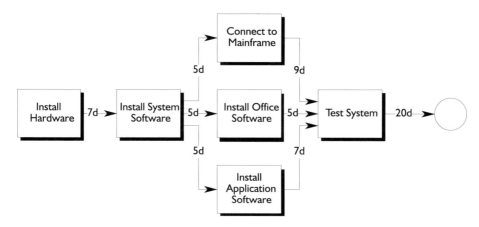

Gantt chart

A Gantt chart provides an alternative way of showing how long the project will take and is also used by managers in deciding who will carry out the various activities. This is named after Henry Gantt (a management theorist from the nineteenth century) and shows the activities down the left side and the project dates across the top. Next to each activity, a line or bar is shown from the scheduled start date to the scheduled end date.

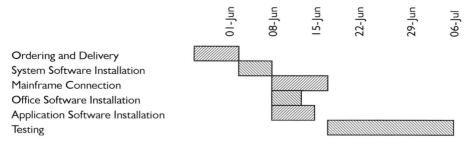

The manager will decide what skills are needed to carry out each activity and put them on the Gantt chart. He or she can then look at the overall picture and see whether there are enough people available with the right skills at any one time. If not, the manager may need to reschedule or to bring in more people with the skills needed.

The skill sets required in this example are the project manager, system support and office support.

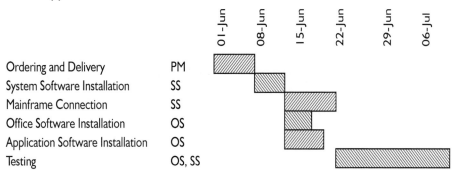

		01-Jun	08-Jun	15-Jun	22-Jun	29-Jun	06-Jul
Ordering and Delivery	PM						
System Software Installation	SS						
Mainframe Connection	SS						
Office Software Installation	OS						
Application Software Installation	OS						
Testing	OS, SS						

Resource histogram

A more formal approach to deciding whether the right skills are available is a resource histogram.

The Gantt chart breaks the project down into time periods (usually weeks or months). It also lists the skills needed to work on each activity. We can draw a histogram showing the total amount of each skill required for each time period. By comparing this with the resources available, we can find out if we have too few people with the right skills available to complete the tasks or if we will have people with insufficient work to do.

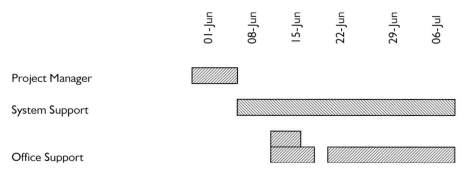

The manager will then decide who will carry out each activity. He or she will need to keep in view that people working on activities on the critical path should not be given other activities at the same time – this will delay completion of the critical path activity and of the project as a whole.

In the example above, two office support resources are needed for the period 13–18 June. Although there is two days float, five days are needed and the project manager will need to bring in a second resource for three days.

Other planning techniques – PERT

There is another form of planning that makes use of the idea of float. This was developed by the US Navy and is called Programme Evaluation and Review Technique (PERT). A PERT chart shows a network of activities, in the same way as critical path analysis, but each activity has four dates associated with it. These are the 'early start', 'late start', 'early finish' and 'late finish' dates.

The early start date is the earliest date the activity can be planned to start – the start date of the project plus the amount of time needed to complete all preceding activities. The late start is the latest date the activity can be planned to start without delaying the project – this will be the early start date plus the amount of float for the activity. The early/late finish date will be the early/late start date plus the amount of time needed to complete the activity.

We can show this on a diagram.

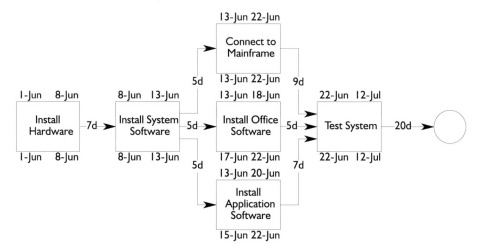

To keep the example simple, weekends have been ignored. Note the difference between the early (above the activity) and late (below the activity) start and finish dates for office software installation and application software installation. Note that the early and late start and finish dates for the other activities, which are on the critical path and therefore have no float, are the same.

7.3.3   Project control

The project manager is responsible for monitoring and controlling the project. The areas of control include:

◆ costs;
◆ timescales;
◆ quality.

The project manager's role involves balancing cost, time and quality to produce the best overall result for the business.

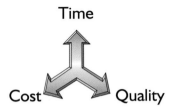

One example of balancing time and cost is 'crashing'. Project managers usually try to minimise total project cost, but crashing techniques allow projects to be completed in a shorter time but at higher cost – for example, by building the use of overtime into the plan. In the example discussed earlier, the project manager could have authorised overtime for the office support resource as an alternative to bringing in a second resource (if any were available) or delaying the project.

Controlling cost

Techniques used for controlling project cost include:
◆ budgets;
◆ timesheets;
◆ earned value analysis.

Budgets are a standard financial control technique. Project budgets can be set and monitored against actual expenditure.

For IT development projects in particular, staff time is the largest controllable cost item and using timesheets to monitor staff time is an effective alternative to using project budgets. This approach ignores non-staff costs as they are either relatively small (for example, travel expenses) or outside the project manager's control (for example, premises costs or equipment costs).

The problem with using budgets for cost control is that they show the costs incurred, but they do not show the amount of work completed. Earned value analysis is a method of assessing this.

Let us consider the example we have been discussing. The total amount of effort required is 53 days (7 days + 5 days + 9 days + 7 days + 5 days + 20 days). If we assume our costs are £100.00 per day, we have a total budget of £5,300.

The first two tasks are planned to require 12 days' (7 days + 5 days) effort and therefore should cost £1,200. If we have completed them while actually spending £1,100, we will be ahead of budget and if we actually spent £1,300, we are behind budget. We cannot get this information from budgets alone – these would continue to show the £5,300 budget cost.

In earned value analysis terminology, the planned cost of £1,200 is the Budgeted Cost of Work Performed (BCWP) whereas an actual cost of (say) £1,300 is the Actual Cost of Work Performed (ACWP). The cost variance is £100 (£1,200 – £1,300) adverse or 8.33% (£100 as a percentage of the BCWP £1,200) adverse. The cost efficiency is the BCWP divided by the ACWP or 92.3% (£1,200 divided by £1,300, expressed as a percentage).

Earned value analysis can be used to provide a range of information about both costs and timescales and is becoming an important project control technique.

Controlling time

Techniques used for controlling time include:

- Gantt charts;
- milestones;
- timeboxing.

We have discussed how Gantt charts are used for project planning, but they are also very useful for project control. A second line can be drawn next to each activity, from the actual start date to the actual end date, and this can be used to identify activities which have started late or taken longer than planned. By drawing a line down the chart, the manager can identify all activities which are scheduled to be in progress and all activities that are scheduled to have been completed.

We have also discussed milestones. Milestones represent physical deliverables, the dates for which have been agreed with the project sponsor. Therefore, the ability to achieve milestone dates is a very visible measure of how well the project is meeting its planned timescales.

Timeboxing is a technique by which each piece of work is given a fixed time in which it must be completed. If it exceeds the time allowed, the piece of work is stopped. The Development Bank of Singapore provides an extreme example of this, where *all* projects must be completed in three three-month timeboxes – limiting each project to a total of nine months.

Controlling quality

Quality control is a major concern of all project managers. Activities poorly completed will generally cause later activities, which are dependent on them, to take longer. This will increase the project time and costs.

When we discuss managing quality, we are really discussing how we manage what functions we will be delivering. The project manager may find it necessary to meet time and cost constraints by delivering slightly less than was originally planned or the delivered system may need more manual work arounds.

It is worth thinking of this in engineering terms. Components are not made to a precise size, but to 'engineering tolerances'. For example, a part may be specified as having a diameter of 8.32 mm, but the engineering tolerances might allow it to be between 8.29 mm and 8.35 mm. Therefore, the part is 'fit for purpose' provided its diameter falls within these limits. Similarly, systems can achieve their objectives quite adequately provided the functions they offer fall within acceptable limits.

Techniques used for controlling quality include:

◆ statements of work;
◆ walkthroughs;
◆ inspections;
◆ testing;
◆ deliverable sign-off.

Some approaches to project management require a *statement of work* to be drawn up for each task. This is a precise definition of exactly what is required to complete the task and of the measures of quality which will be applied to the results. This may form the basis of a legal contract, especially if the task is to be sub-contracted to an outside organisation.

A walkthrough is a meeting at which the developer presents his or her work to an audience which may include other members of the project, IT staff from other projects, business users and IT staff with relevant technical knowledge. The purpose of the meeting is to give the audience the opportunity to ask questions or make suggestions.

An inspection also takes the form of a meeting and has a very similar audience. However, proceedings are controlled by an independent inspector, instead of the developer. The inspector will usually either be a quality assurance specialist or an IT specialist and will have studied the developer's work carefully in advance of the meeting.

Inspections should be more thorough than walkthroughs, both because a second person has had the opportunity carefully to examine the work and because the inspector is accountable for any problems which are found.

Walkthroughs and inspections are usually carried out at the end of each stage of the systems development cycle before system testing. It is common to break large developments down into 'sub-projects' and to carry out separate walkthroughs or inspections on these.

Testing takes place during the development process and is discussed in more detail in Chapter Eight. We can distinguish between two tests.

◆ *Unit testing* takes place during the construction stage and checks that individual system components work as specified. Unit testing is carried out by the developer.

◆ *System testing* takes place as a separate stage and checks that the system works as a whole and that it will not adversely affect other systems. System testing is usually carried out by a designated system tester who may be independent of the project team.

One of the main forms of project control is deliverable sign-off. Deliverables which need to be signed off include the terms of reference and the key outcomes from the development stages. The lifecycle used in the systems development process may also say which deliverables should be produced and signed off for each development stage. This sometimes takes the form or a project deliverables catalogue or a project responsibility matrix.

Once a project has completed a development stage, it should not continue until the deliverables have been signed off. Without sign off, the project team does not have the authority to continue. In practice, this rule is sometimes waived as it would lead to all work on the project being halted, but organisations must ensure that sign off takes place as quickly as possible.

7.3.4   Project management systems

Project management systems are computer programs that will assist the project manager. The project manager will enter the activities, estimates, dependencies and skills/resources. The program will identify the critical path and calculate the float and the early/late start and finish dates for each activity. It will also identify whether resources have been overscheduled (sometimes presenting the results as a histogram). It can produce individual work plans for every member of the project team.

These programs are particularly useful for project control. They usually allow staff to enter their timesheets (often based on the individual work plans) and can apply 'charge-out rates' to calculate staff costs. Some programs can bill users for staff time if necessary.

They can be used to record when individual tasks are complete. If a task runs over schedule, they can forecast a new estimated completion date for the project as a whole. These programs generally also allow a 'percentage complete' figure to be entered against tasks in progress (although people's estimates of how much work remains to be done should usually be treated with extreme caution!).

Perhaps the greatest benefit of these programs is that they capture all the information about the project, including the initial plan, any revisions and the actual time and cost of the project. This information can be used to improve planning and estimating for future projects.

Early project management systems were only effective for single projects and were unable to manage the complex relationships in programmes. The most up-to-date versions of project management systems support programme management. Some project management systems can operate over the Internet, allowing world-wide access to information.

7.3.5   Project closure

Project closure includes the following activities:
- transferring the project into operations;
- the post development review (PDR);
- the post implementation review (PIR);
- maintenance may be covered for a period;
- closing the project accounts;
- releasing project resources.

The PDR, PIR and maintenance are described in more detail in Chapter Eight.

Transferring the project into operations involves handing the system over to operational management.

Closing the project accounts involves balancing and closing the accounts for the project.

Releasing project resources involves redeploying the resources used on the project – which may include equipment and premises as well as people – back into the business.

7.4   Project organisation and accountability

Projects are an example of matrix management, with the project team having both 'line' and 'functional' responsibilities.

To illustrate this, we will start by considering an influence diagram, showing the project manager's lines of responsibility.

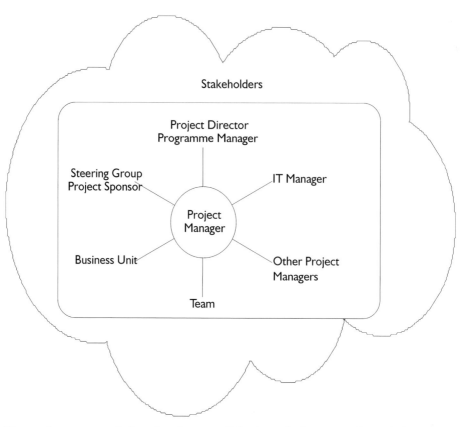

Stakeholders

The project manager's functional responsibility is to the business, through the project sponsor and steering group. There may be a project director or a programme manager who will have an additional accountability to ensure the project achieves the business objectives. The project manager will also have a responsibility towards the business units with which he or she is working.

The project manager's line responsibility is to the IT manager, to other project managers and to the project team.

7.4.1 Project organisation

Projects are organised into project teams. There are two approaches to this:

◆ matrix management;
◆ permanent project teams.

Matrix management

Under matrix management, the organisation would regard its people as a 'pool' of resources with various skills. When a project team needs to be formed, those people who are available and have the most suitable skills will be brought together. A project manager will be appointed from within the project team, who will not necessarily be the most senior member, but who will be the person best able to manage the team. The key feature of matrix management is that project team members will report to the project manager for project work, but will have a separate 'resource manager' for personnel matters such as salaries and appraisals.

Permanent project teams

An alternative is to operate permanent project teams, often specialising in particular areas of work. The size of the project team may vary, depending on the demand for work in which it specialises, but the core group will remain together.

Comparison of the approaches

Matrix management uses resources more efficiently. Permanent project teams allow the development of 'centres of expertise' in particular areas. In practice, most organisations use a mixture of both approaches.

Multi-disciplinary teams

A project team includes people with a variety of skills (a 'multi-disciplinary team') who can contribute towards the current stage of the project. During the systems analysis stage, for example, the project team might include a business analyst (who has a good understanding of the business problem), some systems analysts (who can describe the processes needed to solve the problem in logical terms) and a data analyst (who understands how to describe the data in logical terms).

During the systems design stage, this would change. Some of the systems analysts might be replaced by designers and the data analyst would be replaced by a database designer. These people's skills are in deciding how the logical description produced at the systems analysis stage should be turned into a physical system.

This raises the issue of continuity. As membership of the project team changes, how can we ensure that the project as implemented will meet the objectives from the problem definition? One approach is for the same people to occupy key roles such as project manager, project director and project sponsor throughout.

7.4.2   Project structure

Functional reporting

There will be a steering group for large projects and projects affecting different parts of the organisation. The steering group will be drawn from senior business management and will be responsible for ensuring that the project meets the requirements of the stakeholders. The steering group will authorise changes to the project budget and will sign off major deliverables.

The project sponsor will commission the project and define its objectives. If there is no steering group, the project sponsor will discharge its responsibilities. The project manager will report progress to the project sponsor, typically on a monthly basis.

For large projects, there may be a project director. The project director will represent the interests of the business, but will be involved on a much more regular basis than the project sponsor or steering group. The project director's job is to provide overall direction and to deal with issues and identify those which need to be escalated to the steering group.

The project manager also has a responsibility to the business unit that will use the outcomes from the project. The resulting system must be usable and of acceptable quality.

Line reporting

The IT manager will have overall responsibility for providing IT resources for the project. The split of management responsibilities by which the project manager reports to the project sponsor for project issues and the IT manager for resources and staffing issues is an example of the use of matrix management in project work.

If the project forms part of a programme, the programme manager will co-ordinate the projects.

The project team will carry out the work necessary to complete the project. The project team reports to the project manager, who will plan and organise the work of the team and monitor progress.

The project manager has a responsibility to other project managers in the department to present a professional image and to share best practice.

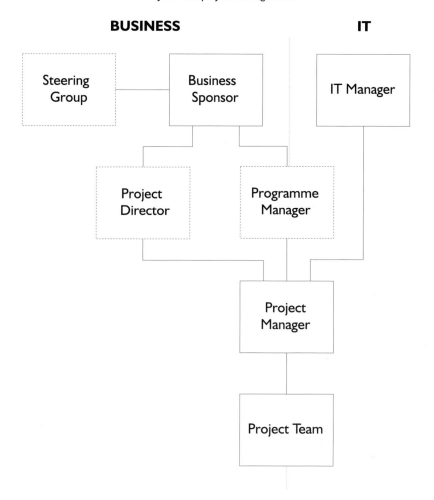

The formal project structure may be as follows:

It is important to understand the difference between project management and project direction.

- *Project management* is concerned with how the project is managed on a day-to-day basis. Project management is a specialist skill and is completely different from 'business as usual' management in a functional organisation. Project managers must be trained specialists and managers drawn from the business often find it difficult to make the transition to project management.
- *Project direction* is concerned with what the project is doing and whether this will meet business needs. Project direction should usually come from the business and there are a number of approaches including the appointment of a project director and/or a steering group. A business project manager is sometimes appointed, whose role will often be providing project direction rather than project management.

Stakeholders

In addition to the formal project structure, any project will have a number of 'stakeholders' who will be affected by its outcome. If we consider a large IT project within a financial services organisation, the stakeholders will include:

- staff in other departments who will be affected by changes in the user department;
- the financial services organisation's senior management;
- the financial services organisation's shareholders;
- those customers who may be affected by the changes;
- finance department;
- inspection/audit department;
- legal department;
- compliance department;
- those suppliers who may be affected by the changes;
- those suppliers who are participating in the project.

Given the number of stakeholders, it is hardly surprising that project organisation is very complex. The interests of stakeholders can be represented through:

- formal involvement in the project;
- 'sign off' of the relevant parts of the project;
- participation at the implementation stage.

The method of representation varies but a typical pattern might be:

	Formal involvement	Sign off	Participation at implementation
Other affected department staff			Yes
Senior management		Yes	
Shareholders			Yes
Customers			Yes
Finance Department		Yes	
Inspection/Audit Department		Yes	
Legal Department		Yes	
Compliance Department		Yes	
Affected suppliers			Yes
Participating suppliers	Yes		

It is worth noting how few of the stakeholders will usually have formal involvement in the project. In particular, it would be unusual for key stakeholders such as shareholders and customers to have any involvement prior to implementation.

7.4.3 Governance

Governance is the process of ensuring that the IT function produces what the business requires. The project director is responsible for governance at an individual project level, but governance across the organisation as a whole depends greatly on the relationship between the business and the IT function. There are two main views of what this should be.

♦ One view is that the relationship is contractual. Systems development is a supplier like any other and should be managed according to terms agreed in a contractual document.

♦ The alternative view is that the business and systems development should operate in partnership. Systems development is not a zero sum activity and both parties benefit by co-operating rather than competing.

Both approaches have their advantages and most financial services organisations fall somewhere between these, moving closer to one or the other as recent experience and management fashion dictate.

The main advantage of the contractual relationship is that of certainty. Both parties are committed to take certain actions and are liable should they fail so to do.

The main disadvantages of the contractual relationship are interpretation and the risk of the systems development function not going beyond the narrow view of the contract.

♦ Interpretation is a source of problems for all complex contracts. During the early stages of the systems development process it is often very difficult to define a precise contract as the objectives of the development and the method of work may be difficult to specify with any certainty.

♦ We have already shown that changes occur naturally during the course of a project. A contractual relationship needs to consider how such changes are accommodated and who will bear the cost. Contracts must specify how responsibility for changes is to be allocated.

♦ A contractual relationship implies that the systems development function will deliver exactly what is specified. This is a disincentive for systems developers to use their knowledge and experience to suggest improvements beyond the contracted minimum.

One approach that relies on a contractual relationship is to use an external supplier for systems development. External suppliers can also be used for operating computer systems, which is called 'facilities management', and for operating business processes, which is called 'outsourcing'.

The contractual relationship is the preferred approach for most financial organisations at the time of writing and many are considering facilities management and outsourcing.

Using external suppliers has the disadvantage that the organisation loses control over its development process. If we regard information as a tradable commodity and source of competitive advantage, we can readily see the disadvantages of outsourcing. There are a number of examples of organisations giving control over the systems development process to external organisations and then buying this back. Further, studies show 80% of such contracts do *not* save the organisation money – the usual justification.

Facilities management does not have this disadvantage and the main issue with facilities management is security of supply – can the supplier guarantee the service levels the organisation requires?

Outsourcing raises similar issues round the security of supply and is discussed in Chapter Seventeen.

Eight

Methodologies and techniques

8.1   Introduction

The systems development cycle or lifecycle was developed by the National Computing Centre (NCC) in the 1960s. A lifecycle is a list of the stages we go through in developing an IT system.

There are various lifecycles in commercial use. The original NCC lifecycle included six stages and lifecycles typically have between five and ten stages.

There are four common approaches to developing IT systems.

- The traditional approach is called 'waterfall development'. This defines the development process as a series of stages through which the project moves. It is called waterfall development because it is not possible to go back up the waterfall – once a stage has started, it is not possible to go back to an earlier stage.
- A popular alternative is to buy a 'package' from an external vendor. Vendors can supply software ranging from full service packages covering industries such as banking and insurance to specialist niche packages covering areas such as payroll or derivatives trading.
- Another alternative is to use an external vendor to meet some or all of the organisation's requirements for systems. Again, this can range from full outsourcing of all systems provision to the more limited provision of 'turnkey' systems in niche or non-strategic business areas.
- Another approach is joint application development, also called 'prototyping' or 'iterative development'. Unlike waterfall development, this does allow us to go back to earlier stages during the development process.

Each of these approaches has its own lifecycle, which will share some stages with other approaches, but which will also have its own unique stages.

8.2 Waterfall development

Developing a system using the waterfall approach involves going through a series of stages in order. Before we can go on to the next stage we must have completed the previous stage and had the deliverables signed off.

We will use a ten-stage lifecycle as a basis for considering waterfall development as follows:

◆ problem definition;
◆ requirements definition;
◆ feasibility study;
◆ systems analysis;
◆ systems design;
◆ construction;
◆ system testing;
◆ implementation;
◆ review;
◆ decommissioning.

8.2.1 Problem definition

The problem definition stage answers the question, what problem are we trying to solve? Although this may seem obvious, it is common to find symptoms and possible solutions confused with the real problem. For example, a manager may define the problem as 'I need this report on my desk at 8:30 every morning' when what is *really* needed is access to the information the manager requires to take decisions. This could be the report asked for, it could be a different report giving more relevant information, it could be online access to the information or it could be access to a decision support system.

It is the responsibility of the business user to define the problem clearly and correctly. This does raise two problems. First, the business user may take a parochial view – only considering the effect on the particular department and ignoring other possible users of the system. Secondly, the business user may not have the skills to analyse the root causes of the problem or the knowledge to understand what IT can achieve.

Business analysts – who have a good understanding of the interaction between IT and the business – can play a useful role here, bringing analytical skills and an understanding of what IT can (and cannot!) achieve to the problem definition. IT specialists may also need to be involved where solutions to the problem are likely to affect other systems or to involve a requirement for additional hardware, system software or telecommunications.

Others who may need to be involved could include organisation and methods specialists and internal audit staff. External consultants may be able to advise on approaches other organisations have taken to the same problem.

A short conference or 'workshop' usually forms an important part of the problem definition stage, allowing all the relevant groups an opportunity to discuss the problem and its impact on them. The outcome of this stage will be a problem definition report which will be used as input to the feasibility study stage.

8.2.2   Requirements definition

Requirements definition looks in detail at what the new system is expected to do. This will include the functions carried out by any existing systems (whether they are manual or on a computer), together with any new requirements.

Interviews and questionnaires are used to identify the requirements. New requirements may be identified using techniques such as brainstorming, workshops and throwaway prototyping (discussed later in this chapter under 'joint application development').

Observation and participation may be used to build up a description of the current system. Workflow within the office is documented and copies taken of forms and reports. Published documentation such as procedure manuals are an important source of information. Business analysts will sometimes work in the department for a period to observe and participate in the business processes. The current system is often documented using techniques such as process maps and flowcharts as these can be easily used in the later stages of the development.

The business analyst carries out the requirements definition, working closely with the business users. At this stage, additional IT staff – systems analysts who will work on the next stage – may also be involved.

The outcome of this stage is a requirements definition report containing a list of requirements and charts describing how the current physical system works. These are supported by examples of forms, copies of relevant documentation and statistics about the number of transactions carried out.

Other lifecycles use the term 'systems investigation' for this stage.

8.2.3   Feasibility study

The feasibility study stage looks at possible solutions to the problem and considers whether they are feasible and how much they might cost. Feasibility includes:

- *technical feasibility* – can the problem be solved given the current availability of technology?
- *fit with existing systems* – how will the technology required fit with our existing systems? In particular, how do we get the information we need into and out of the various possible solutions?
- *fit with strategy* – does solving the problem fit with the organisation's business strategy? Does the technology fit with the organisation's IT strategy?
- *technology risks* – what risks are associated with the technology? How will the organisation manage these risks? 'Leading edge' technology in particular is prone to risks including whether it will work and the risk of obsolescence if it is overtaken by a different technology;
- *cost benefit* – do the expected benefits offer a satisfactory return on the investment required?

The feasibility study starts by identifying different options for solving the problem. This will consider factors such as whether the problem can be solved using a package, how much of the solution should be delivered using technology and what technologies are available. This stage must also include the identification of evaluation criteria and the assessment of the options against these criteria.

The feasibility study stage is usually carried out by a business analyst. If additional hardware, telecommunications components and/or software forms part of the solution, it is likely to involve discussions with potential suppliers and also with the technology strategists within the organisation. Internal audit staff may be involved if there are any security issues.

The outcomes from this stage will include a feasibility study report (outlining options and making recommendations), a cost benefit analysis and (if outside suppliers are likely to be involved) a draft request for information.

A request for information describes the work the supplier will be required to do and asks for an estimate of time and costs – either on a fixed price basis (once the tender is accepted, the agreed price is fixed) or on a time and materials basis (the price may change if the supplier completes the work cheaper or more expensively than estimated). Requests for information are discussed in more detail later in this chapter.

8.2.4 Systems analysis

The systems analysis stage produces a full description of *what* the system will need to do. This is based on the description of the current system and additional requirements developed during the requirements definition stage. It does not consider *how* the system will do it or the constraints under which the system will operate. This is described as a logical model of the system.

The analysis of an existing process usually starts by removing the constraints which affect the physical system. For example, physically, it is usually impossible for two different people to work on the same document at the same time. This constraint would be ignored during analysis. The analysis of new requirements often starts by identifying how they fit into the existing process. A detailed discussion of systems analysis techniques is outside the scope of this book.

This stage is carried out by systems analysts, some of whom may have been involved in the requirements definition stage. The business analyst will usually continue to be involved and may work as a systems analyst – the skills required are similar. A specialist data analyst may be involved in producing a logical model of the data.

The business users will be involved in checking the analysis and confirming that the system would meet their requirements. The analysis stage usually involves specifying screen and report layouts and the business users would be involved in this.

The outcome from this stage will be a systems requirements definition containing models of the processes and data to be provided by the new system.

8.2.5   Systems design

The systems design stage looks at how the system can actually be built – it produces a physical model of the required system. This will include deciding which processes will be carried out manually and which by the computer. This is called the 'man–machine boundary'. The manual component of the system will need to consider how staff will interact with the computer.

It also needs to identify the constraints under which the new system will operate. These are likely to be different from the constraints of the current system – for example, an online system, where up-to-date information can be requested at any time, will be less constrained than a batch system where information is only available as reports printed at the end of the previous day. These constraints are then applied to the logical model from the systems analysis stage to produce a new physical model.

Design of the computer system will depend greatly on technical factors – whether the system will be batch, online or real-time, whether a database will be used, etc. It is important that the computer system design is efficient in the particular environment in which it will operate.

The systems design stage may be carried out by specialist system designers or by systems analysts carrying out a design function. The skills required are more technical than in the systems analysis stage and a common approach is to have one or more specialist system designers working with the systems analysts who worked on the systems analysis stage. One area where a specialist designer is almost always required is database design.

Business users will have limited involvement in this stage, although they may be consulted about the 'user interface' – what the screens and reports will look like – if these were not fully defined during the systems analysis stage.

The outcome from the systems design stage will be an overall systems design report and possibly a set of program specifications. Alternatively, the program specifications may be written during the construction stage.

8.2.6   Construction

The construction stage involves writing the computer programs required. It also involves a certain amount of 'unit testing' to ensure that the programs work properly.

This stage is largely the responsibility of IT staff. Unless a prototyping approach is used, the business users' only involvement may be in producing documentation and forms and in preparation for testing the system.

The outcome of this stage is a set of computer programs.

8.2.7   System testing

The system testing stage involves a far more thorough test than that carried out at the construction stage. Not only does it check that the programs work on their own, it also checks that they work together and that they do not cause any problems for other programs which may be running on the computer. This stage may include a number of tests.

- ◆ *System testing*, to check that all the system components work together.
- ◆ *Regression testing*, to check that the system works with other systems which may be running at the same time.
- ◆ *Volume testing*, to check that the system will handle the required numbers of transactions.
- ◆ *Operational proving*, to check that the system will run on the system for which it is intended and that the operating instructions are complete and accurate.
- ◆ *Acceptance testing*, to check that the system will meet the business requirement and that the user manual is complete and accurate.

Which of these tests are carried out depends on the nature of the system, but system testing (always), operational proving (almost always) and acceptance testing (sometimes) are the most important.

Specialist testers are often responsible for all of these. Business users are involved in the acceptance test and, in some organisations, may have complete responsibility for it. Business users will be involved in drawing up 'test cases' to be system tested and in checking the results.

Another way of looking at testing is the V-lifecycle, which relates testing stages to lifecycle stages:

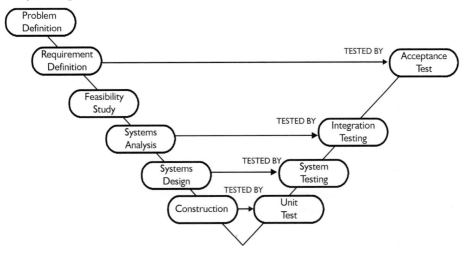

Integration testing includes regression testing, volume testing and operational proving.

The outcomes from this stage will be a set of tested programs with operating instructions and user manuals. Many organisations retain the test cases and results to make it easier to test changes to the system or to regression test other systems.

8.2.8 Implementation

The implementation stage involves making the programs available for use. This will include designing any training programmes, writing manuals and designing forms for the users. There are four approaches to implementation.

♦ *Big bang*, in which the new system is implemented through the entire organisation, all at once.

♦ *Parallel run*, in which the new system and the current system are allowed to run alongside each other for a period. The results from the two systems are compared to check the correctness of the new system.

♦ *Pilot run*, in which the whole of the new system is implemented in part of the organisation – say 2–5% of the branch network for a large retail financial services organisation. A pilot run requires different versions of the software to be used in different parts of the organisation and the technique of allowing changes to be switched on and off is usually used.

When the system has been proved in part of the organisation, it will be 'rolled out' to the remainder. This roll out is often carried out in stages – for example, an initial roll out to 15% of the organisation followed by three further roll outs covering the entire organisation.

♦ *Phased implementation*, in which part of the new system is implemented in the whole of the organisation. For example, enquiries against the database may be implemented first, followed by database maintenance (for example, change of address), followed by transaction processing.

The decision as to which implementation strategy should be adopted is mainly that of the business user. However, IT staff should be involved and the decision may need to be approved by internal audit.

8.2.9   Review

Reviews are very important to allow the organisation to learn from the development. There are two types of review:

♦ post development reviews;
♦ post implementation reviews.

Post development reviews cover the *efficiency* of the development process and are carried out by IT staff. They are usually carried out by someone who was not involved in the original project team and look at whether all of the stages in the systems development cycle were completed correctly and what problems were encountered.

Post implementation reviews cover the *effectiveness* of the system and may be carried out by IT staff, business users or external consultants. They look at the original objectives of the project and determine how well the system meets these. They look at whether agreed service levels are being achieved. They also consider how easy the system is to use and issues such as cost overruns and late delivery.

8.2.10   Decommissioning

Some types of project have a formal decommissioning phase when the main project deliverable reaches the end of its economic life. Obvious examples include projects to build nuclear power stations and off-shore oil rigs where the cost of decommissioning has a substantial effect on the project's business case.

Although this is rare for information technology projects, we must give consideration to when the system will be replaced. As systems get older, they incur increasing costs.

♦ Maintenance costs increase. Changes to the system often have the effect of increasing maintenance costs and it may be expensive to support obsolete technology. We can use the analogy of an old car where it may be hard to find spare parts or find a mechanic who understands how to service it.

- The system may act as a constraint on the business. The limitations of the system may limit the business's ability to enter new markets. This will impose an opportunity cost in terms of lost business opportunity.
- Maintaining the system diverts scarce resources away from the development of new systems to meet business needs. We consider one solution to this – outsourcing system maintenance – later in this chapter.

For an information technology project, it would be very unusual to include a specific decommissioning stage in the initial project plan. However, maintenance costs should be monitored and the decommissioning or replacement of the system should be considered when these get too high.

8.3 Using a package

The decision to use a package does not mean that we can do without a structured approach to the process. We will use a ten-stage lifecycle as a basis for package selection. The first three and last four stages are similar to the corresponding stages in the waterfall development lifecycle. The stages are as follows.

- Problem definition (as for waterfall development).
- Requirements definition (as for waterfall development).
- Feasibility study (as for waterfall development).
- Request for information and vendor shortlist.
- Invitation to tender and vendor selection.
- Procurement.
- System testing (regression testing, operational proving and acceptance testing).
- Implementation (as for waterfall development).
- Review (post-implementation review).
- Decommissioning (as for waterfall development).

During the feasibility study stage we will have used sources such as reference books, the computer press, consultants, competitor information and perhaps customers to identify that a package is a potential solution to our system requirements.

8.3.1 Request for information and vendor shortlist

A request for information (RFI) is a document which typically contains the following.

- A brief description of the main requirements. This may be a summary of the requirements definition report.
- A statement of the constraints under which the system will need to operate. These might be quite specific (for example, a description of the hardware and

telecommunications environment and a requirement that the package must operate within this environment) or they might be more general (for example, a requirement to be able to analyse information using a spreadsheet – it will be the vendor's responsibility to determine how best to move the information from the package into a spreadsheet).

◆ A request for information about the company. This will include financial health and standard terms of business including warranties and the availability of support and consultancy.

◆ An outline of the tender process, including the timescales and the form in which tender documents must be submitted.

The RFI may be produced during the feasibility study stage.

The next stage is to draw up a vendor shortlist from the requests for information.

◆ From the systems investigation and systems analysis stages, identify the criteria that will be used to assess the package. These will include the functions that the package needs to be able to perform and compatibility factors such as whether the package can run on existing hardware.

◆ For each of these criteria, decide whether it is 'must have' or 'nice to have'. An alternative classification takes the acronym MoSCoW from the initial letters of the classification 'must have, should have, could have, want'. Give each of the criteria a 'weighting' which reflects its relative importance.

◆ Assess each package against the selection criteria. A common approach is to give a score from 1 (does not meet) to 5 (meets very well) against each criterion for each package.

◆ Calculate the total score for each package. For each criterion, multiply the weighting by the score. Add up the results to give a total.

◆ Draw up a shortlist of suitable packages. These will be the packages which:
  – meet all of the 'must have' criteria – typically having a score of at least three for each criterion; and
  – represent good value to the organisation, taking account of their cost and overall score.

Before embarking on this process, organisations have to be aware of the problems which might arise during selection. These include:

◆ there may be no package which adequately meets the selection criteria. In this event it may be necessary to consider bespoke development;

◆ available packages may meet some of the selection criteria, but some of the required functions may not be available. Here, bespoke development is an option or it may be possible to tailor the package.

The objective is to reduce the number of potential vendors to a manageable shortlist, usually of between three and six.

8.3.2 Invitation to tender and vendor selection

The shortlisted vendors will be sent an invitation to tender (ITT) which may be prepared during the shortlisting process and will typically include:

◆ a list of specific questions about how the proposed solution will meet the requirements;

◆ information about how any changes to the package will be implemented;

◆ information about 'reference sites' – other organisations which already use the package;

◆ specific proposals about costs, training, warranty, consultancy and support arrangements.

The next stage is to select the vendor.

◆ The shortlisted packages will be examined in more detail. Depending on the type of package, this may well involve talking to and possibly visiting reference sites.

◆ All of the shortlisted packages should provide the main functions required by the organisation. The final selection will take account of other factors such as:
  – performance and response times;
  – ability to handle required volumes;
  – compatibility with existing hardware;
  – compatibility with system software;
  – quality of documentation;
  – availability and quality of support;
  – costs, including operating and maintenance costs;
  – audit trails and security/control features;
  – access to and cost of upgrades and enhancements; and
  – access to source code.

8.3.3 Procurement

The procurement stage is not usually the responsibility of the project team. Finance or a central purchasing function is usually responsible for this.

The objective of the procurement stage is to secure the package on the most favourable terms to the organisation. This will not necessarily be at the lowest possible price as factors such as support, training and security of supply must be considered.

8.4 Outsourcing

Financial services organisations have several options for outsourcing IT.

◆ Full outsourcing of all systems functions.

- Turnkey development.
- Partial outsourcing.
- Facilities management.

Business process outsourcing, discussed in Chapter Seventeen, usually also involves outsourcing the associated IT and systems functions.

Even where the organisation is handing over responsibility for system development, we must still consider this in terms of a lifecycle. Some stages – problem definition and requirements definition – are common and similar to the waterfall development lifecycle. Others will depend on the type of outsourcing adopted.

8.4.1 Vendor selection

The selection of an external vendor is similar to the selection of a vendor for a package solution, involving request for information (also called a request for proposal), invitation to tender and procurement stages.

The evaluation process will consider the ability of the vendor to meet the requirements, rather than a specific solution. This is a long-term relationship and the vendor's financial stability and ability to meet agreed service levels over the long term is of particular importance.

8.4.2 Full outsourcing

If a financial services organisation fully outsources its IT, it transfers all responsibility to a vendor. This is rare in financial services, although it may happen when a financial services organisation meets its needs by buying a package together with a maintenance and facilities management arrangement. Therefore, the lifecycle we use for buying a package applies to this type of outsourcing.

8.4.3 Turnkey development

Turnkey systems development involves the organisation transferring responsibility for the development of some of its systems to an external vendor. Financial services organisations generally use turnkey development for systems that are not strategically important, for example, administrative systems such as payroll and property management.

The problem definition and requirements definition stages are as for waterfall development. The systems resulting from turnkey development will be used alongside the organisation's other systems. Therefore, the later lifecycle stages are needed.

- System testing (regression testing, operational proving and acceptance testing).
- Implementation (as for waterfall development).
- Review (post implementation review only).
- Decommissioning (as for waterfall development).

The most important factor is ensuring that all of the requirements – including any methodologies or standards to be used – are clearly documented. Asking the supplier to make changes during the development will be expensive. The completed system, including any documentation, must also be carefully checked to ensure that it complies with the requirements before sign off.

Although we cannot ensure that the supplier uses our methodology, we can require that they document the system in a way consistent with it and with any other standards we use. An important issue here is who is going to maintain and support the system? If this is the supplier, it may not be necessary for the technical documentation to meet our standards. If we are, it is important that all the documentation is consistent with our own.

Standards are rules to be used in the development process. Standards include:

- *documentation standards*. These define what documentation should be produced and in what format;
- *data naming standards*. These define how data elements should be named;
- *operability standards*. These define how the system should run in the data centre – for example, what action the system should take if it cannot find a file it needs.

8.4.4 Partial outsourcing

We have a number of options for partial outsourcing of the development process. Common approaches include:

- using contract staff as part of the development process;
- outsourcing the construction stage;
- outsourcing the maintenance stage.

None of these approaches has a significant effect on the lifecycle.

The reasons for using contract staff as part of the development process include securing access to skills and knowledge that are scarce within the organisation and coping with temporary peaks in demand for developers.

The reason for outsourcing the construction stage is that it is largely independent of the other stages. One option is to outsource this to another country where computer programmers are cheaper and countries such as India have developed major software industries through this.

Maintenance typically uses up to 80% of an organisation's total spending on information systems and outsourcing this frees resources to use on the development of new systems. The main disadvantage of outsourcing maintenance is that it requires expertise and knowledge of the organisation's existing systems which an external vendor will need to develop.

8.4.5 Facilities management

Facilities management involves the transfer to an external vendor of responsibility for some or all of the following.

- ◆ Operation of the organisation's data centres and mainframe computers or processing of the organisation's work on the vendor's mainframe computers.
- ◆ Operation of the organisation's telecommunications network or transmission of the organisation's telecommunications traffic over the vendor's network.
- ◆ Support for the organisation's telecommunications network.
- ◆ Support for the organisation's 'desktop' – its PCs and terminals.

Facilities management is becoming increasingly important. A few financial services organisations have outsourced their data centres either by floating them as separate companies or by selling them (and transferring their staff) to an external vendor. Outsourcing the telecommunications network and desktop support are more common.

Facilities management has the following advantages.

- ◆ The organisation does not have to pay for upgrades to hardware and software except through the cost of the service. The vendor will be able to spread the cost over a number of clients and will receive discounts as a large user, so the cost of such upgrades is likely to be lower than the financial services organisation would have been able to secure.
- ◆ The vendor may be able to operate the hardware and software at a lower cost, both because of economies of scale and because the vendor specialises in this type of operation and should be able to generate savings through process improvement.

Facilities management has the following disadvantages.

- ◆ It may be expensive if the organisation relies on unusual hardware or software. As the vendor cannot easily spread the costs, the organisation will not achieve any cost savings. This also limits the organisation's ability to delay taking new releases of system software as the vendor may only be willing to support older versions for a limited period.
- ◆ The organisation loses control over its systems. If a contractual dispute arises the organisation's security of supply may be jeopardised if the vendor can withdraw the service offered.

It is important to note that financial services organisations are increasingly outsourcing non-IT operations functions such as cheque clearing.

8.5 Joint application development

Joint application development (JAD) involves a series of meetings or workshops between the developers and the business users to develop the system. This is an iterative process, with new requirements or changes being identified at each meeting and incorporated in a prototype or model of the system prior to the next meeting.

One approach used for JAD is the rational unified process (RUP). This is a four-stage methodology including:

◆ inception;
◆ elaboration;
◆ construction;
◆ transition.

The inception stage defines the scope and requirements through a 'vision' of the end product. This stage also considers the business case, priorities, risks and development process.

The elaboration stage defines and elaborates the vision into an overall architecture. This emphasis on the early development of a robust architecture is the key feature of RUP. This stage also produces a firm project plan and ensures that all risks have been addressed.

The construction stage is broadly similar to the construction and testing stages in the waterfall development lifecycle.

The transition stage is broadly similar to the implementation stage in the waterfall development lifecycle.

An alternative is the dynamic systems development methodology. This has a five-stage methodology:

◆ feasibility study;
◆ business study;
◆ functional model iteration;
◆ system design and build iteration;
◆ implementation.

The feasibility study and implementation stages are broadly similar to the corresponding stages in the waterfall development lifecycle and the business study is equivalent to the requirements definition (system investigation) and systems analysis stages.

The functional model iteration stage involves several cycles of iteration in developing a functional model of the system. The objective of this stage is to work out exactly what the system has to do. The model can be developed using very simple tools – pen and paper can be used to develop prototypes – but will usually use tools such as databases and screen painters (to simulate computer screens).

The system design and build iteration stage again involves several cycles of iteration. The objective is to take the functional model developed in the previous stage and create a system that offers robust and efficient performance.

An important technique used in all JAD approaches is timeboxing. Each cycle of iteration is limited very strictly to a period of time. Timeboxing is important because it allows the development to be kept under control – without timeboxing, developers might be tempted to keep including additional features without going back to the business user to confirm the requirement. Timeboxing can also be used in waterfall development to maintain control over phases such as requirements definition.

We may start JAD by choosing one clearly-defined business function within the system. We will use our prototype-building tools to develop a system which supports that business function. We can then choose another business function and prototype and add it to our original prototype.

When we have built a prototype which covers the entire system, we will go through the prototype with the business user to identify which parts need further development. We will make the necessary changes and go through the prototype again. Only when the user is completely happy that the prototype meets the business requirement can the prototype be considered complete.

There are three things we can do with our prototype. We can implement the prototype as it is. We can throw it away and redevelop the system using waterfall methods. We can 'evolve' the prototype.

Implementing the prototype as it is seems obvious. However, there are disadvantages. The system will have been developed with a single user – will it be sufficiently robust to cope with a large number of users at the same time? Is the system efficient or will it use very large amounts of computer resources? The system will not have been documented – how easy will it be to identify and correct faults or to make changes as the business requirements change?

Implementing the prototype is a common approach where the risks of failure are low – typically, systems with a small number of users. Systems running on a large network or alongside other systems should not be implemented directly without considerable testing.

Throwaway prototyping may sound ridiculous, but it is a common technique. We have used the prototype to design a system that meets the requirements of the business. This means that we have completed the most difficult stages of the systems development cycle. Further, we know that the system works. If we redevelop the system using waterfall methods and a third generation language, we will produce a robust and efficient system, usually at lower cost than if we had used other methods.

Throwing the prototype away is most common when the system will need to be implemented across a large network, where robustness and efficiency are critical factors.

Evolutionary prototyping involves 'tuning' the system to increase its efficiency and robustness. Important components may be rewritten if necessary, possibly using a third generation language.

Evolutionary prototyping attempts to combine the benefits of implementation and throwaway prototyping. Its disadvantage is that the two parts of the system (the original prototype and the rewritten components) have been developed in different ways and may not fit together very well. One situation where this will not usually present a problem is in a client/server system, where the original prototype can be used for the 'client' component of the system and the 'server' component can be re-written for greater robustness and efficiency. Client/server systems are discussed in Chapter Seventeen.

8.6 Comparison

The following diagram covers the main approaches, showing common stages and differences between them.

Customer information management

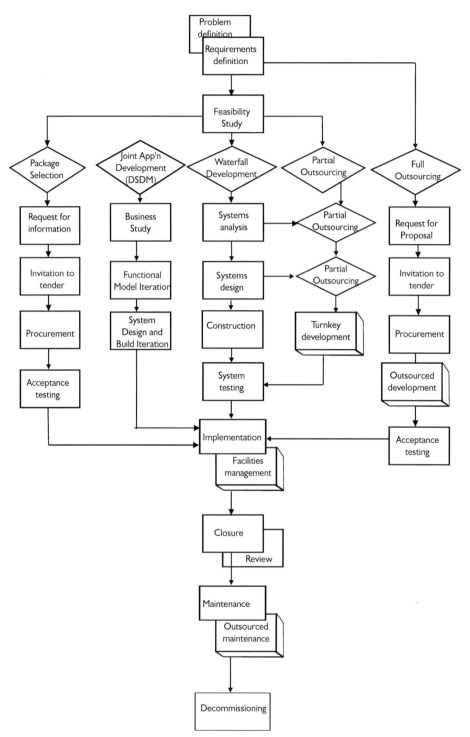

8.7 Methodologies

We have said that a lifecycle is a checklist, telling us what stages we need to go through in developing a system and what we are trying to achieve in each of these stages. It tells us *what* to do during the systems development process.

The word 'methodology' really means the study of methods. In IT, we use this word to describe a comprehensive approach that covers *how* to develop systems as well as what must be done. The following are the main characteristics of a methodology.

◆ It covers the whole of the systems development process from the initial identification of the problem to the period after implementation.
◆ It includes its own lifecycle and it may allow alternative lifecycles to take account of the difference between types of project.
◆ It includes a set of techniques and it may have its own distinct 'notation' for describing parts of the system. The same techniques will usually be used throughout the development process, with additional levels of detail being added during the later stages, and will form the basis for most of the documents produced during the development.
◆ It may include project management techniques and some methodologies, such as PRINCE (projects in controlled environments), are mainly concerned with project management.
◆ It may include a set of computer aided software engineering (CASE) tools specifically designed to support the methodology, possibly also including project management tools.
◆ Training and consultancy in using the methodology will usually be available.

We will consider three examples of methodologies:

◆ structured analysis;
◆ information engineering;
◆ projects in controlled environments (PRINCE).

8.7.1 Structured analysis

A number of methodologies follow the approach described as 'structured analysis'. The important point about these methodologies is that they start by analysing the processes which are required. The data required by the system is defined by the data requirements of the processes within it.

Structured analysis methodologies are very effective for automation – improving existing processes using IT to make them more efficient. Their main disadvantage is that they only consider data used within the processes or defined as an input or output of the system. The value to management of collecting additional data is not considered.

8.7.2   Information engineering

An alternative approach is adopted by methodologies following the principles of information engineering. These methodologies start by modelling the data requirements to produce a 'logical data model'. This ensures that the value of management information is taken into account. It also provides an overall framework (or architecture) for developing systems.

Information engineering methodologies are effective for developing systems that rely on data – for example management information systems. They also provide a good basis for developing an information systems strategy. Their disadvantage is that they are dependent on the quality of the data model they start with. Concern about costs may lead to too little senior management time being spent on this, resulting in a poor quality data model.

8.7.3   PRINCE

PRINCE is a project management methodology and provides a management framework for systems development. It is designed to be used with the UK government's structured analysis methodology Structured Systems Analysis and Design Methodology.

PRINCE has five major components:

◆ organisation;
◆ plans;
◆ controls;
◆ products;
◆ activities.

The organisation component is concerned with the project structure and organisation. The plans component provides a structure for preparing and managing project plans. The control component provides a control structure. Products are what we referred to as 'deliverables' in Chapter Seven and are the outputs from the project. Activities include management activities, technical activities and the quality process.

8.7.4   Computer aided software engineering

CASE is an acronym for 'computer aided software engineering', and a CASE tool can be any computer program or system that can be used as an aid in the development of computer systems. These can be classified as:

◆ workbenches;
◆ generators;
◆ environments;

- meta-CASE tools;
- computer aided software testing tools.

Workbenches

Workbenches are tools that support one part of the systems development process. The main types of workbench are designed to support:

- systems analysis
- data analysis
- systems design
- data design
- construction (programming).

Systems analysis workbenches support the techniques required to describe and analyse logical processes. They provide a diagramming tool (which can also control the levels of diagram) and a glossary of process, flow, data store and external names. They sometimes include data analysis workbenches.

Data analysis workbenches provide similar features for data. They have a glossary, which holds information about the logical data model. They can check that it has been built correctly.

Systems design workbenches can be used on their own or with systems analysis workbenches. Although they hold similar information, they present it in a way which allows it to be used as a 'first cut' design for the construction phase. In particular, they allow the system to be broken down into a hierarchy of programs and modules and show the flow of control between these. This first cut design can then be changed as needed to meet the particular requirements of the organisation.

Data design workbenches are usually used with data analysis workbenches. They use the information about the logical data model together with information about the number of records expected and the order in which they will be accessed to develop a first cut database design. This can then be changed to meet the requirements of the organisation.

Programmers' workbenches allow programmers to develop and carry out some testing on programs. The main benefit of these tools is in their testing facilities, as they allow programs written for mainframe computers or minicomputers to be tested on a workstation in a very interactive way. This is cheaper and easier than using the main computer for testing. When the program has been tested on the workbench, it will still need to be tested on the main computer, but the majority of the errors should have been identified and corrected.

Generators

Generators include program generators and application generators.

A program generator uses an input source file similar to a fourth generation computer language (4GL) or a fifth generation computer language (5GL). Whereas a 4GL or 5GL will either be run directly using an interpreter or compiled to give an object file, the program generator will convert the source file into a source file in another language – usually a third generation computer language (3GL) such as COBOL or C. This can be used as a starting point and the programmer can make further changes to make the program do exactly what is required and to improve the program's efficiency.

An application generator takes this further, often using a systems analysis workbench to identify what is required. This will be translated into a working system, either written in a 4GL or using a program generator to produce a system written in a 3GL.

Environments

Environments include integrated CASE environments and component CASE environments. Both of these support the main stages of the systems development cycle (typically from systems analysis through to construction, although some may also include feasibility study, system investigation and maintenance). This means that they include all the types of workbench discussed above. It is also possible for organisations to use meta-CASE tools to build their own environments.

In an integrated CASE environment, all of these come from the same supplier (who will usually also supply a methodology, consultancy and training). This has the advantage that tools work well together. The disadvantage is that the individual workbench tools may not meet the organisation's needs.

Component CASE environments attempt to overcome this disadvantage. A central repository (similar to a data dictionary, but also including information about processes, computer programs and the computer itself) is used to co-ordinate information from different workbenches (which may come from different suppliers). The disadvantage of this approach is that it is technically quite difficult – workbenches designed to support structured analysis and information engineering will work quite differently, for example.

Meta-CASE tools

Meta-CASE tools can be used to build bespoke development environments designed to fit exactly the methods used by the organisation. This has the advantages of both the integrated CASE and component CASE approaches, but the organisation will incur costs in developing and maintaining such environments.

Both component CASE environments and meta-CASE tools need the ability to exchange information between CASE tools. Two methods of achieving this are the CASE data interchange format and the portable common tools environment.

Computer aided software testing

Computer aided software testing (CAST) tools are a type of CASE tool designed specifically to support aspects of the testing process. The main types of CAST tool are:

- capture and playback tools;
- test scripting tools;
- test data generation tools;
- stress testing tools;
- desktop testing tools;
- test management tools.

Capture and playback tools allow us the 'capture' the keystrokes when we enter test data. If we need to re-run the test, we can 'play back' the recorded keystrokes rather than needing to re-enter the data. This saves considerable amounts of time and ensures consistency between the tests.

Test scripting tools allow test 'scripts' to be run automatically. These typically have features such as requesting external resources and handling errors that may occur during the test.

Test data generation tools allow large amounts of test data to be produced quickly and automatically.

Stress testing tools allow large volumes of transactions to be presented to the system. These are similar in function to some of the programs used for the 'denial of service' attacks discussed in Chapter Nine.

Desktop testing tools allow some testing of mainframe systems on workstations.

Test management tools allow the testing process to be managed and controlled. They are similar in function to the project management tools discussed in Chapter Seven, but are specific to testing. They also allow the test manager to record and track problems and changes.

Nine

Risk management

9.1   Introduction

Risk is an important issue for financial services organisations. The objective of risk management is to balance the risks faced with the cost of managing that risk. The objective is not to prevent all risks at any cost.

Information security is one aspect of risk management. Information is one of financial services organisations' most important assets, so the need to safeguard information should be self-evident. In practice, we are concerned with safeguarding data as this automatically safeguards the information, which we have already defined as data in context. This is called 'data protection' and includes data security and data privacy.

Data security is concerned with ensuring that data is protected from loss or damage and that we can access it when required. We usually consider data security under two further headings.

- ◆ *Data availability* is concerned with protecting data from loss and ensuring that data can be accessed.
- ◆ *Data integrity* is concerned with protecting data from damage and with ensuring that the data held is accurate, up to date and consistent.

Data privacy, also known as 'data confidentiality', is concerned with ensuring that data about customers and data that is commercially sensitive to the financial services organisation is not seen by anyone not properly authorised.

We also need to be aware of the particular threats posed by the nature of IT and what it allows.

- Much more information to be produced, which will need to be stored and disposed of securely.
- Information can be produced in a portable form, for example, CDs, magnetic tapes and portable computers, which will need to be protected against theft.
- Transactions can be entered and enquiries made by anyone with access to a workstation attached to the computer network provided that they know the passwords. Physical security is important to limit access to workstations and automated security checks such as passwords must be kept secret.
- Offices and branches are now almost totally dependent on IT to provide an acceptable level of customer service, so hardware, software and data needs to be protected against damage and plans need to be in place to restore service as soon as possible in the event of failure.
- The Internet provides a route by which hackers and viruses can gain access to the organisation's systems.

9.2   Risk framework

An overall framework for risk would include the following:

- risk identification;
- risk assessment;
- risk management;
- contingency and recovery planning.

It is important to appreciate a number of distinctions between:

- threats and risks;
- business and project risk;
- risk prevention and contingency planning.

9.3   Risks and threats

We will start by drawing a distinction between a risk, a failure mode and a threat.

- A risk is an impact on the business. Therefore, we can quantify risks – usually in terms of their financial impact, although safety risks are often quantified in terms of the likelihood of death or injury.
- A failure mode is a way in which something can go wrong.
- A threat is something that can cause failure – usually, an external event that may or may not happen. We can quantify threats in terms of probability – how likely they are to occur.

Let us illustrate this with an example.

- There is a risk that the authors will not complete this book in time. This has a quantifiable financial impact on the authors (who will not be paid) and on the

Institute (who will need to commission another book).

◆ This could come about in various ways – the failure modes. For example, the authors may not have enough time or they may suffer computer problems and lose their work.

◆ There are various threats that could cause failure. Insufficient time could be the result of additional work or changed family commitments (an external event), but it could also be the result of poor planning. Computer problems could be the result of hardware failure or a virus. We can assign probabilities to these (the probability of the authors being given additional work is close to 100%!).

We can also show this as a decision tree:

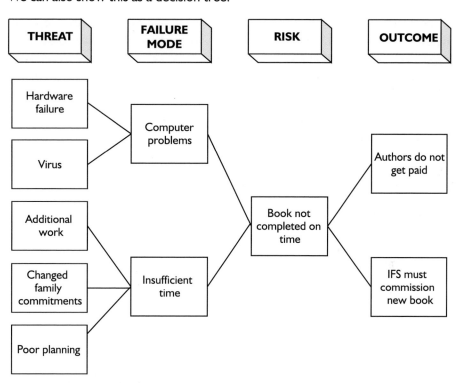

9.3.1 Business risk and project risk

We can draw a distinction between business risk and project risk.

Organisations have no choice about incurring risks in the normal course of business – it is the price of entry to the financial services industry. Projects are an investment and organisations must balance the risk against the expected reward before deciding whether to undertake the investment.

In addition, projects are very much more risky than normal business. There have been various studies on IT project success rates and these indicate the extent of the problem.

◆ Only 2% of projects are implemented without changes.
◆ Less than 16% of projects are implemented to time and budget.
◆ Only one third of projects are judged 'successful' by business management.
◆ 31% of projects are cancelled before completion.
◆ 15% of projects deliver absolutely nothing.

We must be careful not to read too much into these figures. Business requirements do change so we should expect projects to change or even to be cancelled to reflect this. However it does illustrate the uncertainties associated with projects.

We can think of normal business risk as having one dimension – we know what our business is, but we do not know which of the various threats may materialise. With projects, we have two additional dimensions.

◆ *Process uncertainty*. Each project is unique. Although the lifecycle gives us some guidance, there is usually some uncertainty about the best way to do things.
◆ *Control uncertainty*. The control processes associated with projects are not always reliable. Whatever methods are used to ensure quality, it is impossible to be certain that the project will meet the requirement until it is implemented.

Risk management usually only considers the risk of failure, but sometimes the risk of success should also be considered. An example illustrating this is the launch of Egg, where the demand for access through the Internet was so great that the system was unable to cope.

Consultants Gartner Group have suggested a model for classifying project risk that looks at 'team risk' and 'technical risk'. Team risk looks at the knowledge and experience available within the project team. Technical risk looks at factors such as the size of the system and the familiarity of the project team with the technical environment in which the system will operate. A high level of uncertainty on both dimensions suggests a very high level of risk for a project.

9.3.2 Risk prevention and contingency planning

Risk prevention is concerned with ensuring that either threats are never realised or that, if realised, they have no effect on the organisation. Methods of risk prevention include:

◆ counter-measures can be taken to prevent threats from being realised;
◆ failure modes and risks can be monitored. If a risk is detected at an early stage, its consequences can be mitigated to minimise the damage to the organisation. For example, if a financial services organisation detects a fraudulent transaction before paying out against it, this minimises the risk of financial loss.

Contingency planning assumes the threat will be realised and will have an impact on the organisation and manages the consequences to limit the damage caused.

Adding these to our risk management diagram.

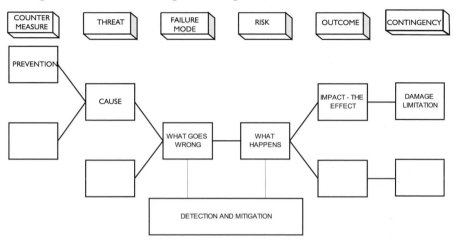

9.3.3   Risk identification

Most approaches to identifying threats and risks rely on using methods such as brainstorming to generate ideas. These methods can be used to identify problems.

- ◆ *Threats*. Brainstorming can be used to identify events that could have an impact. For example, major events such as the UK entering into Economic and Monetary Union (EMU) would be threats to computer systems development, as development resources would need to be diverted to work on EMU.
- ◆ *Failure modes*. Brainstorming can be used to identify the potential weaknesses in the organisation's systems and procedures. For example, a failure mode for payments systems is that the incorrect beneficiary may be entered into the system. Once the failure mode has been identified, the corresponding threats can also be identified. This is the approach used in the failure modes and effects analysis (FMEA) technique for risk management.
- ◆ *Risks*. Another possibility is to identify the risks themselves and use these as a starting point to identify the threats. The failure mode discussed above – incorrect beneficiary entered – corresponds to a risk that the organisation will be unable to recover money paid out.

Another approach is scenario planning. This can be used for business contingency planning, discussed later, or for major events such as the UK entering into EMU. If we were to use scenario planning to consider the potential impact of EMU entry on the organisation's computer systems development projects, we would start by drawing up a number of scenarios relating to the EMU timescale (date of entry and length of transition period, for example). We would then look at the impact of each of these scenarios in turn on the organisation's portfolio of projects. This would help us to understand the failure modes and risks the organisation faces.

9.3.4 Risk assessment

The objective of risk assessment is to determine the significance of the risk to the organisation.

One way of converting threats into risks is to consider the probability of the threat being realised and the expected cost to the organisation if it is. In Courtney risk analysis, the probability of the threat being realised in the next twelve months is multiplied by the expected cost to give an annualised loss expectancy (ALE).

The expected cost itself depends on the possible consequences of the threat being realised and the cost of those consequences. Many threats have a range of possible consequences, some of which are very low risk because their financial implications are small or because the probability of that particular consequence is very small.

Courtney risk analysis assumes that both the probability and the cost can be quantified. This is often not the case and these must be estimated or alternatives must be used.

We have discussed scenario analysis as a method of risk identification, but it can also be used when it is difficult to estimate the probablility – often, when a large number of factors are involved. The usual approach is to look at an 'optimistic' scenario, an 'expected' scenario and a 'pessimistic' scenario. The consequences of these scenarios are then estimated.

Scenario analysis does not give any absolute answers and much of the value of the technique comes from analysing how the organisation might respond to the various threats.

Monte Carlo methods, also called 'stochastic analysis', can be used when it is difficult to estimate the cost. A model of the situation is set up and a large number of examples are put through it. A random number generator is used to change key variables. The results are averaged to give an estimated cost.

Another approach is called 'failure mode effect analysis'. This involves the following stages:

◆ identify the potential failure modes;
◆ for each failure mode, identify the potential effects of failure. These are the risks and the outcomes;
◆ for each failure mode, identify the potential causes of failure. These are the threats;
◆ for each threat, identify how likely it is to occur. This is expressed as a number between 1 (low) and 10 (high);

◆ for each threat, identify how severe a problem it will cause if it does occur. This is expressed as a number between 1 (low) and 10 (high);
◆ for each threat, identify how likely it is that the threat will be detected. This is expressed as a number between 1 (high probability) and 10 (low probability);
◆ multiply the likelihood of occurrence, the severity and the likelihood of detection to calculate a risk priority number (RPN). A high RPN indicates a major threat for which there must be counter-measures.

9.3.5   Risk management

Having quantified the risk, the next stage is to manage it. There are four general approaches:

◆ eliminate it;
◆ reduce it;
◆ ignore it;
◆ transfer it.

Eliminating the risk involves reducing the probability that the threat will be realised to zero. This is rarely possible, although some threats may materialise in a number of ways and it may be possible to eliminate some of these.

For example, we can eliminate the risk of computer viruses being introduced over the Internet by not connecting PCs to it. This is common for PCs that are running critical systems. It is still possible for computer viruses to be introduced as email attachments, however.

Reducing the risk involves either reducing the probability of the threat being realised or reducing the cost, or both. This is a common approach to risk management.

Ignoring the risk is feasible provided that the ALE is small and the cost is not excessive. This approach is common for small risks.

Risks can be transferred, either to a supplier or to an insurer. Should the risk be realised a supplier may have to put things right or pay compensation, or both. This approach is common, with suppliers being expected to provide warranty against failures.

Where a service is provided, for example, where a supplier runs the financial services organisation's computer systems (facilities management, discussed in Chapter Eight) or business processes (outsourcing, discussed in Chapter Seventeen), service level agreements allow the risk of poor service to be transferred in much the same way.

Corporate assurance is similar to a warranty, except that a guarantor (rather than the supplier) provides the assurance. This is common where the supplier is a relatively small organisation and the guarantor has a relationship to the supplier, for example, in providing marketing support.

An insurer would simply pay the organisation's loss. This is common, particularly where the probability of the risk being realised is low, but the potential cost is high.

9.3.6 Contingency and recovery planning

Contingency and recovery planning allow organisations to plan what to do when things go wrong. Contingency planning is used in many situations, but one of the most important is business continuity planning.

Business continuity planning attempts to answer the question, if any part of our systems fail, what will we do? The answer to this question will depend to a large extent on the likely cost of the failure to the organisation. There is no point in making elaborate plans to recover from systems failure if these cost more than the failure would. Techniques such as Courtney risk analysis are important to quantify the various risks and to identify how much should be spent on counter-measures. Business continuity planning is also called 'disaster recovery planning'.

Organisations need to be aware of the time value of different types of information. For example the loss of information about the organisation's foreign exchange position, even for a few minutes, can be very expensive if rates change. The loss of information about customer balances for a very short period would generally be less expensive but would damage the organisation's reputation with its customers. The loss of the organisation's management information system would be very visible and embarrassing, but would not lead to any significant costs in the short term.

Most organisations have disaster recovery plans that cover a large scale failure, perhaps the loss of a data centre or of a major part of the organisation's telecommunications network. There is ample evidence that companies that suffer catastrophic failure such as fire can go out of business if they do not have adequate disaster recovery plans.

Organisations may not bring the same level of planning to more localised failures. Offices and branches are often left to make their own plans for the failure of local components such as workstations and even local area network file servers. Although this approach is valid (a centrally imposed plan may be costly to develop and inflexible to implement), there do need to be checks to ensure that offices and branches have drawn up adequate plans. Although the immediate financial costs of failure within a branch may be small, the effect on customer service and satisfaction – and therefore on the long-term profitability of the organisation – needs to be considered.

A business continuity plan may include the following:

- ◆ responsibilities
- ◆ priorities;
- ◆ communication with staff;
- ◆ backup and standby arrangements;
- ◆ public relations;
- ◆ risk assessment.

The section on responsibilities identifies who does what. Some staff will be required to come into their normal offices, others will need to go to contingency sites, others will report to the nearest local office, others may be asked to stay at home. Some staff will continue with their normal duties, but others will move to dealing with the situation and ensuring recovery from it.

The section on priorities identifies what needs to be done first. The organisation will need to balance operations, to look after its customers, with recovery, to restore normal levels of service.

The section on communication with staff identifies how the organisation will communicate with its staff. This is usually through a series of telephone calls 'cascading' through the levels of the organisation.

The section on backup and standby arrangements identifies what the standby and backup arrangements are. Contingency sites, backup and checkpointing are discussed below.

The section on public relations identifies how the organisation will communicate with the public through the media – television, newspapers etc. This is very important as a loss of confidence by customers or suppliers would threaten the organisation's survival.

The section on risk assessment considers how the organisation will use the experience going forwards by strengthening its risk management processes.

9.4 Threats

We will focus on three main categories of threat:

◆ malicious action;
◆ disaster;
◆ hardware or software failure.

9.4.1 Malicious action

Malicious action is carried out deliberately, either with the intention of doing damage or of committing another crime. The most important types of malicious action are:

◆ hacking;
◆ introduction of a computer virus;
◆ fraud.

Other forms of malicious action are less common and include sabotage.

Hacking is unauthorised access to data or computer systems. There are two main types of hacking.

◆ Use of the Internet to gain access to systems and data. Most people would associate the word 'hacking' with illegal access through the Internet and this is the most common form of external hacking.

♦ Internal hacking. A lot of hacking is internal. Staff access data and systems for which they are not authorised, either taking advantage of poor security systems or using stolen passwords. This is sometimes associated with fraud.

Although hacking is mainly seen as a threat to data confidentiality, it can also threaten the integrity of the data. Hackers are not always content just to look at the data, but may also want to leave messages to announce what they have done. These messages may change the value of (or 'corrupt') data used by the system. Hackers may also change websites.

Computer viruses are computer programs that can duplicate themselves. They 'infect' other programs by adding a copy of themselves to the end of the program. Some viruses are harmless but others can destroy data held on disk or even physically damage the computer. There are a number of different forms of virus, the most important of which are executable viruses, macro viruses and worms.

Executable viruses affect computer programs – for example, .EXE and .COM files on PCs. These are the original type of computer virus. The Internet has increased the risk by increasing the number of different types of executable file that can carry viruses.

Executable viruses work in the following way.

♦ When an infected program is run, the program's first action is to write a copy of itself into memory. It will then go on to complete the program's normal functions.

♦ The copy of the virus in memory is actually a small computer program of a type called 'terminate and stay resident'. It does not do anything until another computer program starts.

♦ When another program starts, the virus will first check to see if it has already been infected. If it has, the virus will not do anything. If not, the virus will attach a copy of itself to the end of the program and will change the first instruction in the program so that the virus is run before the program does anything else. It will then write the program back to disk with the copy of the virus attached.

Viruses check to see if the program has already been infected because they want to stay hidden for as long as possible. If a virus kept re-infecting the same program, the program size would increase (remember that viruses infect programs by *adding* a copy of themselves to the end) and it would soon be obvious by the increase in size that the program was infected.

To see if programs have already been infected, viruses look for a 'signature'. This is a part of the virus that has an identifiable pattern. Some viruses (called 'polymorphic' viruses) continually change the pattern, which makes it harder for virus checker programs to identify them.

♦ Most viruses will not take any other action until a certain amount of time has passed or until they have infected a number of other programs. This gives the virus the chance to spread as widely as possible. Once this has happened, the virus will wait for a trigger – usually a date, such as Frodo's birthday

(22 September) for the Hobbit virus or Friday 13th for the virus of the same name.

◆ When the trigger arrives, the virus will take whatever action it is designed for. Despite the publicity attracted by viruses, many of them do little damage (the Hobbit virus simply displays the message 'Frodo Lives').

Viruses such as this may cause no damage to the data on the computer or they may simply hide files (they are still stored on disk, but the operator cannot see them). Other viruses delete files, but the operator can recover the data fairly simply provided he or she realises what has happened. However, there are viruses that do more substantial damage, over-writing the contents of files with meaningless data or causing physical damage in some way.

Macro viruses affect the macros used with office automation software, especially word processors and spreadsheets. They usually create an AutoOpen macro that will run automatically when the document is opened.

Worms, which affect networks, are now the biggest threat. These used to be relatively rare, but the increasing popularity of email has provided an effective method of spreading them. The virus is usually carried in an attachment to the email and may be a macro virus or a computer program disguised as another type of file – for example, a word processor file, a picture or a music file. Opening the attachment activates the virus, which spreads by emailing copies of itself to people in the recipient's address book.

The original worm was written by Robert T. Morris in 1988. The program exploited several known security holes in the UNIX operating system and gathered user and network information as it duplicated itself and spread from machine to machine. It also employed a dictionary of common and easily broken passwords to access user login accounts. The worm also tried to hide its activity by changing its name to that of a common UNIX program and even tried to erase any trace that it had penetrated the system in the first place.

This program, now referred to as the 'Internet Worm', crashed computers all over the United States of America. Estimates vary, but it was calculated that between 2,000 and 6,000 computers were infected by the program. The financial cost was even harder to calculate, but figures quoted range between $1m and $100m.

By comparison, the Love Bug virus introduced in 2000 is estimated to have reached 45m PCs on the first day and estimates of the damage caused by the virus have been as high as £6bn world-wide. The two Code Red viruses introduced in 2001 are estimated to have caused between £5bn and £6bn of damage between them. This illustrates the growth of the Internet and the consequent increase in risk.

Worms are a particular threat. Because they spread directly, through the email system, viruses can spread very rapidly and cause damage immediately. This also makes it difficult for anti-virus software to be introduced in time to combat the effects of the virus.

Trojans are programs that create security weaknesses. An example might be a program to steal passwords. Trojans are not viruses, but are often spread by viruses – for example, the Love Bug virus installed password-stealing trojans on infected computers.

Trojans can also be used to launch denial of service attacks. These are discussed later in this chapter.

Spyware is software that is intended to monitor how a computer is used. Spyware is intended to collect marketing information about consumer behaviour, but it can also collect confidential information in the same way as a trojan. Spyware is often associated with adware, which causes advertising 'pop ups' to appear on the computer.

In most 'computer frauds' the computer is used only to create the documentation – the fraud takes advantage of weaknesses in the organisation's procedures and controls rather than in its computer systems. For example, the computer can be used to record the receipt of false invoices, but this relies on a failure to reconcile invoices against orders and delivery notes.

Another type of fraud is the misuse of the organisation's computer resources. In 'Datatheft', Hugo Cornwall gives the example of two employees who used their office computer to run a music rescoring business. They were using three quarters of the available storage space before they were detected.

Phishing and pharming were discussed in Chapter Four.

9.4.2 Disaster

Disaster includes various categories such as fire, smoke, flood and explosion.

The effects of fire are obvious and usually result in the complete loss of everything in the affected area – not only the computers, but also magnetic disks, optical disks and magnetic tapes. Smoke can also produce damage over a much wider area, causing electrical short circuits and damaging magnetic disk drives.

Water also causes damage by short circuiting electrical equipment. Water damage can be the result of flooding, burst pipes or sprinkler systems designed to combat fire. In many small office fires the threat of damage to computers from the sprinkler system is greater than the threat due to the fire!

Explosions can be due to gas leaks, chemical explosions, bombs or disasters such as crashes. An explosion can cause great damage to computer equipment in the vicinity, warping disk drives and breaking circuit boards. Debris spread by the explosion as shrapnel may cause further damage. The explosion may be followed by a fire, resulting in additional damage due to the fire and smoke. Water damage may result from pipes fractured by the explosion and from sprinkler systems activated if there is a fire.

9.4.3 Hardware or software failure

The most common causes of hardware failure are wear and tear, and environmental factors such as variations in power supply. Wear and tear includes connections becoming loose, circuit boards cracking and disk drive read-write heads getting out of alignment. Variations in power supply include both electrical 'surges' and power cuts.

Peripheral equipment is equipment attached to the computer and is subject to a wide range of temporary failures including paper jams on printers and 'parity checks' on storage devices. Ionising radiation (such as X-rays or ultra-violet radiation) or magnetic or electric fields can corrupt data held on magnetic storage devices such as disk or tape.

Telecommunications links are subject to various types of failure including lines being cut and electrical interference. Even if interference does not prevent messages being received the amount of 'noise' may make it impossible to interpret the signal correctly or the message received may not be the same as the message sent. Telecommunications components such as modems and multiplexors are also subject to the same causes of failure as other hardware devices.

Software failure is often the result of errors made when the software was written. The software may not have been designed to cope with a particular set of conditions and, when these occur, there will be an error. Alternatively, the software may not work on the particular hardware (perhaps because there is insufficient storage space) or with other systems software components.

9.5 Generic counter-measures

Before we look at specific responses to the types of threat we considered earlier, we need to consider the most important approaches to risk prevention. These are:

◆ contingency sites;
◆ fault tolerance;
◆ backups and checkpoints;
◆ passwords and access security;
◆ encryption.

An additional topic we will consider at this stage is audit trails.

9.5.1 Contingency sites

Contingency arrangements allow financial services organisations to use alternative computer equipment if they have a problem. Many such organisations have spare equipment of their own but it is also possible to make contingency arrangements with specialist disaster recovery services providers. There are two main types of contingency arrangement, hot site and cold site.

Hot site contingency means that the spare computer equipment is fully set up and loaded with the data needed to run the organisation's systems. This may be up to date as at the start of the business day, or data may be copied to the contingency site on a regular basis. If the main computer system fails, the hot site computer can be ready to take over.

This may not be immediate. Unless completed transactions are immediately copied to the contingency site, there will be a need to re-process or re-enter data lost when the main system failed. Even so, it should be possible to restore access to systems and data within a relatively short time.

Cold site contingency simply means that spare computer equipment is available. If the main computer system fails, the cold site computer will need to be loaded with the programs and data required to run the organisation's systems. Data lost when the main system failed will need to be re-processed or re-entered. This may take several hours.

Hot site contingency is much more expensive than cold site. In effect, the financial services organisation needs to pay for two computers, only one of which will be fully used. Some organisations exploit this by splitting their workload between the two computers. If both are working neither is fully utilised, but they are able to carry out additional, lower priority work. If one computer fails, all work is switched to the other and low priority work is discontinued. Even if this approach is not used, some systems are so important that the extra cost of hot site contingency can be justified. An example is a dealing system, where the organisation could lose large amounts of money if it is unable to react to exchange rate changes.

9.5.2   Fault tolerance

An alternative to contingency sites is the use of 'fault tolerant computers'. These are designed so that important components are duplicated – if the original fails, the duplicate can take over. Fault tolerant computers are used where it is very important that computer systems do not break down, such as the payment systems CHAPS and SWIFT.

We can also apply the idea of fault tolerance to magnetic disk storage. RAID, which stands for a 'redundant array of inexpensive disks', can be used to store data. The data can be 'mirrored', with copies stored on two or more separate disks, so that the failure of one disk will not result in the data being lost. RAID allows data to be stored on cheap disks and to be at least as safe as data stored on more expensive, higher quality disks.

An alternative to mirroring is 'striping'. Three disks are used and the data is split between two of the drives. The data on the two drives is compared and the *difference* is written to the third drive. If one of the drives holding the data fails, this can be reconstructed from the other data drive and the drive holding the difference. Striping is possible because the computer can treat data as if it were a series of numbers and this is important for a number of risk prevention techniques.

9.5.3 Backups and checkpoints

Taking a backup involves copying data and programs to a removable storage medium such as magnetic tape, magnetic disk or optical disk. If the data or programs are later lost, the backup copies can be reloaded. This will not completely prevent the loss of data – transactions entered since the backup was taken will still have to be re-entered – but it will minimise the loss. All data and programs must be backed up regularly.

The usual approach is the three generation (or 'grandfather-father-son') backup. Let us use this approach to see how we might take backups over a typical week.

- ◆ Monday's work will be processed. At the end of the day, all data will be copied to magnetic tape (tape 1) and stored in a fireproof container.
- ◆ Tuesday's work will be processed and the data copied to tape 2 which will be stored in a fireproof container. Tape 1 will be sent to another location for safekeeping.
- ◆ Wednesday's work will be processed and the data copied to tape 3 which will be stored in a fireproof container. Tape 2 will be sent to another location for safekeeping. Tape 1 will be retrieved from storage and returned to the building.
- ◆ Thursday's work will be processed and the data copied to tape 1, overwriting Monday's work. Tape 1 will be stored in a fireproof container. Tape 3 will be sent to another location for safekeeping. Tape 2 will be retrieved from storage and returned to the building.
- ◆ Friday's work will be processed and the data copied to tape 2 which will be stored in a fireproof container. Tape 1 will be sent to another location for safekeeping. Tape 3 will be retrieved from storage and returned to the building.

If the data on the computer is found to be corrupt, there are three backups available for recovery – the previous day's work (the 'son', stored on site in a fireproof container), the work from the day before that (the 'father', stored off site) and the work from the day before that (the 'grandfather', on site after retrieval from off site storage). This allows for two types of problem.

- ◆ The backup tapes themselves may be corrupt. Three generation backup provides three chances of finding a readable tape, although if the father or grandfather backups are used some data will have been lost and will have to be re-entered or re-processed.

◆ The problem may have arisen earlier in the week, but may only just have been discovered. Three generation backup allows the organisation up to three days to discover any problems.

We have said that backups can be made to any removable storage medium. The choice of backup medium depend on a number of factors, the most important of which are cost, robustness and the amount of programs and data which needs to be backed up.

◆ *Cost*. Cost can be expressed in terms of cost per megabyte (a megabyte is one million characters of information).

◆ *Robustness*. Robustness is the probability of the backup medium getting corrupted, so that the stored information cannot be read. Robustness can be expressed as the mean time between failures – the average number of hours usage before the medium fails.

◆ *Amount of programs and data*. This is also called 'volume' and is the storage capacity of the medium.

Magnetic tape is one of the oldest media used for backup and is still one of the most important. It is very cheap, quite robust and can store very high volumes.

During the first and second generations of IT, magnetic tape was usually in the form of a reel of tape which had to be loaded manually and was only suitable for mainframe and minicomputers. This has now largely been replaced by magnetic tape cartridges, similar to video cartridges, and a smaller version is used for backing up personal computers. More recently, digital audio tape has been introduced.

The main disadvantages of magnetic tape are that reloading backed up data is slow and that data stored on magnetic tape can be corrupted, especially when the tape itself is heavily used. However, low cost and high capacity still make magnetic tape the most important medium for long-term storage of backed up information.

An important alternative is optical disk. This can be 'write only', which is cheaper and can hold more information, or rewritable. The price of optical disk has fallen greatly over recent years and it is now little more expensive that magnetic tape. It is robust and can store very high volumes.

A major advantage of optical disk is that it can be read randomly, like magnetic disk, and reloading backed up information is much faster than for magnetic tape. Optical disk backup is often provided through 'jukeboxes' having a number of optical disk drives and a mechanism allowing optical disks to be loaded into the drives from an expansion rack.

Integrated storage units are becoming increasingly important. They will usually store current information on magnetic disk, older information to which access is still needed on optical disk and information for which access is rarely needed on magnetic tape. A particular feature of these units is that the user does not need to know where the information is stored to get access to it – the information can be requested using the standard database access language (Structured Query Language or SQL) and the unit will work out where it is stored and will retrieve it.

Removable magnetic disk storage is still often used, especially for personal computers. Floppy disks have been used for many years but their capacity is too low to be used for backing up significant amounts of information. More common is the 'zipdrive', a high capacity disk unit that uses data compression to allow it to store large amounts of data.

Data compression uses patterns in the data to reduce the amount that needs to be stored. The phrase 'the cat sat on the mat' contains 22 characters. If we replace 'the ' with '*' and 'at ' with '#', we can store this phrase as '*c#s#on *mat', which contains 12 characters (note that we have to put 'mat' rather than 'm#' because there is no final space). We have reduced the amount of storage needed by almost 50%.

Removable hard disk is also found, either as an external hard disk unit that can be connected through a Universal Serial Bus (USB) or in the form of a PC card designed to fit into slots in laptop computers. This is usually too expensive to be effective as backup and its main benefit is the ability for individuals to hold personal data and transfer this to any computer to which they have access.

Magnetic disk storage is generally more expensive than magnetic tape and only zipdrives offer cost or capacity comparable to optical disk. It is also less robust than the major alternatives. Information backed up onto floppy disk or removable hard disk can be read directly, with no delay while the data is reloaded, and this can be of benefit.

Differential backup, which only backs up the program and data files which have changed, can be used to reduce the amount of storage required. The disadvantage of differential backup is that reloading the computer requires every differential backup to be applied in turn – a very time-consuming process and vulnerable to corruption affecting any backup in the series.

A more sophisticated version of the differential backup is checkpointing, which is used on mainframe computers. Instead of copying the whole of a data file, only the items of data that have changed are copied. This is much faster than copying the entire file and checkpointing can be used to recover from errors while processing individual transactions.

Compare this with other forms of backup, where we have to recover from the start of the business day (or a previous business day if differential backup is used or there is a problem with the most recent backup). This would mean that almost an entire day's work might need to be re-entered if there was a problem towards the end of the business day. Checkpointing avoids this problem.

Checkpointing can store 'before' images, allowing the database to be 'rolled back' to a safe point before restart, or 'after' images, allowing a database backup to be restored and the database to be 'rolled forward' without the requirement to re-enter or reprocess transactions.

9.5.4 Passwords and access security

We can restrict access to systems by asking for a code to gain access. Each user will typically have a 'user ID' (which defines who the user is) and a 'password'.

The user ID is not necessarily secret. John Smith, employee number 12345678, may have a user ID of JohnSmith, SmithJ, SmithJ1 (if there is another J Smith in the organisation) or 12345678. The user ID will not change and its long-term secrecy cannot be guaranteed.

The password must be kept secret. The user chooses a password and must change it regularly, usually on a monthly basis. The password must typically include between six and thirty two characters and the system may check to see that the new password is not too similar to the previous password. To gain access, the user must enter both the user ID and the current password correctly. To protect the secrecy of the password, the system will not show the characters of the password on the screen, but will usually show a character such as '*' instead to prevent onlookers from identifying the password.

If the password is wrong, the user will usually be allowed to enter it again, but many systems allow a maximum number of tries (typically three) and may prevent the user ID, the workstation itself or both being used after this maximum has been reached.

For each user ID, the system will store a security profile saying what the user can do and what data he or she can access. This usually gives a level of authority. For example, counter staff may be able to enter transactions or make changes, whereas staff working in open plan areas may be restricted to making enquiries and opening products.

Variations on passwords include code books and personal password generators. Both of these generate one-time passwords.

♦ Code books can be used to validate messages sent over a network by customers. Each customer has a unique list of codes. Whenever the customer wants to send a message he or she will use the next code in the list. The computer processing the message has a copy of the list of codes and will check that the correct code has been used. The code book itself is kept securely under lock and key.

♦ Personal password generators such as Watchword and SecurID. These are credit card sized calculators that can generate a one-time password based on a Personal Identification Number (PIN) and either a challenge from the main computer system or the date and time. These are usually used by staff to authenticate highly secure transactions.

The advantage of both code books and personal password generators is that the password is never used again, so it does not matter if it becomes public.

Passwords can also be used to restrict access to hardware, for example, workstations or terminals. Most personal computers have a 'power on password' that must be entered correctly to use the PC. Power on passwords apply to the computer itself and are not specific to a user or associated with a user ID. Workstations or terminals can have a security profile, for example, to restrict which terminals can enter certain types of transaction. This is useful for ensuring that transactions such as money transfers can only be entered in secure areas. We can combine terminal profiles with individual profiles to provide a further level of security. We can also restrict who is allowed to use certain terminals by checking the terminal against a list of valid user IDs.

It is common automatically to 'log off' terminals from any systems to which they are attached if a period of time passes without anything being entered. This ensures that staff do not leave terminals in a position to enter transactions when they go to lunch or go home, for example.

An alternative is to use screensaver passwords. Screensavers are computer programs that put some form of moving pattern on the computer screen when it is not used for a period. The purpose of the screensaver is to protect the screen – if the same image remains on the screen for too long, it will leave a permanent imprint. A password can be assigned to the screensaver and this will protect the system if it is left unattended.

Alternatives to user IDs and passwords include badges and biometrics. Badges can be required in order to activate terminals – this could be combined with a system where staff need badges to gain access to the premises. The badge is usually a magnetic strip card or a smart card, which is swiped through or placed in a reader attached to the terminal. Another alternative is the active badge or radio badge, which activates the terminal when it is within a certain distance of a sensor attached to the terminal.

A variation on this is often used for office banking. The customer uses a smart card that not only proves his or her identity to the system, but also provides a key for coding and decoding messages sent to and from the bank. A new smart card is sent to the customer on a regular basis, changing the key used for encrypting messages.

Biometrics were discussed in Chapter Four.

9.5.5   Encryption

Encryption is used to encode messages or data and is another technique that relies on the computer's ability to treat data as a series of numbers. When the computer encrypts data, it carries out a mathematical operation using the data and an encryption key.

The mathematical operation usually used is the 'exclusive OR' (XOR), but we can illustrate the principles using multiplication. If our encryption key is 67 and the data we wish to encrypt is 12345 we can multiply these to get 827115. It is impossible to get back to the original data without knowing the key.

In practice, encryption keys are much larger than 67! 'Weak' encryption uses a key of 40 binary digits – allowing numbers of over one million million to be used. 'Strong' encryption starts at 56 binary digits – 72 thousand million million – and systems used to encrypt financial transactions may use 128 binary digits – three hundred million million million million million million.

Financial services organisations have two main requirements for encryption.

♦ To encode data held on portable computers. This is important as staff increasingly use portable computers when visiting customers' premises, to store information about both the customer relationship and any new business. This protects sensitive information if the portable computer is lost or stolen.
♦ To encode messages containing confidential information or carrying instructions for the transfer of value.

The example we have used is an example of symmetric or secret key encryption. We use the same key to encrypt and decrypt the data. Therefore, we must ensure that the encryption key is kept secret. The Data Encryption Standard is a symmetric key encryption standard.

The difficulty with using symmetric encryption to encode messages is that the sender needs to have access to the encryption key. If a financial services organisation provides thousands of its customers with the key, how can this be kept confidential?

One possibility, which we have already discussed, is the use of smart cards to provide customers with encryption keys. However, issuing new smart cards every month is too expensive to be practical for the retail market. There is also a risk that some of these will be intercepted in transit.

An alternative approach is to use different keys for encoding and decoding the message. The key used for encoding is called the 'public key' and the key used for decoding is called the 'private key'. Together, the public and private keys are called the 'key pair' and there is a mathematical relationship between them. This is called 'asymmetric' or 'public key encryption'. Asymmetric encryption was developed by Rivest, Shamir and Adleman, after whom RSA encryption is named.

Asymmetric encryption is slower than symmetric encryption, but provides better security. If someone wants to send a message to us, they will encrypt it using our public key. We then use our private key to decrypt it. If we want to reply, we use the other person's public key to encrypt the message and they will use their private key to decrypt it.

We can encrypt data using either hardware or software. Hardware encryption uses a special computer chip that automatically carries out the encryption process. It is faster than software encryption and is used where large amounts of data need to be encrypted. Software encryption is more flexible and keys and algorithms (the method of encrypting the data) can more easily be changed.

There is also a form of encryption called 'steganography', in which the encoded message is hidden in a picture file. This is makes it difficult to detect whether an email contains a coded message at all.

9.5.6 Audit trails

Audit trails keep a record of everything that happens in the course of processing a transaction. The most common form of audit trail is a system 'log' which records all attempts to access systems and data. Attempts that are unsuccessful may well be shown on a separate security report for later investigation.

In addition to the system log, most systems in financial services organisations maintain their own audit trails. These systems usually require different people to enter and authorise transactions and maintain an audit trail by recording who entered and authorised each transaction, when it was entered and authorised and sometimes the terminals on which it was entered and authorised.

Audit trails do not prevent breaches of data protection, but they make it easier to detect and identify who is responsible. Audit trails may also be needed to comply with the Police and Criminal Evidence Act 1984 and the Civil Evidence Act 1995.

9.6 Specific counter-measures

Let us return to our three main categories of threats:
◆ malicious action;
◆ disaster;
◆ hardware or software failure.

How can we apply the risk prevention methods we have discussed to these and what other methods can we use?

9.6.1 Malicious action

Some of the approaches to risk prevention we have discussed above apply to the threats due to malicious action. For example:
◆ backups allow programs and data to be recovered to their state before the malicious action took place;
◆ passwords and access security prevent access to systems by hackers or those intending to introduce a computer virus;
◆ encryption prevents hackers from intercepting messages, either to breach data confidentiality or to alter the message with the intention of committing fraud. Encryption also prevent thieves from reading the data stored on a stolen portable computer.

In addition to these general measures, there are some specific measures financial services organisations can take to protect themselves against malicious action. These include:

- ◆ virus protection measures;
- ◆ authorisation.

Virus protection measures include restrictions on sources of software, firewalls and virus checking programs.

Restrictions on sources of software usually require that all software is obtained from reputable sources and is still sealed in its original packaging when it is delivered. Cheaper sources of software such as shareware are sometimes infected with computer viruses. If software media are not sealed in their original packaging, there is a risk that the software may have been pirated and may be infected with a virus. There are also licensing implications, as discussed in Chapter Three.

Firewalls are used to reduce the risk of infection over networks, especially the Internet, and are discussed later in this chapter.

Virus checking programs look for the signatures of known viruses. With worms now presenting the greatest threat, anti-virus software vendors monitor threats around the clock and distribute updates to signature files over the Internet. This has proved effective and recent viruses such as the Sasser Worm (2004) have been less destructive than the Love Bug or Code Red viruses.

Another approach is to prevent any data being written to the area where computer programs are stored. This may take the form of setting up a separate area on the hard disk for software and preventing any changes to this data, or at least warning if such an attempt is made. This approach is often used to protect programs stored on the file servers of local area networks.

Authorisation involves another person – often a supervisor – checking the data back to the original input instructions and authorising it. Authorisation is used for transactions such as payments and new accounts where an error could be expensive for the organisation.

9.6.2 Disaster

Some of the approaches to risk prevention we have discussed above apply to the threats due to disaster. For example:

- ◆ contingency sites allow rapid recovery of the most important systems and data in the event of disaster;
- ◆ backups allow programs and data to be recovered to their state before the disaster took place.

In addition to these general measures, there are some specific measures financial services organisations can take to protect themselves against disaster. These include:

- Fire prevention
- Flood prevention.

Fire prevention measures include the use of smoke detectors, fire alarms and fire doors. Fire extinguishers should be available and should use carbon dioxide or powder instead of water-based foam. Copies of back-up data stored on site should be kept in firesafes or fire resistant cabinets.

Sprinkler systems should not be used near computer equipment as the water will cause damage. 'Halon gas' systems, which spray gas to smother a fire, are usually used near mainframe computer equipment.

Flood prevention measures include the use of false floors provided with drainage to allow small amounts of water (for example, from a burst pipe) to drain away. Computer facilities such as data centres should not be sited where they are likely to be subject to flooding.

9.6.3 Hardware or software failure

Some of the approaches to risk prevention we have discussed above apply to the threats due to hardware or software failure. For example:

- fault tolerance allows hardware to continue to operate even if some components fail;
- backups and checkpoints allow programs and data to be recovered to their state before the failure took place.

In addition to these general measures, there are some specific measures financial services organisations can take to protect themselves against hardware or software failure. These include:

- uninterruptable power supplies;
- preventative maintenance;
- parity checking and data correction.

Computers are very sensitive to variations in power. Some of the most sensitive equipment is protected by capacitors. In the event of power failure, these supply power for long enough for the equipment to close down safely, preventing any damage. Another method is the use of surge protectors to prevent a power surge causing damage.

Uninterruptable power supplies are more sophisticated and can be used to ensure that voltage does not go outside the range acceptable to the computer. Large data centres will usually also have a standby generator, allowing rapid restoration of power in the event of power loss.

Computers, like cars, need regular maintenance to detect and sort out problems. This is called 'preventative maintenance' because it helps to prevent the computer from failing when it is processing the organisation's work.

Parity checking is used to identify corruption in data read from magnetic disk or tape or received over a telecommunications link. It again relies on the ability of the computer to carry out mathematical operations on data. The results of these operations are stored as additional characters with the data. When the data is read or received, the computer repeats the calculations to see if it gets the same answer. If not, this shows that the data has been corrupted.

Errors in data sent over telecommunications links can be corrected automatically. When the receiving device gets a block of data it checks the parity. If this is correct, it will send an acknowledgement back to the sending device. If the parity is incorrect, it will send a negative acknowledgement back, and the sending device will send the block again. A system of this type is called an 'automatic repeat request' system.

9.7 Internet security

It has been said that the problem with the Internet is 'security, security and security'. Why is this and how can we overcome it?

The problem is that the Internet is an open network. Anyone can connect to the Internet and the standards and protocols are widely published.

Security breaches are usually a result of weak links, weak services or internal threats.

- ◆ *Weak links.* Breaches are normally attributable to several factors occurring individually, but when they all occur together, then mayhem usually ensues. For example, an easily-broken user password can let in a would-be hacker to cause damage and if this user account is held on a computer system with known security holes (that have not been corrected), then the problem is easily compounded – even more so if the compromised account is the root or system administrator's account.
- ◆ *Weak services.* Internet services themselves are not 100% secure – they were never designed to be so. They were originally developed for the rapid exchange of information, not to prevent hostile attacks. However, Internet services can be made secure easily enough in a number of ways, for example, integrating a security module, using encryption, understanding the weaknesses, deploying best practice, staff training and education, etc.
- ◆ *Internal threats.* By far the biggest threat to computer systems is not, as one might first think, from an external hacker lurking somewhere on the Internet, possibly on the other side of the world. In fact, the biggest threat to computer and network security comes from staff internal to an organisation. It is estimated that over 80% of security breaches originate from a company's own personnel. These staff members usually have the biggest motivation for causing such damage: they may have been ignored for a pay rise or job promotion, or may not get on well with their boss, or may have social

or personal problems that increase the chance of them causing vicious or hostile damage to a corporation's valuable resources. They also have the best opportunity – staff are already inside the organisation and do not need to gain physical access to the data and resources.

The main security weaknesses are in services, data and communications.

◆ *Services*. In theory, all Internet services are under possible threat of attack. This includes internal and external email, company websites, file transfer facilities, remote logins, networked (shared) file resources, etc. While all these services have the ability to introduce loopholes, careful deployment of the technologies and a firm understanding of their limitations should ensure all is relatively risk free.

◆ *Data*. Corporate information and data is probably the greatest company asset, and it should therefore be protected. However, it can still be compromised; a troublesome staff member may decide to copy, destroy, sell or otherwise tamper with this information. Such actions should be planned for and suitable counter-measures introduced.

◆ *Communications*. This same corporate data could also be intercepted as it travels from one computer to another (either on the same Local Area Network or over the Internet). Software applications and hardware devices are available that allow such 'sniffing' or 'snooping' of information when it is in transit. One possible solution to this problem is to encrypt all data as it travels across the internal network as well as out onto the Internet.

There are many types of attack that can be used and directed towards computers, networks and other resources. These four are probably the most common.

◆ *Denial of service*. This type of attack involves a user or intruder taking up so much of a system resource that none is left for other legitimate users. The attack itself can take several forms: destructive attacks (re-formatting hard disks, deletion of system-critical files, cutting power or network cables, etc), overload attacks (continually querying a server so that it cannot process valid requests, etc) and file system attacks (filling up all available disk space thus not allowing others to save data/files, etc).
Denial of service attacks over the Internet are sometimes called 'cracking'. Trojans are planted on innocent systems that will, on activation, query the target server. This makes the source of these attacks very difficult to identify.

◆ *Spoofing/impersonation*. Both computers and individuals can be impersonated and forged. Computers can easily be configured with fake or forged IP addresses that can subsequently allow access to specific networks, resources and information. Similarly, individuals can use 'social engineering' techniques to try and obtain privileged information. The classic example is someone telephoning the technical support desk and saying: 'Hi. This is Fred over in accounts. I've forgotten the password to access the payroll data. Can you let me have it please?' Pharming and phishing, discussed in Chapter Four, are both intended to obtain privileged information.

◆ *System intrusion.* If corporate resources have succumbed to an attack, then it's likely that an intruder will be able to wander around the networked systems and resources. What they do while they're on their 'electronic stroll' is open to question depending on how they feel at that particular time. They may be kind and leave everything untouched, or they may be particularly nasty and delete files, tamper with user accounts, crash machines, leave backdoors to gain future (unnoticed) access, send fake emails, corrupt websites – the list is endless.

◆ *Data corruption and disclosure.* Corporate data is valuable and must be safeguarded and protected – otherwise, it may well be destroyed and/or duplicated by an intruder. The integrity of the data will come under question – how can the organisation be sure that it was not edited, tampered with, or changed in some other way? How can the organisation now control who gets to see it? Will it be sold to a corporate competitor?

9.7.1   Identification and verification

A particular problem with carrying out a transaction electronically is, how to identify the parties.

This is similar in some ways to the problem of 'card not present' credit card transactions. Cardholders receive a measure of protection in these transactions through indemnities, rules on delivering goods to the cardholder's registered address and expert systems which can identify attempted fraud. These measures are not generally available for electronic transactions.

One approach is to use a digital signature. This allows an individual to establish that he or she sent the message – provided the recipient knows the sender. In many cases the recipient will not know the sender personally.

An alternative is to use a public key Infrastructure. This allows the sender to be issued with a digital certificate to establish his or her identity.

9.7.2   Digital signatures

We discussed asymmetric encryption earlier in the chapter. With asymmetric encryption the message is encoded using the recipient's public key, with the recipient using the private key to decode it on receipt.

A digital signature works the other way round – the sender uses his or her *private* key to encrypt the signature information. The recipient will use the *public* key to decode it. This proves the identity of the sender as the only person to know the private key. We call this the 'signature key' pair to distinguish it from the encryption key pair.

9.7.3   Digital certificates

A digital certificate is an electronic identity document issued by a certification authority and corresponding to a physical identity document such as a driving licence or passport used to identify the parties in a physical transaction. A digital certificate may contain information such as:

◆ identification information (for example, name and address) for the certificate holder;
◆ the certificate holder's public key;
◆ information about the certificate (for example serial number and validity dates);
◆ identification information about the certification authority who issues the certificate;
◆ the certification authority's digital signature. This allows the parties to the transaction to authenticate the digital certificate.

The certificate must be issued through a 'trusted third party' in which all parties to the transaction have confidence. There will be a 'certification hierarchy' by which a certification authority of undoubted probity can certify others to issue digital certificates. This infrastructure is sometimes called a 'public key infrastructure'. Financial services organisations could act as certification authorities or trusted third parties.

The integrity of the certificate issuing process must be clear. Certification authorities must only issue certificates to parties whose identities they are certain of and must have systems for tracking certificates in issue. There must be a certificate revocation list to identify unauthorised and expired certificates.

Digital certificates are generally issued as software at present. This creates a potential security weakness and the security of the digital certificate can be compromised if the keys are known. In future, it is likely that smart cards will be used to store digital certificates, providing additional security.

9.7.4   Digital envelopes

Another security device is a digital envelope. This combines symmetric and asymmetric encryption. The system generates a random symmetric key that is encrypted using the recipient's public key. The message is then encrypted using the symmetric key. The symmetric key (encrypted with the public key) and the message (encrypted with the symmetric key) are sent to the recipient in a digital envelope.

This has two advantages. First, symmetric key encryption is faster than public key encryption, so a large message can be encrypted and decrypted faster if this method is used. Secondly, if the message is being sent to a number of people, then it only needs to be encrypted once. The symmetric key will need to be encrypted once for each recipient (as they will have different public keys), but this is faster than encrypting the message several times.

9.7.5 Secure electronic transaction standard

The Secure Electronic Transaction standard (SET) was developed by Visa and MasterCard as a method of protecting financial transactions over the Internet. It makes use of encryption and digital certificates. As SET is restricted purely to financial transactions, it is not subject to the US government restrictions on the export of encryption technology. SET also allows brand differentiation between the Visa and MasterCard payment networks.

SET meets five major business requirements:

♦ it ensures the integrity of the data;
♦ it protects the confidentiality of payment and other information forming part of the transaction;
♦ it provides authentication of the cardholder's identity and status as a legitimate user of a payment card account;
♦ it provides authentication of a merchant's identity and ability to accept payment card transactions through an acquiring financial institution;
♦ it creates a set of rules that is independent of the security mechanisms used.

Integrity is ensured through a 'message digest'. Mathematical operations are carried out on the message to produce a 'checksum'. The message digest is encrypted using the signature key. The recipient can make sure that the message has not been altered by decrypting the message digest and then repeating the checksum calculation.

Confidentiality is preserved through encryption. We may want different parts of the transaction to be accessed by different parties – for example we may want a financial services organisation to have access to the payment details and the counterparty to have access to the commercial details. SET allows a 'dual signature' by which different parts of a message can be kept confidential. There is one dual signature which covers both parts of the message. This includes the message digests, allowing the parties to have confidence that the messages have not been altered.

Digital certificates are used to authenticate the identity of all parties to the transaction. As well as the purchaser and merchant, these will include the payment gateway and the acquirer. The certification hierarchy is used to verify these certificates.

Although the account number is needed to validate the cardholder's certificate, the account number is not held on the certificate and cannot be calculated from it.

An alternative approach, which also uses both public key encryption and digital signatures, is the Secure Sockets Layer (SSL). SSL is widely used in the US for e-commerce.

9.7.6 Identrus

Identrus provides stronger security as digital certificates are issued on smart cards and are authenticated in real-time.

Identrus provides a public key infrastructure for the issue of digital certificates. Identrus is the highest level certification authority and financial services organisations participating in Identrus can act as certification authorities (issuing digital certificates to their customers) or as registration authorities (outsourcing the certification authority role).

Identrus meets five major business requirements:

◆ *authentication* – assurance that the parties to the transaction are legitimate;
◆ *authorisation* – assurance that the individuals representing the parties to the transaction are acting within their authority;
◆ *confidentiality* – assurance that the transaction will only be seen by the party for which it is intended;
◆ *integrity* – assurance that the message is not altered;
◆ *non-repudiation* – assurance that the agreement is binding and recourse if the other party disputes the agreement.

We can show this as a diagram:

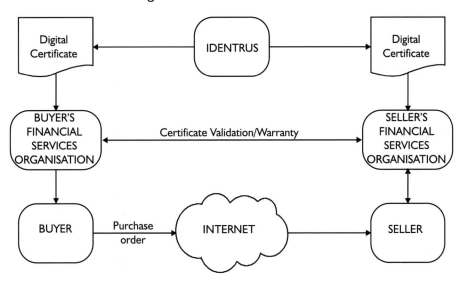

Entrust is another organisation offering similar services.

9.7.7   Firewalls

A firewall includes software, and sometimes hardware, and protects the organisation from viruses and other forms of malicious action. If the firewall does not have its own hardware, it is installed on a router. There are two types of firewall.

- ◆ *Filtering firewalls.* A filtering firewall only allows specified types of data through. For example, a filtering firewall can be set to allow Internet access for email only.
- ◆ *Proxies.* A proxy is more sophisticated. Instead of allowing data through, the proxy 'pretends' to be the organisation's systems to anyone trying to access them externally and pretends to be the external network (for example, the Internet) to anyone trying to access it from inside the organisation.
  This allows the proxy to examine the data much more thoroughly than with a filter firewall and proxies are better at detecting and eliminating attacks such as viruses.

In practice, most firewalls combine both approaches.

Firewalls also provide other services.

- ◆ Providing an audit trail of all data passing through the firewall.
- ◆ an alarm about apparent attempted security breaches.
- ◆ supporting network address translation (NAT). NAT allows us to use different addresses within and outside the organisation. This is very important if we want people to be able to send email over the Internet to people within the organisation – it hides the real address and also allows us to register a single IP address rather than one for each server.
- ◆ Some firewalls allow authentication of security devices such as smart cards
- ◆ Some firewalls can operate a virtual private network (VPN). A VPN uses public links, but messages are wrapped in a digital envelope to provide a very high level of security.

9.7.8   Handshaking

Handshaking allows two computing devices to recognise each other. This involves an exchange of information between the devices before any sensitive information is sent. The concept is similar to that of a digital certificate, but it identifies devices rather than individuals.

This was used in ATM networks operating on a remote batch basis to ensure that the ATM was connected to the financial services organisation's mainframe before sending details of any ATM transactions.

It is also used in the Mondex system. Mondex only allows e-cash to be transferred between Mondex cards and the cards go through a handshaking routine before any transfer. This could also be used in transferring e-cash across the Internet.

9.7.9 Cookies

A cookie is a small text file stored on the PC's hard disk. When we access a web page it may update the cookie file.

Cookies are used to store identification information about the PC. This is similar in principle to handshaking, but is for convenience rather than security. It can be helpful as the website will not need to ask again for information it already has. Cookies are particularly useful for holding registration information as the web site will know that the user is already registered the next time it is accessed.

Cookies are text files and cannot carry viruses. A cookie can only be accessed by the website that created it and cannot be used to trawl for information about what sites the PC has accessed. Current versions of browsers allow users to request a warning before cookies are created or to refuse to accept all cookies.

Ten

Understanding customers: customer knowledge management

10.1   Introduction

Most financial institutions would list their top three assets appearing in their balance sheet as:

◆ employees;
◆ physical network of branches, call centres and processing centres;
◆ investment in Technology.

There is, however, another asset which does not (at least currently) appear in the financial assessment of an organisation – the value of the customer information the organisation holds and its ability to use this information to enhance the customer experience and create value. This is the essence of customer knowledge management. It is insufficient just to hold information it must be structured and connected to enable its use for the benefit of both the customer and the organisation.

Customer knowledge management brings together external macro-economic research and links it to demographics with the goal of applying this insight with individual customer behaviour to predict likely future needs of each individual customer.

External and market research information

Individual customer behaviour

10.2   Understanding external forces

a restructuring financial world

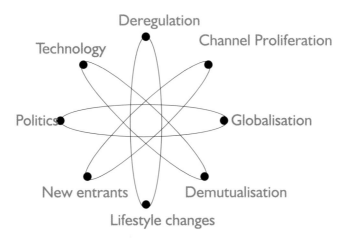

The types of external forces and agents of change, which need to form the backdrop to effective knowledge management, are shown in the diagram above.

10.2.1   Deregulation

The increasing desire of governments to create a level competitive playing field to encourage active competition, while creating a mix of self and statutory regulatory bodies.

10.2.2   Channel proliferation

The growth in the number of different ways in which a business and consumers can interact and the removal of geographic boundaries through 'virtual' channels such as the telephone and Internet. The growth in use of plastic cards and the demise of cheques.

10.2.3   Globalisation

Virtual channels and an increasing desire to exploit economies of scale are leading to businesses (and individuals) thinking and acting beyond traditional borders.

10.2.4   Demutualisation

The need for the ability to move quickly and dynamically to embrace opportunities is making some corporate structures such as mutuality appear cumbersome. This is further fuelled by the desire for short-term returns and 'financial windfalls' for members on conversion.

10.2.5   Lifestyle changes

Traditional life patterns are changing rapidly with increasing mass wealth and an ageing population giving access to more consumer goods and lifestyle options.

10.2.6   New entrants

Financial services products are, in most cases, virtual rather than physical and with the removal of barriers to entry (such as the branch network) together with increasing demand and good historic margins, new players are appearing almost daily. The growth in specialist direct providers.

10.2.7   Politics

The growth in desire (from all major parties) for individuals to take on more personal responsibility for their lives and financial well being and the gradual removal of the state 'safety net' to a basic level.

10.2.8   Technology

The rapid development and innovations created by the merging of computers with communications and multimedia challenging traditional methods of delivery. The widescale availability and adoption of high-speed mobile Internet access.

10.3   Demographics

Demographic information enables financial organisations to understand how the population of customers will change over time and therefore predict likely needs and consumer demand for products and services.

10.3.1   Ageing, maturing – demography of the UK

There will be more elderly people and fewer young people in the population of 2010. Increased longevity – the outcome of better nutrition, greater health awareness and improved healthcare – is a prime indicator of our success as a society of relative plenty, prosperity and protection. On current evidence, there will be substantial increases in the older age groups – with the 85 + age group growing the most. The shifts by age group from 1991 to 2011 are shown in the chart:

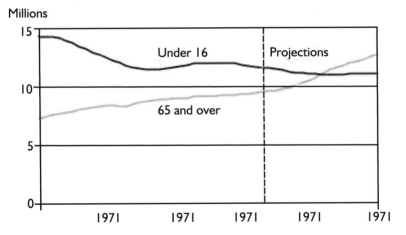

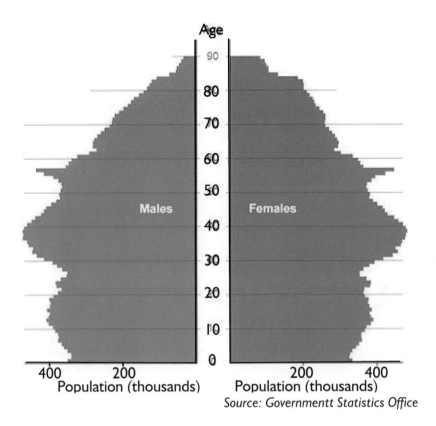

Source: *Governmentt Statistics Office*

Some medical commentators are predicting life expectancy of 130 years for children born in the first years of the new millennium, which means that the pensioners of 2060 might have a further 70 years of active life to fill and finance. Of course, by 2060, retirement may well have changed so radically in form and function that the idea of it being a quiet 'twilight time' is far from relevant, but looking towards a nearer horizon, the Future Foundation Group estimate there could well be five million healthy and active 65+ year-olds in 2010 – half the total of this age group.

This information alone is likely to lead to:

◆ increasing demand for:
  – medical and life care insurance;
  – pensions;
  – flexible investment plans;
  – home visits;
  – easy access to services (increased proportion of population with disability).
◆ decreasing demand for:
  – personal loans (most taken out by 20–29 age group);
  – mortgages for first time buyers;
  – starter homes.

10.3.2   Changing household composition

Thousands

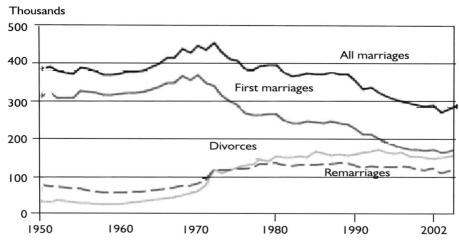

A reduction in married couples and growth in single person forecast will change the demand for housing provision and design with probably fewer bedrooms and more flexible living space to accommodate home working, etc. As the Internet plays a greater role in serving domestic consumers, it is anticipated that a modern-day version of the traditional neighbourhood milkman could re-emerge as part of the social fabric and informal support structure of communities. Delivery agencies, for example, may be charged with alerting health services if a single or elderly client fails to open the door at a pre-agreed delivery time.

10.4   Technological advances and usage

Percentages

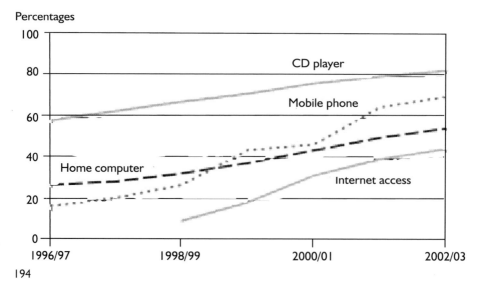

It is now 20 years since information technology was first parachuted into schools and there has clearly been an appreciable and accelerating growth in technological confidence among young people. There is no doubt that new communications technologies have already had a revolutionising impact on the way information is accessed and shared, as well as on working and learning methods.

Students are the group of the population with greatest exposure to new media and new communications technology. Today's school students can have experience of creative play, networking and remote contact and collaboration in, for example, virtual school exchanges. They can also learn how to plan and manage their time, using real-time and deferred contact through e-mail, multi-player games, etc. This raises questions about how this generation will respond to directed work in the future and what value will be placed on communications in the global networked society.

Taking the forecasts for numbers of young people together with trends in access and usage of the Internet and new media, Future Foundation group estimates that, by 2010, there will be a technologically literate population of 40 million in the UK.

Some 30% of these will be 'functionally literate' – ie, they will be capable of finding readily-accessible public domain information and shopping via simplified games console-type digital TV interfaces. This group will typically be those who have adopted new technology in adulthood. A further 60% will have grown up regarding new media as today's middle-aged would the TV – these will tend to be younger people. While not experts in information technology, they will be adept at using it for all types of transactions, games, networking and as the 'default medium' for contact with their family and peers. They will naturally gravitate towards jobs in the service sector which can capitalise on their familiarity with communications technology. A further, much smaller group will be expert users, including developers, engineers and architects of integrated systems.

10.4.1 Internet access

Highest in London and South East

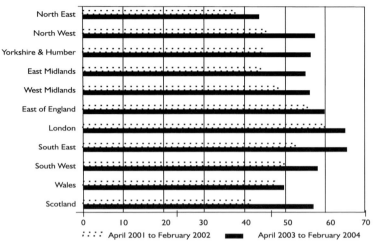

Adults who have used the Internet in the last three months: by government office region and GB country

In 2003/04 the proportion of adults that had used the Internet in the three months prior to interview was highest in London and the South East (both 64%) and lowest in the North East (43%). The highest percentage increase in Internet access between 2001/02 and 2003/04 was in Scotland (16%), followed by the North West and Yorkshire and the Humber (both 12%).

In 2003/04, 58% of adults in Great Britain had used the Internet in the previous three months. This was 9% higher than in 2001/02. Men are more likely than women to use the Internet, but the gap between men and women closed over the two years to 2003/04. Among women, the proportion increased by 12 percentage points to 54% compared with a seven percentage point increase among men (to 61%).

Internet use also varies by age. It is highest in the 16 to 24 age group (83%) and lowest in the 65 and older age group (15%). In the two years to 2003/04 the greatest percentage increase was among adults aged 45 to 54, increasing by 13% to 63%. The lowest increase was among those aged 65 and over (6% to 15%).

In 2003/04, half of all adults who had used the Internet in the previous 3 months had used it for buying or ordering tickets, goods or services. A higher proportion of men (53%) than women (46%) had used it for purchases. Adults aged 25 to 44 were the age group most likely to purchase goods over the Internet (55%), while the least likely age group was those aged 65 and over.

Annual data from the ICT module of the NS Omnibus Survey released on
29th June 2004.

Eleven

Customer relationship management

11.1 Introduction

Customer relationship management (CRM) is a key initiative in many financial organisations today. Proliferation of delivery channels such as the Internet, TV and mobile phone together with increased competition and customer sophistication, continue to increase the competitive pressures on finance institutions. Such pressures have revolutionised the way we do business and nowhere is this more apparent than in the need to understand customers as individuals and draw as much value as possible from the information generated during every interaction.

This view is reinforced by Graham Flower, head of Customer Management at HSBC:

> 'CRM is our corporate glue; as custodians of our customers' information, we are obligated to use this information wisely and to make it available when and where they need it and to help customers understand and solve their financial needs.'

Today, organisations are finding that they no longer have the initiative. Customers are now empowered by ready access to information and have greater access to businesses than ever before. According to Peter Soraparu, Managing Director for Retail Financial Services at the Bank Administration Institute: 'CRM is a passé concept. It assumes customers can be managed. That is no longer the case. It is the customers who are managing their own financial services'. This increasing consumer awareness only adds to the pressure for organisations to organise, protect and deliver information as required by the customer.

Customers are demanding access and treatment on their terms, not the firm's. More than ever, it is essential for a company to excel at each customer contact point, be it in the field with mobile sales forces, traditional face-to-face interaction at branches or in the contact centre by phone, fax and e-mail correspondence. The acceptance of the web has further changed this landscape as customers and channel partners increasingly interact in a self-service environment. Businesses are faced with adapting to this new reality or becoming irrelevant. The mantra is increasingly about understanding, managing and enhancing the 'customer experience' rather than just reducing the cost of delivery.

There are increased requirements (often regulated) to prevent money laundering, terrorism, tax evasion and social security fraud through identifying who is behind transactions. This, together with requirements under Basel II, also drive the creation of integrated customer databases.

Finally, the increasing incidence and concern over identity fraud (where a criminal is able to assume the identity of a customer and gain access to their accounts) heighten the need for customer data to be protected both physically and from electronic attack.

11.1.1 A definition of customer information management

'Customer information management involves the collection, synthesis and secure delivery of the right information at the right time to the right person or delivery channel in order to optimise the return for both the business and the customer.'

11.1.2 A definition of CRM

'CRM is the intelligent use of information and people to identify, predict and learn from customer behaviour and contact in order to initiate appropriate action to develop and maintain a relationship with the customer to achieve commercial benefit.'

The fundamental difference in these two definitions is the concept of a 'relationship' between the organisation and the customer, largely as a result of the historic relationship manager concept in banking. The word 'relationship' has an almost unique definition in banking which causes confusion. In this book, relationship is always discussed and seen through the eyes of the customer NOT through the eyes of the organisation, ie it is up to the customer to determine if they have a relationship, whether they have an 'allocated' relationship manager or not. Relationship is therefore made up of the total customer experience through all channels, both electronic and human.

11.2 Identifying customers

It may seem obvious, but if you are unable to identify a customer as a customer and understand the products, services and interaction the customer has with your organisation, then tailoring that experience is going to be very difficult.

11.2.1 Defining a customer

In structuring information, the key is to understand who your customer is. This may sound obvious, but defining a customer does require an organisation to make some fundamental decisions. For example, a person holds a personal account and a business account with a bank. How many customers are there? Logic would lead you to believe there was one customer: however, many banks would define this as two customers despite there being only one legal entity. Reasons for this may be that the bank wishes to hold separate behavioural and attitudinal information in order to aid segmentation or business reporting. However, frequently, it is because either the commercial and personal systems are separate or incapable of holding two addresses (ie one for the business and one for the person). If the customer were a director of a limited company, then would the answer be different? Obviously, in law, we now have two separate legal entities. The bank's systems must reflect this for accounting purposes, but what about for marketing and analysis purposes?

Similarly joint accounts can give a problem. You have two customers sharing a product, but if either also holds a sole account, then the other party to the account has no right of access to information on the other's sole account unless specifically granted through a mandate from that customer.

11.3 Customer types and relationships

Most organisations resolve the above dilemmas by defining certain customer types and then through defining relationships that can link customer types together, eg

11.3.1 Customer types

Personal	Personal customer (who has or has held a product or service with the organisation)
Personal prospect	Customer who has no products with the bank but has been targeted or received a marketing approach (eg direct mail)
Business customer	Sole trader or other unincorporated business
Incorporated business	Separate legal entity

11.3.2 Relationship types

Parent/child	Linking a parent to a child
Personal/business	Linking personal customer to a business
Partner/partner	Husband/wife
Household member	Live at the same house

The importance of getting the definition right and consistent should not be underestimated as these definitions form the basic building blocks of a customer orientated data structure/data model.

For example, take two customers, Mr and Mrs Jones, who hold a joint current account and each holds a sole deposit account. This gives two customers and three accounts open on the system. What is the cross–sales ratio? If you take two customers and three products, the answer is $3/2=1.5$.

However, each customer has access to two products (the joint account and their sole account) so, from a customer viewpoint, the cross–sale ratio is actually 2. Which is correct? Well, they both are depending on if your starting point is a product or customer focus, highlighting the need for a consistent approach and set of definitions across the business.

In customer to customer links, further problems can occur and restrictions exist in data protection as to the use bank's can make of such links. For example, a poor credit history on a member of a household cannot be used in the assessment of creditworthiness of another member of the household.

The next stage in the development of CRM is to answer the following question:

11.3.3 Who are my customers?

In most organisations, this involves the pulling together of data from so-called 'legacy product systems' and to create a customer (rather than product) driven view of the world. Obviously, in start up situations such as 'Egg' or 'Virgin one', this is easier as the systems architecture can be built from this viewpoint, but equally they start with little or no data. Traditional organisations have basically two options. They can either re-engineer their systems totally (as in the case of the Woolwich [see the case study]) or connect and evolve their existing systems into an integrated CRM system (HSBC have followed this approach) . The decision on which (or any) approach to follow will involve an assessment and balancing of the following points.

- *Risk*: does revolution or evolution offer the lower risk to the business?
- *Functionality*: is it a better investment to build on existing (often rich) functionality or better to start from scratch (or buy a package)?
- *Who 'owns' the data?* Often third party organisations that provide products sold by the bank (for example, house insurance) maintain customer data and the underlying terms and conditions/contract may need to be revised to permit consolidation.
- *Development cost*: can the organisation fund the development in terms of skills and resources required?
- *Financial cost* : can the organisation afford the investment
- *Executive sponsorship*: is the commitment there to develop CRM?

The basic structure of the customer database could be as outlined in the diagram below.

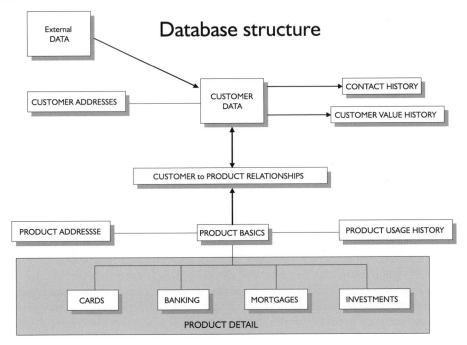

The customer database pulls together information on the customer (for example, name, address, age, income, customer value, customer preference, propensity to purchase and channel/contact history) which is then linked to the product holdings (for example, type, balances, transactions, interest rates, etc).

201

It also takes in external data from suppliers such as Axciom or Experian who can provide demographic and credit data at a household or individual level to enhance understanding of the customer's needs.

The detailed structure of relational databases is covered elsewhere in the text and more detail on building a data warehouse is covered later.

11.4 Single customer view

Businesses need to form a single view of customer information to enable relationship building. A single view of information helps a business identify its most valuable customers and understand the value they get from the business. When a business understands its customers, it can show customers that it cares about them and their needs.

Also, while revenue growth through new customer acquisition was possible in a silo organisation structure, the current objective of 'value growth for the existing customer base' requires the integration of customer knowledge and cross-channel contact management for an intelligent and seamless sales and service capability. At the same time, financial services regulators demand that a bank demonstrates that it is effectively managing risk, anti-money laundering, financial accounts and corporate governance across the whole enterprise.

CRM helps address this challenge by connecting delivery channels to the hub of a CRM plan. Additionally, the focus moves from viewing the various transactions that occur with customers as single transactions to viewing all of the transactions as a continuing dialogue with each customer.

Critically, this includes the customer's channel preferences and permission to use the channel to contact the customer. The increasing quantities of poorly-targeted (in terms of customer need) direct mail, email (spam) and unsolicited telephone calls have led to increased consumer protection through central 'no mail' and 'no telephone' (for example, telephone preference service in the UK) registers restricting the ability to make contact. Businesses must also realise that different channels require different etiquette. For example, people tend to be more informal with email than they would ever be by phone or written letter. Businesses need to consider all of the dynamics of new access channels. CRM can address the need to find and integrate access channels. Additionally, CRM can help businesses capture information about consumers at all access channels.

Many finance companies are organised along the lines of various functions, like marketing, customer service or by product line, rather than along customer lines. Too often, the various vertically-organised departments have different measurements and objects. For example, learning about customers and what they need and want is a task assigned to marketing, but creating the things customers need and want falls to the product areas. Customers are brought into a company by marketing, but the area that is charged with keeping customers happy are the various channels which are often run as separate business areas.

Every time information about a customer transaction moves from one department to another, it runs the risk of being lost in the process. There are several inefficiencies in the process.

- Strategies and plans are developed by each department independently.
- Information sharing and joint problem solving are limited.
- Accounting, measurement and reward systems are separate and unsynchronised.
- Customer relationship is fragmented.

The result of this process is that customers are often frustrated and always looking for a better deal from another provider. CRM should help companies create seamless customer experiences so that no matter where customers interact with the company – on the Internet, by telephone or in person – they receive the same experience. Additionally, all departments are working toward common goals, sharing information and viewing the same information. The (hoped for!) result is that if companies create a seamless customer experience, customers will want to do business with them on a continual basis.

More recently, the inclusion of both structured and unstructured information (ie content management) has enabled forms, images, news feeds, videos and other content to enhance conclusions drawn from analysis, but also ensure the availability of this important support information for sales and service processes.

Having outlined the primary reasons for deploying a single customer view, the bank also needs to consider in more depth the most typical new business scenarios to be supported, also, which key components are required.

As banks strive to grow the value of their existing customer base and improve their customer experience, while achieving all aspects of regulatory compliance and good business management, the transformation scenarios that are attracting most executive interest include account opening, cross-selling and retention, loan origination and risk pricing, digital media marketing, Basel II and other regulatory compliance issues.

Each of these relies on seamless 'closed loop' learning operations, from analytics and decision making, through to multi-channel connectivity, ongoing fulfillment of sales and service, with integrated measurement and improvement.

11.5 Consumer managed data – the future?

Making the most of customers who use multi-channel connectivity most effectively may actually pass the ability to link and maintain customer data back to the customer. The following is extracted from an article written by Bryan Foss of IBM:

'During a recent project where a major European bank assessed its separate sources of customer data before integration into a new customer file, it seemed that the only data with sufficient accuracy and currency was provided from profiles maintained by the customers themselves via Internet services. Unfortunately, this was a very small proportion (perhaps less than 1%) of total data, and it had not previously been available for use when managing customers through other channels.

Recent research by Gartner confirms that customers who use online channels to maintain their data and to research related product options have more valuable interactions with branch and contact centre staff than those consumers who make little use of self-service channels.

This suggests that there could be a strong case for differentiating the services provided to customers who use the multi-channel environment more effectively, as they are likely to be more valuable to the bank. In a recent IBM project experience with a credit card company, it became clear that customers maintaining their own profiles through e-business channels had improved data accuracy. The consumer usually recognises that the bank normally benefits more from this house-keeping effort than they do and yet little incentive is offered by the bank for the consumer to continue with this effort. However consumers that prefer to be in control have a preference for this approach.

Smart banks also recognise that it is far more effective to re-focus on meeting the needs of each customer as their needs change through major life events or event stages. In some relationships (for example with a trusted financial advisor), the customer has learned that it is beneficial to share information on expected or planned events as good advice can be obtained in return. Unfortunately, few consumers see the bank as an advisor, able to add value at key life events. Most do not yet trust banks through sharing knowledge of their intentions and plans as they know that very few banks can store and use this information properly.

Rather than maintain a separate profile with each bank, some commentators foresee the time when the consumer will manage their data in one place and allow access to selected providers to specified sub-sets of this data – for example, to enable the bank to provide quotations or services. However, it is not clear what would cause such a major shift in the way data is managed, who would provide the central storage and access methods required and whether banks would be sufficiently prepared to work in this way.

In at least one European country, health data is now being stored centrally and access permissions can be granted to multiple institutions by the patient. Once such a precedent is available, it becomes a far smaller step to enable access to a sub-set of this health data for your insurer or bank to provide more customised pricing, underwriting or claims services. Perhaps early moves like this in other industries will change the way that consumers expect data to be shared and used within financial services too.

In an associated trend, anti-money laundering regulation and other terrorism controls are increasing the focus on identity management, which may evolve fairly quickly to the provision of a central or shared identity validation service in some countries. Not only could this approach address some regulatory issues, but it could also facilitate improved service for consumers. Alternatively, it may be possible for a financial institution that has already validated the consumers' identity to verify this identity to others, making account opening and other processes far more efficient. Companies that already provide data pooling services and external sourced data to the financial services sector may also have a role to play in identity management, especially as they are already familiar with the need to separate validated data (such as electoral rolls and credit history used for credit scoring and underwriting) from the preference, behavioural and other less well validated data more often used for prospecting. Of course, some of these changes may be supported and encouraged by consumers and other proposals rejected as potentially too intrusive and counter to consumer privacy expectations.

Within the last few weeks, I have needed separately to provide photo ID and proof of address documentation to at least four institutions: to open a mortgage account, a stock trading account with a broker, engage a conveyancing solicitor and to transfer funds abroad. Typically, it is not only the initiation of new relationships that are made more difficult and costly as a result of these regulations, but sometimes even new products may require the same identity validation when the relationship was initiated before current regulations came into place. As a result, some banks are finding an increased drop out rate of new business applications through their account opening processes; as the marketing and sales expenses are already spent to recruit the customer, this can dramatically reduce the efficiency and effectiveness of the recruitment process. Other associated industries are affected by the same regulations. For example, in some countries, it is now not possible to purchase a new car with cash to reduce the opportunity of laundering money (whether terrorism or tax avoidance related) through the consumer economy. Payments from recognised banks that have validated identity are acceptable instead.

At the same time, the best banks have already understood that the effectiveness of outbound marketing is waning, especially where the bank has been able to prepare itself to be more effective in the management and response to inbound contacts and opportunities. If the consumer is provided with the opportunity, incentive and confidence to maintain and share current preferences information, then the balance moves even further toward maximising the value of inbound contact opportunities, especially when we know that specific consumers are most valuable through their use of the multi-channel mix. While this inbound consumer contact is often real-time and the initial response may be as well, additional follow-on contacts could also be at the 'right time' for best effect, combining outbound and inbound capabilities to optimise both value and customer experience.

As consumers emphasise their ability to manage the level of relationship that they desire, increasingly, they will also manage the data they share with their chosen financial services providers. Probably, the effects and initiatives described here will start to combine, enabling the smart bank to transform its customer management operations to open up 'clear blue water' from competitors.'

11.6 Linking CRM to corporate objectives

In essence, any organisation with customers is trying to achieve an optimal mix of the following.

11.6.1 Customer acquisition

- ◆ Which customers do we wish to acquire?
- ◆ What do they need?
- ◆ How should we go about it?
- ◆ How much is it worth spending to achieve the acquisition?
- ◆ What is the predicted return?

11.6.2 Customer growth

- ◆ Which customers offer the best prospects for cross–sales?
- ◆ What do they need?
- ◆ How should we contact them to achieve this with maximum return on investment?
- ◆ How do we build the product and delivery to suit the customer?

11.6.3 Customer control

- ◆ Which customers are likely to destroy value (for example, potential bad debts or negative customer value)?

- ◆ What actions should we take to minimise this risk?
- ◆ Which customers do we wish to lose?
- ◆ How do we lose them with minimal damage to brand and reputation?

11.6.4   Customer migration

- ◆ Which customers are going through (or about to go through) a life event (for example, student to graduate, single to family former, working to retired, etc)?
- ◆ What do they need?
- ◆ How should we contact them to achieve this with maximum return on investment?
- ◆ How do we build the product and delivery to suit the customer?

11.6.5   Customer retention

- ◆ Which customers are we vulnerable to losing?
- ◆ What actions should we take to minimise this risk?
- ◆ How should we contact them to retain our return on investment?

Obviously the best way to answer these questions is to understand deeply the customers you already have and use this to:

- ◆ look after and 'grow' your best customers;
- ◆ acquire more like them!

Using customer knowledge

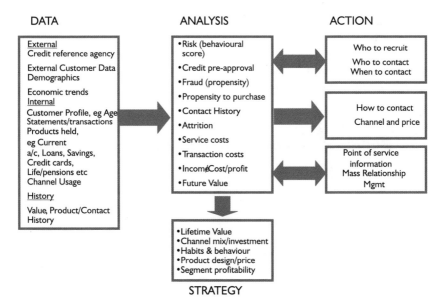

The above diagram gives an overview of how the interaction between data from internal and external sources can be linked ,with insight gained from individual customer interaction, to provide an analysis of the business and answer some of the questions above.

11.7   Key customer management components

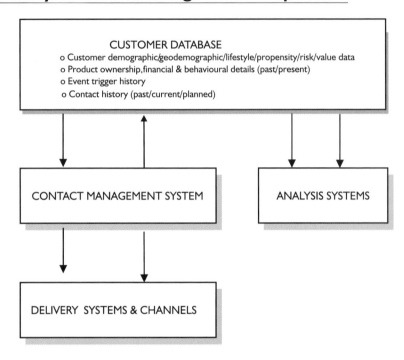

The above schematic gives an overview of the various components that will be described in the following chapters.

11.8   Building the customer database: creating the corporate memory

11.8.1   Data warehouse

Definition: 'database' and 'data warehouse' tend to be used interchangeably. The primary difference is the assumption of scale and integration that is implied in a data warehouse, ie it is a large database pulling together information from other product and transaction systems. At its simplest, a data warehouse is a very large database which is used for the long-term storage of data likely to be of continuing value to the organisation. As with any warehouse, the data is only of value if it can be accessed when it is needed and the other aspect of a data warehouse is some form of query language.

Data warehouses have been made possible by two main developments.

◆ Improvements in the size, performance and cost of storage devices and relational databases.

An example is the development of tiered storage. This allows the most frequently used data to be stored on hard disk and less frequently used data to be stored on optical disk or tape cartridge. The user does not need to know where the data is stored and can use a single instruction to access the data irrespective of its physical location.

We can show this as a diagram.

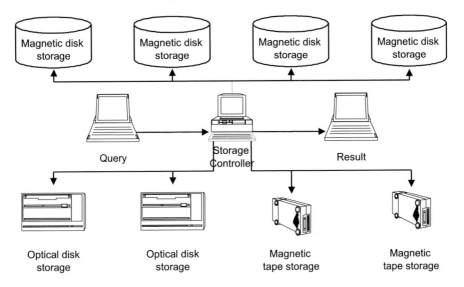

◆ Improvements in the technology available to access data. This includes developments in computer hardware and software.

An example is the database machine. This spreads the data over a number of different storage devices, each of which has its own processor. This allows very rapid access to data as each processor will look for the data requested on its own storage device. In simple terms, if there are a hundred processors, the database machine will find the data one hundred times quicker than a conventional computer.

We can show this as a diagram.

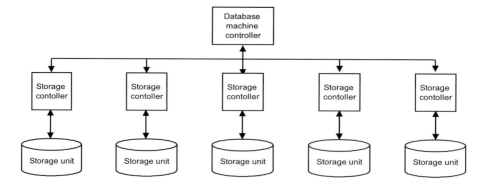

There are three things we can do with our data warehouse:

◆ We can run enquiries against the data. We can use a standard query language, but there are also a number of query languages designed to be used in a data warehouse environment. It is also possible to use software such as spreadsheets and electronic office databases and link these to the data warehouse using database connectivity tools.

◆ We can extract some of the data into one or more datamarts. These are discussed in the next section.

◆ We can analyse the data. This is discussed below under Online Analytical Processing.

11.8.2 Datamarts

A datamart differs from a data warehouse in that it only includes the data relevant to a specific function – often, a single department or line of business. The advantage of a datamart is that it is much easier for the business users to find the information they need as, by definition, the datamart only contains the data relevant to them and can be organised in the way that best suits their needs. The users can retrieve this information using a query language or database connectivity.

In contrast, the traditional approach to management information took a series of data extracts from the operational system databases and loaded this into isolated databases for each function within the organisation. The problem with this was that the data could be inconsistent between the various users. Different functions (for example, finance, credit and risk, marketing) with access to different information could take different and even contradictory decisions.

If a data warehouse is used, all data is first loaded into the data warehouse. Extracts are then carried out against the data warehouse to load the individual datamarts.

The data warehouse presents a 'single image of business reality' and helps to ensure consistency between the various sources of management information. Datamarts are designed round the needs of their business users, presenting the data needed in the format needed, but because the information is drawn from a single source, it is consistent and comparable.

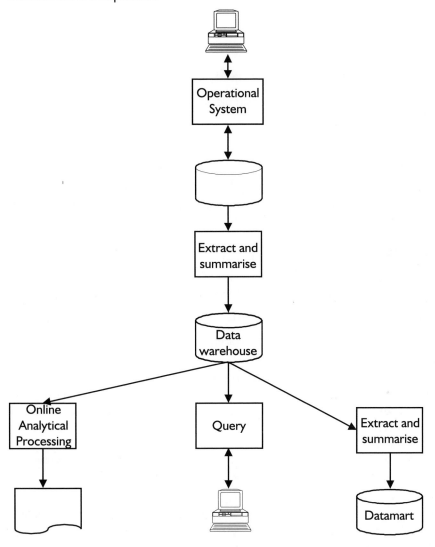

11.8.3   Building the data warehouse

First-generation warehouses – batch orientation

First-generation data warehouses batch-process data useful for supporting decisions about pricing, market positioning, business development and so on. For example, a first-generation data warehouse implementation might be to perform list selection and extracts for direct mail and telemarketing campaigns. However, these list pulls are largely initiated by human intervention or predefined scheduling criteria that are largely independent of individual customer events.

Next-generation warehouses – one-to-one relationship orientation

The next generation of data warehouse implementations support real-time analytics to assist in managing the customer relationship at any and all touch points and in understanding the customer as an individual. This approach is particularly important in light of the impending tidal wave of e-commerce. Conducting business over the web will eliminate traditional channels of relationship building. The self-service model of e-commerce reduces operational costs of customer service.

However, marketing organisations in astute corporations are already grappling with the impact of losing direct contact with the customer.

Thus, the trend toward integrating the data warehouse with customer interactions will be adopted even more aggressively and evolve toward more sophisticated use of information as corporations explore ways of developing a CRM strategy such as event-based triggering for conducting business in the face of e-commerce.

Examples are NCR Teradata and IBM DB2.

An overview of a simple customer data warehouse structure.

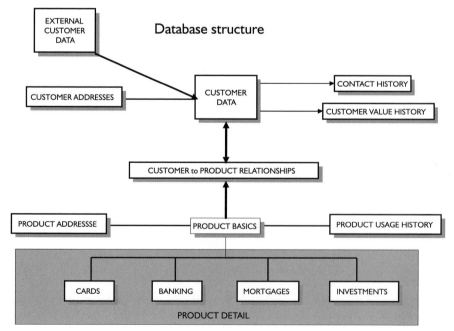

11.9 Data management: obtaining and integrating data in the warehouse

The process of identifying and cleaning data is fundamental to creating a usable data warehouse and is often the most challenging part of creating the CRM system. Keeping data up to date, together with data integrity, is a continuous and major endeavour.

Tasks include the following.

- *Data parsing* – extracting specific data items from a mixed domain field. For example, extracting multiple names from mailing labels or removing product codes from a comment field.
- *Data conditioning and domain integrity* – modifying data when values are missing or in error. Changing data from one set of codes to another ensures that values of specified fields fall properly within defined ranges.
- *Attaining entity integrity and data integration* – ensuring that only one set of attributes reference a particular entity and that only one occurrence of each key entity exists. Data integration resolves character-level anomalies such as spelling errors, abbreviations and conflicting data.
- *Data conflict resolution* – finding multiple records that refer to the same entity, but possess conflicting attributes – for example customer records that list the same name and address, but have different social security numbers.
- *Data enrichment* – adding data from external data sources.
- *Data moving and routing* – moving legacy data to their proper locations within relational tables.
- *Data-rule embedding* – embedding business rules to influence how data is integrated, moved, changed or filled.

Products such as Trillium or Integrity provide an automated means to transform imperfect data from multiple legacy and external sources into a consolidated view of the business across systems, departments and business lines.

The customer database provides the central corporate 'glue' for holding together a record of a customer's interaction with an organisation. The campaign management system helps to turn this knowledge into proactive customer contact with the aim of increasing net customer value.

Twelve

Customer differentiation

Having created the single customer view, the next stage is to identify what different customers are worth to the bank and how their needs differ now and in the future. The key to this is to use traditional research techniques and then integrate them with the individual customer data.

Ideally, this should be achieved at individual customer level, however, sometimes, this can only be achieved at customer segment/cluster level to enable the bank to differentiate its service/products to optimise return.

12.1   Integrating traditional research

Many financial organisations undertake their own (or are partners in) bespoke research. This is either quantitative, where the objective is to achieve a statistically acceptable number of responses to specific questions, for example, there are now more mobile phones in the UK than people, or qualitative, where the research explores the reasons why consumers have an opinion or have made a decision.

There are many quantitative techniques, including the following.

- ◆ Habits and practices (questionnaire used to find out how, where and when a product or service is used).
- ◆ Image and attitude (respondents attribute importance rankings to several product or service attributes then rate brands on those attributes. Helps assess strengths and weaknesses compared to competitors and key product attributes).
- ◆ Trade-off study (measures the relative importance of features of a product or service which assists in both the design and marketing of a product).

◆ Market segmentation study (defines market segmentation for product positioning/characterisation of target audiences to help define customer segments).

◆ Purchase motivation (understands consumer motivations for purchase and usage decisions).

◆ Needs research (understands the key emotional and product performance consumer needs and how those are currently being met).

◆ Post purchase or contact surveys (understands customer experience in a quantitative way after an experience).

◆ General satisfaction surveys (consumer's view of brand/product/service based on experience and general market/media exposure).

An example of quantitative research.

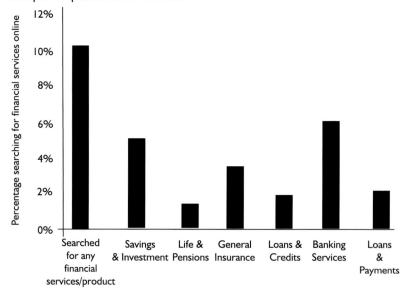

Source Datamonitor

Qualitative techniques include the following.

◆ Focus group interviews (groups of eight to ten consumers discuss motivations, attitudes, beliefs and feelings via group discussions, normally with a facilitator).

◆ One-to-one interviews (generate in-depth information to understand behavioural, cognitive and emotional reasons).

◆ In-home observations (understand how consumer uses product/service in real life context).

◆ Post-purchase or contact surveys (understand customer experience in qualitative way after an experience).

◆ General satisfaction surveys (consumer's view of brand/product/service based on experience and general market/media exposure).

- Special panels and consumer boards (group of customers selected, tracked and interviewed over time to help assess changing attitudes, etc. Group may contain segment representatives or experts).[1]

An example of qualitative research:

Customers' views

Customers want	Banks are
An 'adult to adult relationship'	Self serving, rip you off
To be known and valued	Act as if they can survive without you
Intelligently proactivity	Uninterested in the customer
Qualified, accountable staff	Under pressure to sell
A 'sense of trust'	Seeing customer as 'guilty until proven innocent'
	Lacking personal touch

Source: 'Banking is useful, bank's are not', IFS Cambridge Seminar.

12.2 Customer insight: understanding customer experience

It is also vital for companies to test and understand the customer experience through a mix of techniques such as:

- customer focus groups: gathering together customers to discuss particular aspects of products and/or delivery;
- customer satisfaction surveys: by post, phone or the Internet to gather general satisfaction feedback and/or feedback on recent purchase or contact experience;
- contact recording and sampling: ongoing coaching linked to actual experiences for example call recording;
- back to the frontline: encouraging all staff and executives to experience customer contact directly.

The following is an extract from an article by Bryan Foss, Global Customer Insight Solutions Executive, IBM Banking Industry, Financial Services Sector.

'Too frequently, banking executives are so focused on prescriptive (or push) marketing, sales and service activities that they forget to understand the customer's experience as the key to their success. Perhaps you have had one or more of these experiences from your bank:

- your bank offers you a product you already have with them;

217

- you receive a loan offer, but have cash and never use loans;
- you stop (or don't start) using your credit card, but they don't notice or react;
- as a '20-year valued customer' they don't seem to spot you have left them;
- your bank keeps making the same mistakes, whatever you tell them;
- ... when if they tried this service themselves, they would have left long ago!

As a customer, do you feel that your feedback is accepted? That your bank listens, learns and improves its customer value and service?

Of course, the best banks are way ahead of the rest in understanding the customer experience and continually improving to break away from the pack. More recently, the leading banks prefer to compare themselves to best practice customer experiences, whichever industry sector provides them. This becomes ever more important as customers have a much wider choice of financial services distributors, including retailers and more.

Some of the keys to success are emerging from our best practice assessments.

- Ensuring executives and non-customer facing departments are in touch with the customer's perceptions. One financial services company provides executives with a taped summary of recent service calls to play in their car on the way to the office, a general manager elsewhere joined us in a 'listening-in' call centre audit.
- Use, evaluate and comment on your own company's services, 'seed' your own employees into mail, phone and other campaigns for an experience shared with your customers.
- 'Close the loop' using analytics to understand and improve the acceptance of new offers and services, supported by specific customer and employee feedback.
- Implement 'touch point' research to understand the customer's perception of different offer and channel combinations – one offer may work through the branch, but not on the web, at least in its current form.

It's no surprise that a bank operating without 'customer insight' fails to understand and address its customers' needs and perceptions, operating expensive and multiple channels well below an optimum level of business performance.

Does your bank have a customer insight capability and does it deploy it well to improve customer experience?'

12.2.1   Understanding individual customer behaviour and applying it to individual customers

The external forces and market research gives a good picture of how groups of customers or segments may behave. There is, however, another rich source of customer knowledge which can be drawn form the information held by financial organisations on individuals or purchased at individual or household level from data brokers (for example, Claritas, Experian, Axiom).

The information falls into five broad categories.

Transactional

This includes all basic product purchases or transactions on accounts. For example, a bank will have access to all transactions on the current account or credit card. This information can give a very clear insight into the lifestyle of the customer. The timing, amount and payee enable a picture of the customer's life to be established, for example, payments to a garage indicate vehicle ownership.

Personal

Facts about the individual, age, address, income, sex, etc. These can be enhanced by linking the individual to a household (through address and postcode) to help assess socio-economic class, life stage and lifestyle.

Attitudinal

This is normally obtained through individual customer survey which can either be at an attributable individual level (ie consumer gives their name) or at a segment level where the attitudes are attached to a type of customer. (for example, customers over 85 much prefer access to a branch than through email).

Channel usage

Understanding which delivery channels customers use and for what type of transactions. This can be obtained through transactional information and tracking the types of delivery channels customers have access to (for example, their home has access to digital TV). Understanding this information not only gives a view on how customers prefer to contact an organisation, it can also give an insight into how the organisation should contact the customer. It will also provide an insight into how the customer undertakes complex transactions. For example, in purchasing a mortgage, the customer may go to the Internet first to obtain some quotes, but will then want to visit a branch to complete the transaction with a financial planning manager.

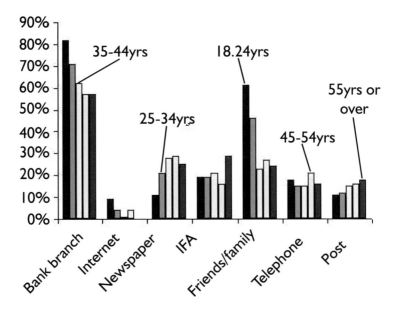

Source: Datamonitor: Customers' preferences for obtaining information on savings and investments.

Risk assessment

Assessing probability of default is a key factor in agreeing and pricing risk products such as loans and overdrafts. Information on individuals' risk history can be built up internally from previous lending successfully repaid and externally from credit reference agencies (for example, Experian).

12.2.2 Customer differention and segmentation

In the previous section, we examined the sources of customer information and how this could be combined to provide a powerful knowledge base for understanding and predicting customer behaviour. Ideally, this can then be applied in a one to one interaction with the customer to help identify the correct needs and solutions.

However, most organisations still make use of customer segmentation models which look to collect customers into groups which will have common needs. It is important that these common needs exist or the segmentation grouping is useless.

12.2.3   Types of segmentation

By product

This is the most traditional analysis method where each product is managed independently and the analysis takes a product (rather than customer) view of the portfolio. For example, a bank's personal loan portfolio could be segmented by:

◆ purpose of loan;
◆ length of loan;
◆ amount of loan;
◆ interest rate applied, etc;
◆ age of loan;
◆ loans in default.

By geography

This is a customer approach where customers are segmented by geography. It useful in the assessment of areas for the building of branches or their redesign to match the types of customer the organisation wishes to attract in an area. Companies such as GMAP and Experian specialise in this type of segmentation to assess:

◆ type of housing by postcode;
◆ customer demographics by postcode;
◆ transport routes;
◆ competitor branch locations.

Lloyds TSB used this type of segmentation analysis in assessing the viability of the merger with the TSB.

By socio-economic grouping

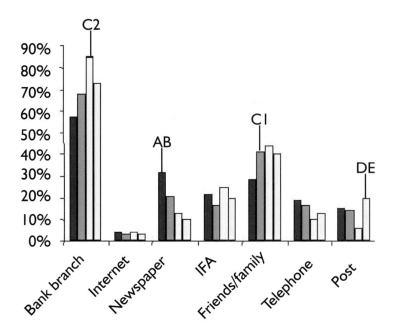

Source: Datamonitor.

By segmenting customers by their socio-economic grouping where A is the most affluent and E the least. Depending on the type of customer the organisation wished to contact, this analysis will help, for example, if you wished to attract AB customers for an investment product then the Datamonitor research would imply that marketing through the branch and newspaper was likely to be the most successful.

By lifestage

A customer's age has been used widely as the single best predictor of likely financial needs. However the changes in lifepath resulting from the changes in society mean that this is a less reliable segmentation method. Many retail organisations are now moving to 'lifestage' segmentation where they try to place each customer in a lifestage, for example, young single, young worker, family former or family with older children. This method offers the flexibility that matches changes in society where a person may get married, get divorced and then remarry to create a second family. Each lifestage will carry high propensities for certain financial needs, for example.

Segmentation by socioeconomic group and lifestage

Socioeconomic group:

◆ Professional and managerials (AB)

◆ Junior managers and non-manual (C1)

◆ Skilled manual (C2)

◆ Semi-skilled and unskilled (DE)

Lifestage:

◆ Young singles

◆ Pre-family

◆ Family formers

◆ Older families

◆ Older singles and child-free couples

◆ Empty nesters

◆ Retired

Lifestage: young single (18–24).

◆ Credit card = high propensity.
◆ Personal loan (for transport) = high propensity.
◆ Investment in equities = low propensity.
◆ Pension = low propensity.
◆ Short term savings = high propensity.
◆ Saving for house deposit = medium propensity.
◆ Internet based current account = high propensity.
◆ Cash machine access = high propensity.

By life event

This is a far more dynamic approach and aims to identify and/or predict the time a customer will be going through a 'life event', for example, moving house, going to university, changing job, getting married, buying a car, etc.

It is based on the fact that most (if not all) financial products are bought to achieve an objective in life either now or in the future. As such, the product is a means to an end and will be considered only when the time is right for the customer.

For example, car insurance is typically renewed annually, so a customer is unlikely to consider purchasing car insurance from a competitor outside a period of around a month before renewal is due. So identifying this date for each individual customer is critical to improving response rates and reducing marketing costs. Some events are easier to predict than others. Typically, knowing a customer's age gives a lot of insight into events such as likely university start and finish dates or retirement.

However, predicting when a customer may move house is a lot more complex. The most sophisticated banks will blend centrally-obtained insight on customers determined from the behaviour of customers deemed similar (through clustering and segmentation) with transactional data and information captured directly from the customer. This last source is often overlooked and yet is most likely to offer the most accurate response!

By customer value

This is the opposite type of approach to product segmentation. Here, the total product holdings a customer has with an organisation are used to assess the customers value. Most organisations are keen to move to this type of segmentation, but it does require detailed information on all of the customer's products and a robust customer database. In the 1990s some banks and credit card providers started to do this analysis and were shocked to find that their initial assessments indicated that 80% of their income streams were being generated by less than 20% of their customers. Further refinements by banks such as Citicorp have shown that, having taken costs into account, the top 20% of customers generate over 100% of income, the next 50% contribute about 30% and the bottom 30% lose or 'destroy' value of about 30%.

This type of segmentation, while very powerful, does have risks. Financial organisations need to retain customers over a long period to maximise return and customers may be loss making in the early years (for example, students and customers with 'special offer' discounted mortgages), but they will offer significant future potential.

The most sophisticated segmentation by customer value is now made up of many dimensions, for example:

- *customer risk*: short-term probability of default;
- *current value*: calculation of actual customer profitability based on current products and services used;
- *future value*: an estimation of future potential based on an analysis of customer lifestage, previous history, socio-economic group and size of 'wallet' or wealth.

By customer attitudinal or behavioural segmentation

This another fairly recent approach to segmentation and it again requires an in-depth knowledge of the customer. Here, customers are grouped by their common attitudes and behaviour. For example, 'early adopters' of technology indicating that these customers will be more receptive to (or even demand) access to the latest technology. FirstDirect has a high proportion of 'early adopters' who joined the bank when it was created as the first telephone based 24 x 7 x 365 bank. Because of this, their customers are much more likely to want Internet, 3G and other new delivery channels compared to, say, the customer base of a small building society or traditional high street bank. This type of segmentation has led to a number of companies offering to group customers into 'pen portraits' or 'stereotypes' with some amazing names like 'lemons' and 'oranges'.

Attitudinal segmentation can be very important in understanding the buying preferences of customers, for example, it can be used to discover which type of customers would prefer a traditional relationship with a member of staff and those who would prefer to make decisions on their own.

An example of analysis based on customer behaviour.

Next purchase intention

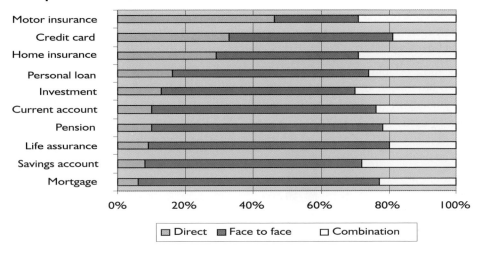

Source: Prospektus 2000

The above is an example of quantative research where the customer is asked 'how do you intend to buy your next XXXXX ?' It demonstrates how, depending on the product, the customer will wish to go through the purchase experience. What you can see is that the majority of customers would not consider a branch as a logical starting point to buy car insurance and would start through either the telephone or the Internet. This gives great insight into what the main role of each of the delivery channels is and how they need to work together to achieve the product sale. It also shows how less complex products are becoming commodities with speed, ease of access and price being more important to the customer than advice.

12.3.4   Which segmentation to choose?

No single segmentation method will provide all of the answers required. This is one of the reasons why financial organisations have built large databases pulling together external and internal information to provide insight into customer behaviour.

Each of the above segmentations (and there are many more) provides a way of helping to answer a particular set of business questions. For example, product segmentation is vital in understanding the profitability and dynamics of a product portfolio. Whereas channel usage segmentation will help understand which customer is likely to want to buy a product through which channel.

225

12.4   Customer value and potential

Having established a single customer level view, undertaken customer research and chosen one (or many) approaches to segmentation, it is then possible to analyse and interrogate the database to understand what individual customers have in common and how they differ.

For most established mass retail organisations such as banks and building societies who have been used to a 'one size fits all' approach with maybe some limited segmentation (such as a special youth or first time home buyer packages) this analysis can come as a shock.

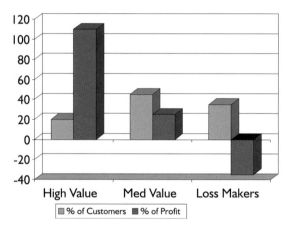

The above diagram is a typical analysis of customers by individual customer value that banks in America and Europe have discovered. Finding out that 20% of your customers generate over 80 – 120% of your income and that 30% of your customers are currently destroying value (or losing you money) is not a message that many financial services organisations' CEOs are happy with!

At this stage, the organisation is not undertaking one to one marketing, but can start to tailor its marketing and contact approach at a portfolio level. In other words, you can identify a large number of customers with a similar profile and approach them with the appropriate product. It also helps the organisation to understand the answer to two fundamental questions.

◆ Who are my most valuable customers (current value)?
◆ Who are most likely to be my most valuable customers in the future (future value)?

12.4.1   Calculating current value

Answering the first question, once you have built your single customer view, is simply a matter of mathematics adding up the net income stream from all of the products owned by the customer and subtracting the costs of the organisation's resources used by the customer:

◆ Customer current value = sum of net income – sum of costs.

This can be done over a period of time typically calculated each month as part of a 12-month moving average.

Whilst the calculation looks easy, the obtaining of the data on transaction costs and income is often far from easy. Few large banks are able to calculate unit transaction costs or separate out the variable element from the fixed with sufficient accuracy to enable the application at an individual customer level. Similarly understanding the 'net income' on some products (for example, life policies and other insurances) is a lot more complex than calculating net interest on a deposit account. However, spread between most and least valuable customers is such that accuracy only needs to be in relative terms for this information to become actionable.

12.4.2 Calculating future value

This is potentially much more of a challenge as this seeks to assess the opportunity to increase business (for example, balances on accounts) or cross-sale future products to the customer. There are many ways to create this score and they are generally made up of some or all of the following techniques:

◆ appreciation of the customer's demographic profile;
◆ calculation of the propensity of the customer to buy a product or services;
◆ understanding of the customer's use of competitor products;
◆ collection of data on the future plans and events of the customer.

12.5 Analysis systems: data mining and predictive modelling

Predictive modelling is a process used in predictive analytics to create a statistical model of future behaviour. Predictive analytics is the area of data mining concerned with forecasting probabilities and trends. A predictive model is made up of a number of predictors or variable factors that are likely to influence future behaviour or results. In marketing, for example, a customer's gender, age and purchase history might predict the likelihood of a future sale.

To create a predictive model, data is collected for the relevant predictors, a statistical model is formulated, predictions are made and the model is validated (or revised) as additional data becomes available. The model may employ a simple linear equation or a complex neural network mapped out by sophisticated software. The Data Mining Group, a vendor consortium, uses an XML-based language called the Predictive Model Markup Language to enable the definition and sharing of predictive models between applications.

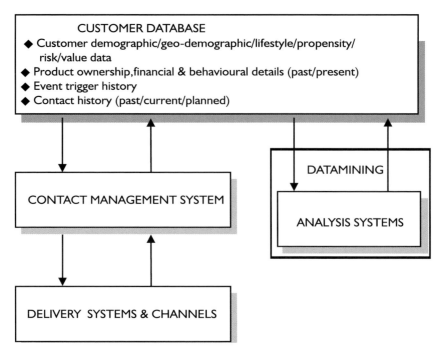

Data mining is the technique using software tools to detect unique patterns or trends in data automatically. This is accomplished by sifting through large amounts of data to create data dependent relationships.

Data mining identifies hidden relationships, new trends and previously undetected patterns hidden within data. It helps decision makers to make intuitive, yet strategic, decisions regarding customer contact, for example, SAS Enterprise miner or IBM's Intelligent Miner software (www.sas.com, www.ibm.com).

Data mining has been defined as:

> 'The non-trivial extraction of implicit, previously unknown and potentially useful information from data.'[2]

It uses machine learning, statistical and visualisation techniques to discover and present knowledge in a form which is easily comprehensible to humans.

To exploit the data warehouse fully an automated analysis tool is used which can rigorously interrogate the data. Typical data mining questions that could be answered are:

◆ What product categories or groups of products do our customers most commonly own?
◆ What products or product categories are owned by specific customer segments (customers with similar characteristics)?

◆ What are the characteristics that delineate this purchasing segment from segments that they do not purchase?
◆ What are the product propensities for the segments?
◆ What is the attrition (churn) of certain products for specific segments?

In addition to answering specific business questions as outlined above, the overall goal of data mining is to improve marketing, sales and customer support operations via a more complete and better understanding of the customer. This is accomplished by detecting meaningful and relevant behavioural patterns through automated exploration and analyses of large quantities of data.

A simple example of a behaviour pattern would be 'customers with children purchase savings plans, while customers without choose a different type of mutual fund'. Data mining encompasses the ability to evaluate customer information either automatically or semi-automatically. This knowledge discovery consists of pattern recognition. The explanation of these patterns is used to explain past events and to predict future events.

The process of directed knowledge discovery includes selecting specific variables or fields and explaining the relationships in data. This process consists of searching large volumes of data and looking for current behaviour patterns that can accurately predict future behaviour in customers. This can be accomplished by using online analytical processing (OLAP) tools with or without statistical tools. The objective is to confirm a hypothesis, ie that a relationship exists between the predetermined variable(s) and the results.

Instead of manually choosing and assessing variables that may be predictive, data mining can go through undirected knowledge discovery where no prior assumptions are made and the data speaks for itself. This type of knowledge discovery consists of 'recognising' relationships in data instead of 'explaining' the relationships. This will require a statistician to interpret the findings and confirm whether the relationships are viable, ie the key component is a good understanding of the data and the statistical significance of end reports and analysis produced by the data mining tool. Although not always intuitive, the relationships identified by the data mining tool helps marketing improve their understanding of customer behaviour. This, in turn, allows them to target marketing campaigns more accurately and to align campaigns more closely with the needs of the customers.

12.5.1   Front end analysis (targeting/querying)

This incorporates the functions that result in the derivation of targeted lists of customers from the data warehouse, ie identification of the targets. These functions include generating target customer counts, producing standard reports to profile the targets and developing statistical models to assess the probabilities of response creating actionable targeting tools to assist in sales and evaluation of the customers/ clients, for example, customer relationship scores, product propensities, etc.

12.5.2   List processing (list creation) and execution

This incorporates the functions that follow once the decision has been made to make the list selections, ie processing the final criteria, scoring statistical models, pulling list, list suppression/de-duplication, creation of contact groups (cells), sales procedure integration (co-ordination of follow up or stages), quality checks, data security and execution (shipping of mail tape).

12.5.3   Non-statistical approaches

In addition to standard or traditional direct marketing, the contact/campaign management system must support the automation of complex, multi-stage, multi-channel programmes/campaigns, using any media. Specifically, the ability to create programmes/campaigns based on the following types of marketing methodologies.

◆ *Event-driven marketing* is based on the calculated recognition of key events affecting customers, for example, a lease that becomes due, an upcoming birthday or a major holiday. The marketers must have the ability to define significant events – the marketing response – and then automate the execution of those efforts.

◆ *Velocity marketing* is based on the rate of change in customer/household/account activity. Marketers must have the ability to respond effectively to gradual or sudden shifts in customer behaviour and to compare changes over multiple periods of time.

◆ *Longitudinal marketing* combines within the same or a series of programmes/campaigns multi-stage marketing efforts with event-triggered marketing to support continuous, multi-stage programmes in which each stage is customised (or governed) by the customer's response to the previous marketing initiative.

◆ *Threshold marketing* establishes absolute or relative thresholds or parameters that govern marketing communication strategies. A relative threshold methodology would simply alert marketers when certain boundaries are breached (for example, balance exceeds certain amount).

◆ *Liquid marketing* is the evolution to 'real-time' one to one marketing. With liquid marketing, a specific offer, promotion or programme/campaign is created on-the-fly for a specific customer/household/account based on certain pre-defined rules and parameters. The offer might exist for a very brief period of time and, in fact, might never be recreated in the same way for another customer.

12.5.4   Decision trees

Decision trees are a way of representing a series of rules that lead to a result or value, ie, in deciding a type of loan.

- ◆ If amount required > 20,000, then loan, else overdraft.
- ◆ If loan and age <65, then mortgage, else special loan.

The first component is the top decision node, or root node, which specifies a test to be carried out. Each branch will lead either to another decision node or to the bottom of the tree, called a 'leaf node'. By navigating the decision tree, you can assign a value or class to a case by deciding which branch to take. Decision tree models are used in data mining to analyse the data and create a tree and its rules that will be used to make predictions. A number of different algorithms may be used for building decision trees including CHAID (chi-squared automatic interaction detection), CART (classification and regression trees), etc.

12.5.5 Neural networks

Neural nets differ in philosophy from many statistical methods. First, a net normally has more parameters than does a typical statistical model. For example, a net with 100 inputs and 50 hidden nodes would have over 5000 parameters. As a result, many of the combinations will result in similar predictions and the net serves as a 'black box', which means it is not necessarily clear as to what combination of events has led to to the result. However, in CRM, this may be acceptable to a bank, for example, just wanting to detect potential credit problems, the historic cause being of less immediate interest.

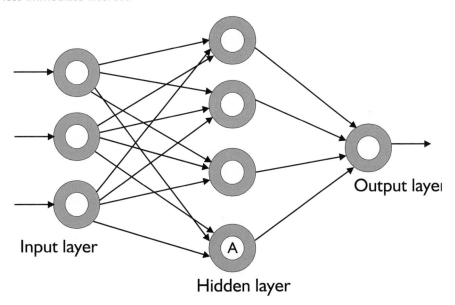

In this example example, node A has three inputs. Each is multiplied by a weighting factor and then aggregated to form the output.

Neural nets start with an input layer where each node corresponds to a predictor variable. These input nodes are connected to a number of nodes in a hidden layer. Each input node is connected to every node in the hidden layer. The nodes in the hidden layer may be connected to nodes in another hidden layer or to an output layer. The output layer consists of one or more response variables. After the input layer, each node takes in a set of inputs, multiplies them by a connection weight, adds them together, applies a function (called the 'activation' or 'squashing' function) to them and passes the output to the node(s) in the next layer.

The goal of training the neural net is to estimate the connection weights so that the output of the net accurately predicts the test value for a given set of values. The most common training method is backpropagation.

The most successful implementations of neural networks involve very careful data cleansing, selection and preparation.

12.5.6   Clustering

This technique uses gravitational spatial modelling to group the database into different clusters. The goal is to find groups that are very different from each other and whose members are very similar to each other. Unlike traditional segmentation and classification, you do not know what the clusters will be before you start. It is the characteristics of the data that determine the clustering. Consequently, after clustering, a business analyst is required to interpret the meaning of the clusters and therefore the business insight this gives. For example, clustering could show that customers with a telephone line are less likely to default on personal loans.

12.5.7   Bayesian logic

Named after Thomas Bayes, an English clergyman and mathematician, Bayesian logic is a branch of logic applied to decision making and inferential statistics that deals with probability inference: using the knowledge of prior events to predict future events. Bayes' Theorem provided, for the first time, a mathematical method that could be used to calculate, given occurrences in prior trials, the likelihood of a target occurrence in future trials. According to Bayesian logic, the only way to quantify a situation with an uncertain outcome is through determining its probability.

Bayes' Theorem is a means of quantifying uncertainty. Based on probability theory, the theorem defines a rule for refining an hypothesis by factoring in additional evidence and background information and leads to a number representing the degree of probability that the hypothesis is true. To demonstrate an application of Bayes' Theorem, suppose that we have a covered basket that contains three balls, each of which may be green or red. In a blind test, we reach in and pull out a red ball. We return the ball to the basket and try again, again pulling out a red ball. Once more, we return the ball to the basket and pull a ball out – red again. We form a hypothesis that all the balls are, in fact, red. Bayes' Theorem can be used to calculate the probability (p) that all the balls are red (an event labelled as 'A') given (symbolised as ' | ') that all the selections have been red (an event labeled as 'B'):

$$p(A|B) = p\{A + B\}/p\{B\}$$

Of all the possible combinations (RRR, RRG, RGG, GGG), the chance that all the balls are red is 1/4; in 1/8 of all possible outcomes, all the balls are red and all the selections are red. Bayes' Theorem calculates the probability that all the balls in the basket are red, given that all the selections have been red as .5 (probabilities are expressed as numbers between 0. and 1. with '1.' indicating 100% probability and '0.' indicating zero probability).

12.5.8 Fuzzy logic

Fuzzy logic is an approach to computing based on 'degrees of truth' rather than the usual 'true or false' (1 or 0) Boolean logic on which the modern computer is based. The idea of fuzzy logic was first advanced by Dr Lotfi Zadeh of the University of California at Berkeley in the 1960s. Dr Zadeh was working on the problem of computer understanding of natural language. Natural language (like most other activities in life and indeed the universe) is not easily translated into the absolute terms of 0 and 1. (Whether everything is ultimately describable in binary terms is a philosophical question worth pursuing, but, in practice, much data we might want to feed a computer is, in some state, in between and so, frequently, are the results of computing.)

Fuzzy logic includes 0 and 1 as extreme cases of truth (or 'the state of matters' or 'fact'), but also includes the various states of truth in between, so that, for example, the result of a comparison between two things could not be 'tall' or 'short' but '.38 of tallness'.

Fuzzy logic seems closer to the way our brains work. We aggregate data and form a number of partial truths which we aggregate further into higher truths which, in turn, when certain thresholds are exceeded, cause certain further results such as motor reaction. A similar kind of process is used in artificial computer neural network and expert systems.

It may help to see fuzzy logic as the way reasoning really works and binary or Boolean logic is simply a special case of it.

12.6 Propensity scoring and modelling

Ultimately, customer intelligence is about scores and segments. Scores are numbers that express the probability a customer will behave in a certain way – that he will default on a loan or respond to mail, for instance. Segments are groups of similar customers. Typically, these customers are grouped because they have similar scores. The calculation of scores and segments is important for improving business processes both for risk management and the marketing of products.

Using, as an example, risk management (similar processes can be applied to marketing management), the processes that benefit from credit customer intelligence include the following.

◆ *Application approval.* Here, customer intelligence is used to reduce bad debt, increase approval rates, streamline the approval process and offer risk-based prices. To achieve these goals, application scores are used for new customers and behavioural scores for existing customers. Customers are often segmented into approve/refer/reject segments or into interest rate classes.

◆ *Risk monitoring and control.* In risk monitoring and control, customer intelligence helps set credit limits, perform risk-adjusted performance management and calculate required regulatory capital. Behavioural scores (probabilities of default) are calculated and customers are grouped into limit classes or rating grades and pools.

◆ *Collection management.* In collection management, scores are calculated to predict the expected recovery from delinquent customers. This type of scoring helps to increase recovered amounts and streamline the recovery process by assigning customers to collection groups.

On the marketing side, customer intelligence benefits from both outbound and 'inbound' communication efforts. When used in outbound cross-sell and retention campaigns, customer intelligence helps with pre-approving marketed products and selecting optimal campaign targets and channels. Here, segments are based on a variety of different scores, such as behavioural risk, mail and call response, product uptake, activity and attrition scores, all to calculate optimal combinations of customer, channel and product. Inbound interaction management activities use customer intelligence to prioritise services and to offer the best product at every customer contact.

For this task, risk and uptake scores can be combined to form service priority groups and define segment-specific portfolios of target products.

12.7 Development of scoring models and decision rules

12.7.1 Credit scoring models

The traditional credit scoring model is a scorecard. A scorecard is a table that contains a number of questions (called 'characteristics') that applicants answer. For each question, there is a list of possible answers (called 'attributes'). For example, one characteristic may be the age of the applicant. The attributes for this characteristic might be a series of age ranges into which an applicant could fall. For each answer, the applicant receives a certain number of points – more if the attribute is low risk, fewer if the risk for that attribute is higher. The resulting total score reflects the probability that the applicant will default on the credit product. For example:

- I   age $< 23.5 = 20$.
- $23.5 <= $ age $< 27.5 = 27$.
- $27.5 <= $ age $< 35.5 = 38$.
- $35.5 <= $ age $< 45.5 = 43$.
- $45.5 <= $ age $<$ high $= 53$.

The scorecard model, apart from being a long-established scoring method in the industry, still has several advantages when compared with more recent data mining types of models, such as decision trees or neural networks. First, a scorecard is easy to apply. If needed, the scorecard can be evaluated on a sheet of paper in the presence of the applicant. The scorecard is also easy to understand. The number of points for one answer does not depend on any of the other answers and, across the range of possible answers to any question, the number of points usually increases in a simple way. Therefore, it is often easy to justify to the applicant a decision that is made on the basis of a scorecard.

Unlike the scorecard, a decision tree detects and exploits interactions between characteristics. In a decision tree model, each answer that an applicant gives determines which question is asked next. Thus, a decision tree model consists of a set of 'if-then-else' rules that segment applicants based on their sequence of answers. Their greater flexibility makes trees potentially more predictive than scorecard models. Trees can, however, become quite complex. They are also unstable when updated with new data in the sense that their structure can change dramatically with a change to the first question asked.

Neural networks are even more flexible models that account for interactions and combine characteristics in a variety of ways. They do not suffer from sharp splits between possibilities as decision trees and scorecards sometimes do. They also do not suffer from structural instability in the same way as decision trees. However, it is virtually impossible to explain or understand the score that is produced for a particular applicant using a simple method. It can be difficult to justify a decision that is made on the basis of a neural network model. A neural network of superior predictive power is therefore best suited for certain behavioural or collection scoring purposes where the average accuracy of the prediction is more important than gaining insight into the score for each particular case.

Example of propensity score card

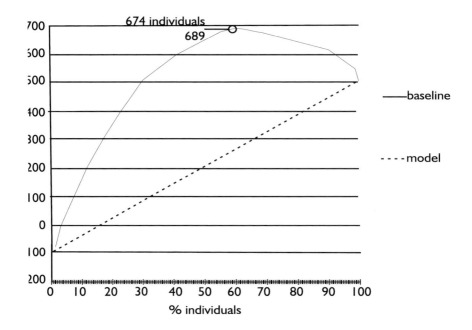

Source: e-piphany campaign manager.

The above shows how a scorecard works. In this example, we are looking at a campaign that will cost £100k in fixed costs (ie the base income point is –£100k). The lower line shows the expected response if we applied no propensity model (ie we contact all customers in a random order).

The top line shows what will happen if we contact customers in decreasing propensity, ie if we contact the top 10% of customers with the highest propensity to buy, then we will achieve an income level of around +£100k, compared to a random 10% contact result of –£50k.

The optimum return is achieved by contacting about 65% of customers (ie the top 65% of the scorecard) which is predicted to achieve a net return of about £690k.

The objective of the score builder is continually to improve the score performance by testing against results and using data mining techniques to identify and refine the data items that determine the probability of purchase.

References and further reading

[1] Recommended Text: Consumer Insight, Stone, Bond and Foss ISBN 0-7494-4292-1.

[2] W Frawley, G Piatetsky-Shapiro and C Matheus, *Knowledge Discovery in Databases: An Overview*. AI Magazine, Fall 1992, pp 213–228. 'State of The Art' in Byte Magazine, October 1995, contains three articles on data mining and data warehousing.

W H Inmon and S Osterfelt, *Understanding Data Pattern Processing*, QED Technical Publishing Group, 1991, Wellesley, MA.

Cheryl Gerber, *Excavate Your Data*, Datamation 42(9), May 1996.

Usama M Fayyad, Gregory Piatetsky-Shapiro, Padhraic Smyth and Ramasamy Uthurusamy, *Advances in Knowledge Discovery and Data Mining*, AAAI Press/The MIT Press.

Herb Edelstein, *Data Mining: Exploiting the Hidden Trends in Your Data*, DB2 Online Magazine. http://www.db2mag.com/9701edel.htm.

Thirteen

Customer contact: contact management system

13.1 Introduction

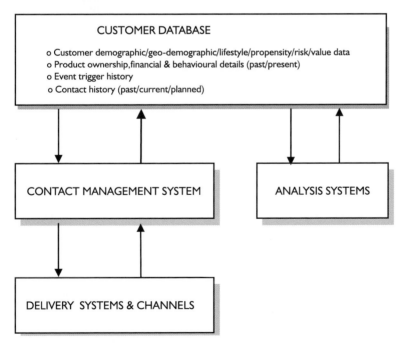

With an integrated single customer view and an analysis platform, it is now possible to start to allocate inbound and outbound resources in alignment with the value and potential of each customer or customer segment through a contact management system.

Contact management is the blending of outbound or 'push contact' where the organisation wants to interrupt or make contact with the customer with inbound 'customer pull' contact data where new information gathered by staff or directly through the Internet is used to optimise the contact with the customer.

13.2 Integrated contact management system: closing the loop

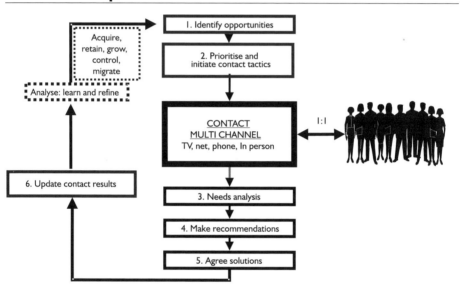

The above diagram provides an overview of how an integrated CRM system enables an organisation to translate strategic objectives of customer acquisition, growth, control and lifestage migration into action.

1. The central data warehouse is used to synthesise customer transactions and behavioural information to identify opportunities.
2. These opportunities are then prioritised and a series of contact tactics created based on knowledge of the customer's channel preferences.
3. Contact takes place (either initiated by the customer or the organisation) and the customers needs are matched with the existing customer knowledge.
4. This generates product and service solutions.
5. Agreement or rejection of the offers.
6. The central data warehouse is updated with the results of the contact and 'learns'. This then enables the process to start again using refined knowledge and rules based on experience.

13.3　Contact management

Note:

◆ Campaign management: traditional outbound.
◆ Contact management: inbound interaction management.

Marketing is undergoing a fundamental transformation. This revolution is driven by a number of factors: increased consumer resistance to traditional marketing methods, the proliferation of communication channels and ever-changing legal constraints. In response, leading consumer-oriented companies are dramatically adjusting their marketing mix to take better advantage of less traditional – but ultimately more effective – consumer interaction channels. They are also evolving the role the department plays in the enterprise, recognising that marketing can help make every interaction more intelligent. As a result, these companies will be able to deliver more timely and relevant marketing messages and will ultimately create stronger and more valuable customer relationships.

Marketing transformation will occur in four phases.

◆ *Increased inbound marketing.* Marketers will make greater use of inbound customer contacts as a channel to present offers.
◆ *Smarter outbound marketing.* Marketers will replace many batch campaigns with more relevant event-driven campaigns.
◆ *Seamless customer conversations.* Once marketers have mastered inbound and outbound contacts as separate functions, they will begin to co-ordinate their activities across channels to create seamless customer conversations.
◆ *Marketing everywhere.* The final phase of marketing transformation will occur when marketing not only makes offers, but also enhances all customer interaction channels with marketing guidance to make each contact more intelligent – and more valuable.

Good marketing begins with a solid, cohesive marketing strategy. This should not be confused with tactics and branding. A real marketing strategy provides a roadmap to creating and delivering true value to target groups of customers. All successful marketing strategies must begin and end with the customer. Customers cannot be an afterthought or taken as given – as such, marketers must test their assumptions about their customers constantly.

Ultimately, it is how well the customer experiences each of these during every customer interaction that makes up your brand and drives customer growth, profitability, and loyalty.

13.4　Campaign management system

The campaign management system (CMS) is a system for launching, controlling and monitoring customer contact strategies.

The campaign manager is a complete, integrated application component that provides powerful database marketing functionality.

Database marketing – a definition:

'The use of information technology and analytical techniques to facilitate customer relationship management and the on-going development, implementation and monitoring of marketing strategy.

NB. Those who are able to use information with superiority and cleverness are certain to achieve great results. This is the essense of strategy.' (Sun Tzu – *The Art of Strategy*)

The CMS consists basically of three components which align with stages of 1, 2 and 6 of the closed loop process.

1. *Opportunity spotting*: detecting the right customer to contact at the right time with the right product or service.
2. *Campaign prioritisation and delivery*: which opportunity to pursue and through which delivery channel or combination of channels.
7. *Contact management*: what was the result of the contact and how should that influence future contact?

13.4.1 Analysis systems: identifying the opportunity

Having selected a customer for potentially multiple contacts/campaigns, the CMS will then use rules to establish the order and priority of execution. Clearly, just initiating all campaigns for a customer simultaneously is likely to cause customer confusion and very probably dissatisfaction!

Techniques for prioritisation include:

◆ *organisational need*: this is where the organisation is in need of a certain business mix (for example, it needs more loans) and therefore priority is given to campaigns that will generate this mix. This is not a customer-centric approach and is often linked to organisations with a product push target led culture;
◆ *value added*: this is where the likely value of the product or service prioritises the contact. For example, the potential sale of a mortgage, being a high income product, would take precedent over the potential sale of, say, car insurance;
◆ *probability of success*: this is where prioritisation is based on the likely probability of the individual customer taking the product or service on offer. For example, if the probability of taking a personal loan is 65% and of taking a credit card 40%, then the loan campaign would take priority for that customer. This is a more customer centric approach.

In reality, a combination of the above is normally used. Capital One bank uses a combination of value added and probability of success as its prime prioritisation methodology.

13.4.2   Campaign delivery

Having identified and prioritised the contact, delivery can now take place. This will, ideally, take into account customer preference for channel (for example, e-mail versus direct paper mail) and take into account appropriate cost of contact for the likely value to be generated from success.

For example, sending a relationship manager to see a customer at home with the hope of selling household insurance is not likely to be an economic proposition as the margin on the product would be outweighed by the cost of delivery.

This requires the organisations' front office systems to be linked to the campaign and contact engines.

13.4.3   Contact history

Having undertaken the campaign, the CRM system needs to collect the result and store this within the customer contact history for the customer. Capturing this information can be done in a number of ways.

Automatic contact history update

This is done normally as the result of a successful contact where the customer has taken the product or service. The physical taking of the offer generates a product opening within the product system which is then fed back to the data warehouse.

Manual contact history update

This requires a physical input to the customer contact history either by the customer directly (for example, customer clicks 'no thanks' when offered an increased credit card limit over the Internet) or by staff following a conversation with the customer. In order to achieve this, it is vital that the customer contact system is available and integrated with front office processes.

The strategy is to gain and secure customers' confidence via targeted communication that relays a co-ordinated single source entity. The organisation will contact customers only when there is a perceived 'need' to be filled. The co-ordinated effort encompasses the different customer touch points, centralised direct marketing (direct mail, telemarketing, Internet, mobile phone and call centre), and localised efforts (branch, telephone, direct mail, walk in, ATMs, etc). This includes taking advantage of the information available and combining them with a contact and campaign management strategy.

CMS is a tool to co-ordinate and synchronise the central and branch 'push' marketing process, suppressing or de-duplicating customer lists and automating the process of running event driven campaigns. In a centralised marketing context, the 'automated leads' and 'individual solutions' can become simultaneous campaigns that will need to be co-ordinated and synchronised (across channels) to ensure customers do not acquire 'contact fatigue' (over contacted). Campaign response and impact can be assessed with results fed back to the data warehouse to assist future campaigns. The introduction of continuous event driven and large numbers of simultaneous campaigns mean that an integrated system is required.

How is this co-ordinated to the customer is such a way that the customer perceives the organisation as a single touch point and not a series of disjointed channels and contacts?

This is achieved by keeping a perpetual history of customer contact and using this information in a co-ordinated effort between centralised and local efforts.

13.5 Campaign manager: an example of how it works – 'e-piphany'

The campaign manager is a complete, integrated application component that provides powerful database marketing functionality while remaining easy to use. Typically, campaign management functionality breaks down into four categories of activities.

- ◆ *Customer targeting*: using filters to define the universe of customers, a campaign will target and break that population into segments and sub-segments.
- ◆ *Campaign planning*: splitting segments into test and control groups, describing offers and assigning those treatments to the various test cells. Setting global permission-based business rules to ensure policies are met. Getting counts and estimating campaign ROI. Planning multi-wave, event driven and longitudinal campaigns.
- ◆ *Campaign execution*: scheduling the campaign and extracting from the database the relevant customer information in the correct format for each offer and channel.
- ◆ *Closed-loop analysis*: tracking all information about the campaign in the analytic datamart and providing tools to analyse post-campaign effectiveness.

13.5.1   Customer targeting

Test and control cells: once segments are created, they can be split into multiple test and control cells.

Permission-based business rules: the system supports permission-based marketing by letting managers define global business rules that automatically apply across all campaigns. Once a rule is created and applied to a user, there is no way to execute a campaign that would breach the business rules.

 The campaign manager provides a highly expressive business rule editor that allows sophisticated 'if-then' rules such as:

◆ 'for all campaigns, do not contact anyone on the global suppression list or anyone who has requested not to be contacted';
◆ 'if this is an e-mail campaign, then only send people e-mail if that is their preferred channel and if we have an e-mail address; otherwise, send them direct mail';
◆ 'if this campaign contains financial information or is targeted towards children under 18, only contact customers who are opt-in'.

Rules can also handle cross-campaign co-ordination, such as 'do not contact people over the telephone more than twice every six months'. Users can update suppression and opt-out lists in real time.

Treatments: each cell is then assigned a treatment, which can consist of the collateral materials that you use to package the offer, the terms of the offer itself (discount, expiration and so on), the channel by which you deliver that offer to members of your target audience and the methods you provide for those members to respond. It can also optionally contain a key code.

Treatment strategies: the system lets users create segmentation schemes – called 'treatment strategies' – that can be reused and shared across users. Treatment strategies can assign one or more attributes of the treatment a customer may receive, including the output file assignment. Then, when a treatment strategy is applied to a campaign, it creates a matrix with existing segments on one side and the treatment strategy segments on the other and then automatically creates a new segment for each cell in the matrix.

For example, assume you have three treatment strategies: one that defines the product being promoted (for example, Product A or Product B), one that defines the offer (for example, 10% off or £20 off) and one that defines the channel and output file (for example, direct mail or e-mail). In each case, there will be list filters that decide which customers are assigned which treatment attribute, for example, customers who have e-mail addresses and who have not opted-out will receive e-mail, others will receive direct mail. When all three treatment strategies are applied to the campaign, there will be eight cells and eight treatments, one for each possible combination of product, offer and channel.

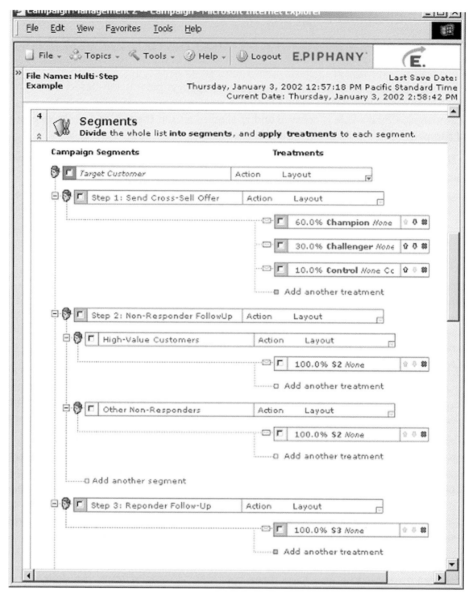

Each treatment is also assigned a unique treatment ID. This ability to create orthogonal segmentation schemes allows users to build complex campaigns quickly: if there were ten segments in each of three treatment strategies, the result would have 1000 treatments and cells.

Multi-message campaigns

Marketing users can create customised newsletters and other treatments that contain multiple messages. This enables the Epiphany campaign management for e-mail engine to send newsletters by e-mail. Other channels, such as direct mail, can also take advantage of 'multi-message' campaigns.

Optimisation

Users may use the integrated data mining in the system to select the 'optimal offer' for each customer automatically, where 'optimal' can be defined as 'most likely to respond', 'highest expected profit' or some other user-defined metric.

Detailed ROI estimates

Users may also assign fixed and variable costs to each treatment and estimate response rates for each cell. Combined with the fast counting capability, the system uses this information to estimate detailed cell-level and rolled-up campaign economics, including costs, revenues, profits and ROI.

Complex campaign types

The system allows users to plan single-shot, multi-wave, triggered and longitudinal campaigns. For example, a user in a credit card company may create a campaign that sends all new customers a welcome letter. Then, three months later (just as the first introductory rate expires, perhaps), a retention offer is sent. Any customer that attrites is sent a new series of communications. For customers that stay, an additional communication is sent on the customer's birthday. Also, if the customer's spending goes above a pre-set limit at any time, an offer to upgrade to the gold card may be sent. Finally, one week before the anniversary of opening the account, customers are segmented by profitability and high-value customers are sent an additional incentive, while low-value customers see their annual fee raised.

Marketing process support

The campaign manager supports complex marketing processes, including specifying custom campaign objectives and using security privileges to restrict who has the authority to approve and execute a campaign. Users with scheduling authority can still design campaigns, and then e-mail the campaign design to another user for approval.

13.5.2 Campaign execution

Custom output formats

Once the campaign is created, users define one or more output files for the campaign. Output formats contain treatment information, such as campaign code, cell code and key code, as well as demographic information such as segment, name and address.

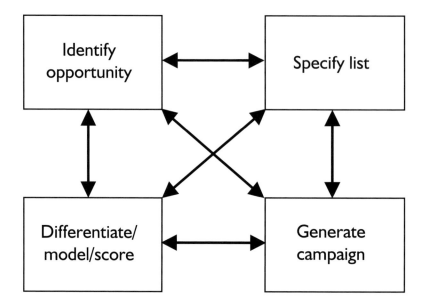

Exclusions

Exclusions prevent individuals or groups from receiving excessive or redundant offers. The campaign manager provides users with an option to exclude any members of the current campaign who have been sent the same treatment or a conflicting treatment in an earlier campaign, either for a specific period of time or for all time.

Campaign scheduling

Once the campaign is completed, it can be scheduled to execute once or repeatedly on a daily, weekly or monthly basis. The status of all scheduled campaigns can be viewed using the integrated campaign calendar, which also provides access to modify running campaigns while maintaining an archive of each campaign definition.

13.5.3 Benefits of CRM

CRM is intended directly to affect the bottom line of organisations. While the use of software associated with CRM strategy enables productivity gains, the biggest benefits of CRM arise from business expansion; doing more of the right things. This is in contrast to the focus of many organisations, which has been on doing more things right.

Business expansion is made possible by CRM because a holistic view of customers enables the organisation to:

◆ develop the most attractive products and services according to customers' needs and requirements;
◆ market and sell to a smaller, but better qualified group of prospects;
◆ retain profitable customers

CRM entails taking a long-term view – to pay more attention to the lifetime value of a customer than to the value of each transaction. It is this emphasis that makes one holistic view of the customer necessary. First, it enables profitability analysis. Secondly, it is only possible to continue to do business with a customer who is satisfied with all aspects of their interaction with a company.

Customer satisfaction is a good thing in its own right, but it is also important in the context of CRM because it is crucial to retaining customers. Even a small increase in retention can have spectacular effects on profitability.

There have been a number of studies in and around the subject of customer retention. *The Loyalty Effect* by Fredrick Reichheld shows that it costs six times as much to acquire a new customer as it does to keep a customer. He went on to show that loyal customers refer new prospects to the business, which then tend to be more loyal.

It is normal for a company to experience a certain amount of churn in its customer base. Reichheld's study indicates that where churn is reduced by x%, then the cost of winning new business to replace lost customers is decreased by six times. These savings have two effects.

1. They decrease cost of sales directly.
2. They free resources to expand the business. Rather than spending time and effort replacing lost customers to maintain revenues, that time and effort can be spent either increasing the number of customers overall or increasing the value of sales to existing customers – hence, the business grows.

Another effect of customer satisfaction is preventive. Dissatisfied customers do not just leave, they also tell their family and friends about their negative experience. This further increases the cost of winning new customers.

Software employed in the pursuit of CRM directly contributes to customer satisfaction by:

- using business intelligence tools to discover what is required and therefore targeting customer needs more directly;
- its ability to provide all employees with all information that is required to service the customer. This means that needs can be more easily met at interaction time.

Customer retention and satisfaction leads to loyalty. Loyalty not only means that the customer prefers to do business with a company, it also means that the customer may not even consider other options. This has two effects on margins.

- Customers are less price sensitive, so a higher price than a competitor's is still considered good value for money due to the better service provided.
- The cost of winning more business from existing customers is less. Hence, profitability can be greater at a price that is equal to, or even less than, competitors' prices.

A holistic view of the customer makes it possible not only to retain customers and win business that might otherwise have gone to competitors, but also to increase the value of business with each customer through cross-selling and up-selling.

This can be achieved in two ways:

- opportunistically, where, in every interaction with a customer, a holistic view provides information that aids selling activity. This includes customer-specific data, such as previous transactions, service history preferences and interests. Other types of information are also useful both to employees serving customers and to customers directly, for example, information about the company's products and services, competitors' products and services, pricing lists, delivery schedules, discounting policy and other related information as appropriate; or
- by planning, where cross-selling and up-selling information are discovered by performing analysis to determine what product and service combinations will be attractive to customers.[1]

13.6   Six requirements for a successful CRM strategy: a summary

13.6.1   1–Create a customer-focused organisation and infrastructure

Internal cultural barriers can inhibit communication and co-ordination among divisions and defeat corporate-level market objectives.

Management must align sales and service behaviours around customer relationships rather than around groups or products. To help remove departmental/channel/product silos, the executive management needs to keep a view toward overall customer profitability rather than in discrete segments of the business.

On the analytical side, it is critical to have a single, enterprise-wide view of the customer, spanning all touch points and systems.

Customer data must be assembled from every contact point – call centres, mail, person-to-person, the web and beyond – to construct an accurate, consistent view of customers across all available channels.

Data and key metrics from diverse departments must be aligned, shared and integrated in a common arena.

Information about customers, which now exists in various databases across the enterprise, must be combined and compatible before meaningful analysis can take place.

13.6.2   2–Gain an accurate picture of your customer categories

To have effective target marketing, you have to have a target. To anticipate customer needs, improve customer retention and identify opportunities to cross-sell and up-sell. You have to understand the unique characteristics of each market segment in an increasingly fragmented marketplace.

Market segmentation in the banking industry has been a 'soft' art based on intuition and experience, looking at characteristics generally believed to predict buying patterns. To pinpoint the best opportunities for marketing, sales and service, financial institutions must adopt a much more rigorous analytical framework.

13.6.3   3–Accurately assess the future value/potential of your customers

In a research report commissioned by SAS, bankers expressed the need to gauge lifetime customer profitability, not just present value. Customers just starting out from school might be marginally profitable right now but very profitable later when they are established in their careers.

Without understanding lifetime value, banks face the potential to take short-sighted actions that unwittingly drive away customers along with their potential value.

According to research conducted by Gartner Inc, about one in five small banks and about half of large banks already work to estimate lifetime value.

However, the accuracy of their analysis is often hampered by missing inputs and variables. For instance, the bank may have data on customer deposit, loan and credit accounts, but not on investment and insurance relationships and third-party products. Or they might rely on industry-average information to compensate for data they do not collect in their own systems. In short, despite their best efforts, many banks still do not have an accurate picture of customer profitability.

13.6.4   4–Maximise the profitability of each customer relationship

As competition and churn reach new heights in the banking industry, banks are looking more than ever toward increasing profitability from existing customers, rather than expecting new customers to account for growth. Retaining existing customers is easier and less costly than attracting new ones. Naturally, that means banks are keenly interested in cross-selling a variety of financial products and services to existing customers. Cross-selling can substantially increase customer profitability, especially if a bank targets valuable customers who are likely to purchase multiple financial products, but how does a bank identify those prospects? How can a bank effectively cross-sell without cannibalising other product lines?

13.6.5   5–Understand how to attract and keep your best customers

The maturing financial services industry is being reshaped by deregulation. Organisations can now offer complete ranges of products in new geographic areas and by the Internet. Customers and prospects have point-and-click access to a stunning array of competing offers. Together, these industry changes make it easier than ever for customers to jump ship and they are doing so in record numbers.

Acquiring a customer can cost from £100 to £300, but if you retain that customer, the investment will be repaid tenfold or more. Given the cost of acquiring customers, banks cannot expect to grow the business simply by attracting more customers. They must retain their business longer and build the customer base by looking more closely at the other end of the customer lifecycle attrition.

Airlines understood this early on and created programmes that rewarded loyalty with flight credits and premium levels of service. Banks have partially adopted this concept by offering tiered levels of service based on account balances. This is a start, but it is important to get a tighter rein on attrition. Who leaves, and why? In a multi-product environment, it is hard to measure attrition. Is this a customer who cancels a single product but still possesses other products, or is this a customer who ends the entire relationship? It is harder still to predict and prevent attrition, which is influenced by a combination of qualitative and quantitative factors. Why do some customers leave? Why do others stay? What do they value? How can you change their minds? A successful CRM approach enables customer service organisations to create the knowledge they need to implement the right retention strategies and minimise defection of valuable customers.

13.6.6   6–Maximise rate of return on marketing campaigns

To increase rate of return on marketing campaigns, market strategies must be based on an accurate and comprehensive understanding of the bank's customers across all functional areas and contact channels. The CRM model of campaign management calls for:

◆ incorporating customer information from all touch points to generate a single customer view;

◆ creating 'smart' campaigns that are tightly targeted to the highest-value customers or the customers most likely to respond, for the most relevant opportunity, through the desired channel, at the most appropriate time;

◆ co-ordinating systems and processes so market programmes can be generated more quickly and so feedback from previous campaigns can be used to fine tune future activities.

Each of these key business requirements is an integral part of a CRM value chain. Once a bank understands its customer base, it can segment those customers into groups to which it targets tailored service and marketing activities. Using analytics, the bank can quantify shifts in behaviour, predict long-term value, and identify prime cross-sell and up-sell opportunities. This type of information forms a basis for creating highly-targeted market campaigns and offers. Information from market campaigns is then cycled back into the CRM system to fine-tune its effectiveness.

13.6.7   The implications of these six imperatives

Legacy banking systems reflect a traditional process- and product-oriented view of the business. The architecture uses a host of independent systems on different platforms, which share information in a limited way. As mergers and acquisitions reshape information networks, it is common to see multiple, incompatible platforms even within a single functional area.

The key business requirements of a CRM strategy necessitate a different infrastructure, one that supports a unified, relationship-based view of the customer. Does that mean that the banks' investment in traditional transaction-based systems is obsolete? No. Those systems just need to be able to share their information through a data warehousing and analytic structure that brings the parts into a unified whole. The glue that binds functions and processes together into true CRM is a decision support system. Unlike transaction-oriented computer systems, decision support systems offer an integrated set of warehousing, analytics and campaign planning and execution modules that address relationships, rather than product-oriented views.

13.7   Technology component of a total CRM strategy

The technology component of CRM offers banks a comprehensive understanding of its customers through data analysis and predictive modelling to support sales and marketing strategies.

13.7.1   Single customer view

A managed and integrated view of the customer, drawn from all contact points and product purchases, enables financial institutions to understand customers better and therefore serve them more effectively.

13.7.2   Predictions for profit

Banks can accurately predict which products and services will appeal to an existing customer and which they are most likely to purchase.

13.7.3   Customer lifetime value

Banks can calculate the probable profitability of a customer over their lifetime, ensuring that they do not alienate low-value customers with high-value potential.

13.7.4   Personalised services

Businesses can segment the market into specific target groups by demographics or purchase types. With a closer understanding of customers by small segments, banks can adopt individual marketing approaches rather than relatively ineffective mass marketing.

References

[1] *Zero Defections: Quality Comes to Services* by Frederick R Reichheld and W Earl Sasser, Jr, September 1999.

Fourteen

Customer customisation and experience

14.1 Introduction

Having invested in the various CRM components many organisations fail to achieve the benefits envisaged. Whilst there can be many reasons for this, often, it is in the customer's experience of the contact that the process fails.

In essence, there are only three points at which the contact strategy can fail to deliver:

- ◆ incorrect targeting of the customer (ie the data modelling and scoring mechanisms (covered earlier) incorrectly predict a customer need);
- ◆ uncompetitive product or offer (ie the customer needs the product and is happy to buy but the product design/features/price make it unattractive to the customer);
- ◆ customer experience breaks down (ie the customer needs the product, would buy it, but the contact process fails either in channel or across channel).

It is the latter which contributes more to lost business and is often overlooked as marketing departments typically measure only response rates against different creatives, not the whole purchase experience. This is understanding and personalising the customer experience at point of contact to provide an appropriate product or service.

In this section, we will cover:

- ◆ contact relevance and real-time campaigns;

- creating the 'virtual' relationship manager;
- customisation of customer channel contact preferences;
- customer experience management;
- alignment of goals and measures of customer facing staff.

14.2   Contact relevance

The key to effective outbound communication is in the relevance to the customer. This is relevance in the customer's eyes, not the organisations. For example, many credit card operations are very happy with 1% response rates to their campaigns in terms of return on investment for that campaign. However, they seldom consider the customer experience for the customers who did not respond, which could range from 'the mail was relevant, but I decided not to respond' to 'junk mail from THAT company again!' Clearly, if the latter is the majority, then the ability for the organisation to appear relevant for any products diminished impacting both the brand and loyalty on existing products.

Contact relevance can be broken down into three categories based on:

- the behaviour of 'similar' customers. This is the traditional scorecard and propensity modelling approach;
- actual customer behaviour (an event) deducted from transactional or other data provided by the customer;
- responding to a customer's interest or request in real time.

Typically, the response rates rise exponentially based on the relevance and timing of contact. The chart below highlights research by the Gartner group.

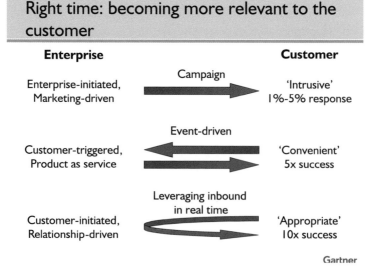

Right time: becoming more relevant to the customer

Enterprise		Customer
Enterprise-initiated, Marketing-driven	Campaign	'Intrusive' 1%-5% response
Customer-triggered, Product as service	Event-driven	'Convenient' 5x success
Customer-initiated, Relationship-driven	Leveraging inbound in real time	'Appropriate' 10x success

Gartner

14.3 Blending central campaigns and real time customer intelligence

In the previous section, we discussed how campaign management systems operate by selecting customers and then deploying campaigns to customers. In the following example we look at an example of how real-time campaign software can used to adjust offers and contact as new information becomes available to customise the customer experience.

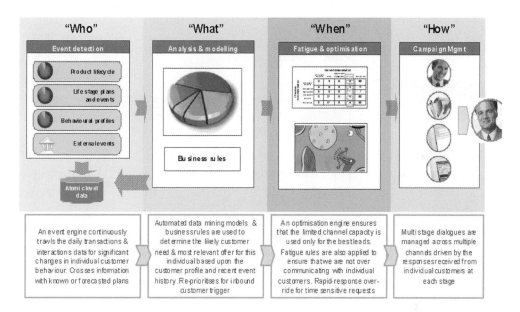

"Who"	"What"	"When"	"How"
Event detection	Analysis & modelling	Fatigue & optimisation	Campaign Mgmt

An event engine continuously trawls the daily transactions & interactions data for significant changes in individual customer behaviour. Crosses information with known or forecasted plans

Automated data mining models & business rules are used to determine the likely customer need & most relevant offer for this individual based upon the customer profile and recent event history. Re-prioritises for inbound customer trigger

An optimisation engine ensures that the limited channel capacity is used only for the best leads. Fatigue rules are also applied to ensure that we are not over communicating with individual customers. Rapid-response over-ride for time sensitive requests

Multi stage dialogues are managed across multiple channels driven by the responses received from individual customers at each stage

Interaction advisor: schematic overview of real-time personalisation of offers

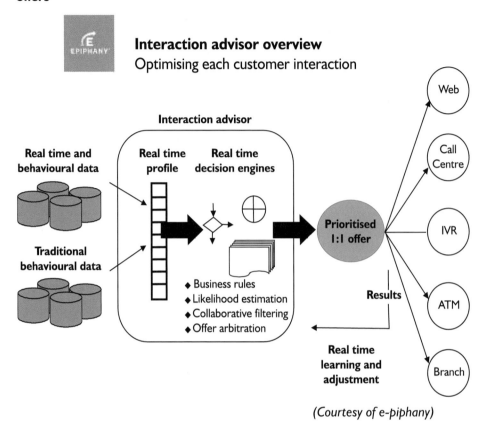

Interaction advisor overview
Optimising each customer interaction

(Courtesy of e-piphany)

Real-time marketing (also called 'next best action') effectively manages inbound interactions with customers when they proactively engage with an organisation via an interactive environment, such as the web, contact centre, ATM or physical branch office. During these inbound interactions the system uses a combination of historical, personal and contextual data to create a real-time customer profile, and then applies a unique combination of real-time analytics and business rules to deliver the highest-impact offers to a customer in real time. The system then measures the results and continuously applies self-learning to improve its effectiveness over time.

The software examines customer characteristics each time an offer is accepted, building an refined profile of customers likely to accept the offer. Each time a new customer is a campaign target, the software measures how closely the customer's characteristics match the aggregated profile for each campaign offer and assigns a likelihood of offer acceptance. The acceptance likelihood is used in targeting criteria to determine whether to extend a particular offer to a particular customer.

The characteristics of customers who accept offers may be discrete values, like occupation, or numerical and continuous values, like income, age, account balance, etc. Collaborative filtering uses an individual's purchase history or preferences to find people with similar tastes, and predicts what else the person will like, based on the collective purchase histories or preferences of other like-minded people. The list of products liked by similar people is sorted according to a score calculation based on closeness to the customer in question and product popularity. The final output of this analysis is then used to determine which products to recommend.

14.4   Customisation of relationship

Once you are able to understand the breadth and depth of the customer relationship with the organisation and have this information available whenever and however the customer chooses to contact then you are in a position to start customising the relationship, a view endorsed by Irene Dorner, General Manager at HSBC: 'This is when it gets exciting. Used wisely, you can now start to build your bank around the customer'.

14.4.1   Relationship management as a process

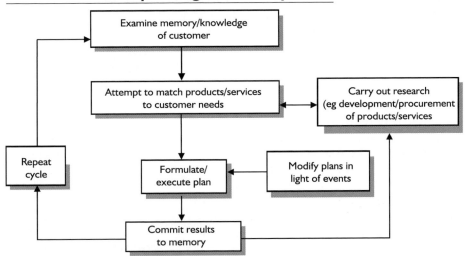

The term 'relationship management' is used to cover a wide variety of activities. The above flow chart tries to rationalise these into a process which helps to understand how a traditional relationship manager (for example, branch manager or account manager) undertakes their role.

For example, consider a branch manager of a bank in the 1950s. All of the knowledge of interactions with the customer would be kept either in the manager's memory or on paper in the form of interview notes or correspondence. Before meeting the customer, the manager would review this information and then try to predict the likely needs of the customer and therefore the products and services to introduce.

The meeting would then take place and the manager would listen to the customer's needs (refining and matching this to previous knowledge) and then propose some solutions.

An agreement would then be reached and the appropriate actions taken to provide the products and services.

The manager would then update the customer's file with any new customer knowledge.

The cycle would then repeat.

Traditionally, banks have offered this method of relationship management to a few customers. However, the massive expansion in customers needing (and able to afford) financial services together with a highly competitive market with consequent reduction in margins, has challenged the viability of this model.

To make matters worse, the ability to understand the customer through contact has been made increasingly complex with the ever-increasing number of delivery channels and the relentless drive towards 24 x 7 x 365 service. In short, organisations cannot afford to deploy the traditional human relationship manager unless the value and complexity of the customer relationship warrants it.

14.4.2 Creating the 'virtual' relationship manager

Having understood the process, it is easy to see how the simple relationship management model described can be automated either in its entirety or in part. This 'virtual' style of relationship management offers the 'holy grail' to industries where high levels of customer interaction are required to understand and provide service. This approach is also sometimes referred to as 'mass relationship management'.

If we now re-run the previous example, then the interaction may go as follows: a customer accesses the bank through the Internet and browses some products and services. The system tracks his passage through the website and matches this to knowledge already held in the central customer database. The system prompts and guides the customer through his needs to some appropriate solutions. The customer either completes the transaction or requests to speak to a person in the bank's call centre or arranges an interview in a local branch. The database records are updated accordingly.

The underlying process is the same as in our 1950s example but the relationship management responsibilities are spread across different channels (for example, the Internet, call centre and branch), the CRM system providing the 'corporate glue' to hold the customer experience together.

14.5 Customisation of customer channel contact preferences

The explosive growth in outbound direct marketing, and the deployment of technologies such as predictive (power) diallers (a mechanism for dialling calls automatically and handing them to agents for completion once the called number has answered. The dialler makes more calls than there are agents available on the predicted basis that not all calls will connect) has led to consumers demanding the ability to block such approaches.

This consumer pressure has led to the creation of central registers such as the TPS (telephone preference service) where consumers can register and block such unsolicited marketing approaches. In many banks, the number of customers so registered is in excess of 25%. These customers also tend to be the most valuable or those having the most potential, so not being able to market to these customers in a proactive way is a real barrier to business growth.

There are two solutions to this and both require an integrated customer database and view:

◆ to collect and record the individual contact preferences in dealings with your organisation (this explicit consent overrides the TPS register, etc);
◆ to maximise inbound customer contact.

14.5.1 Collecting individual customer preferences

In essence, at the most complex level, you allow the customer to define:

◆ content of communication (for example, products/services);
◆ method of communication;
◆ time of communication.

This involves defining the methods of contact (for example, paper mail, e-mail, SMS, telephone, etc) and then asking the customer for their preferences.

So, for example, the customer may accept telephone calls in the evening, but not at weekends or during the day. The data collected will be logged in the customer record and used as a campaign restriction or filter in delivering any outbound communication.

Maintaining customer contact preferences is an ongoing task and research shows customers are pleased to keep information up to date if they are given easy access (for example, via the web) and that they can see that the organisation is able to fulfil their preferences. Collecting customer preferences that cannot be acted upon through the campaign management system is both dangerous and fool hardy!

14.6   Customer experience management

So what is the customer experience?

> 'Emotions set our highest level goals, including how much and well we work and buy. By creating the right emotions in employees and customers, the phenomenon of emotional engagement is the next economic force in the highly competitive marketplace ... a blend of a company's physical performance and the emotion evoked, intuitively measured against customer expectations across all moments of contact.

> In other words, it is the culmination of all of a customer's moments of contact (truth) or touch points with your organisation.

> Make it hard for your customers to do business with you, they'll NEVER come back...no matter how much advertising you do.'

> *Beyond Philosophy, Curt Coffman, co-author 'First Break All the Rules'.*

So in order to measure and understand the customer experience, you first have to define it. Surprisingly, few large organisations systematically design their contact processes and then measure and adjust these in light of real customer experience.

There are many techniques for mapping the process flows and some of these are covered in this book under 'process mapping' and 'business process re-engineering'.

Having mapped and understood the customer experience intention, it is then vital to measure and understand how it performs in reality.

There are many techniques to understand the customer experience, such as:

- ◆ traditional research (focus groups, etc, covered earlier in the book);
- ◆ general customer satisfaction surveys;
- ◆ specific post event/purchase satisfaction surveys;
- ◆ mystery shopping and sampling of contacts.

14.6.1   General satisfaction surveys

General satisfaction surveys help establish a bench mark for how the organisation is perceived by its customers both from their actual experiences and from their perception of the organisation created by external factors from the media, friends, etc.

Trended over time, they can give an insight into the macro perception of the customer experience. Often, they can be carried out by third parties in syndicated research on a number of organisations, such as banks, and provide a competitive comparison dimension. Companies such as NOP and MORI provide such services.

14.6.2   Specific event surveys

Specific post event or purchase surveys can be carried out interactively or by post or e-mail following a contact or interaction. Typically, they involve a number of questions exploring both the rational elements of the contact (did the customer get what they wanted?) and the emotional elements (how did the customer feel during and after the contact?). Provided they are carried out either immediately following the experience or within a short time after, they can provide insight into how the intended experience is actually being received and identify key weaknesses to be investigated.

14.6.3   Mystery shopping and sampling of contacts

Mystery shopping is the collection of information from retail outlets, websites, showrooms, etc by people posing as ordinary members of the public. It is a method of gathering an end-to-end experience. However, it is more difficult in financial institutions as most products require customer identification and hence make the completion of the transaction more difficult.

A variation is to sample actual telephone calls or web sessions and then use this to understand where the experience is working and where it is breaking down. This can be particularly powerful if senior executives take part in the sampling and listen in to calls or take part in direct customer contact on a regular basis.

14.6.4   Alignment of goals and measures of customer facing staff

Having put in place a programme for monitoring and measuring the customer experience, it is vital to link these to the goals and measures of customer contact staff. For example, HSBC tracks each customer contact input into the CRM system and is able to build 'value chains' showing how each individual customer's purchase was made either in channel or across channel. By analysing those chains that did not complete, it is able to pinpoint breaks in the customer experience. Similarly, staff are rewarded for chains that complete which drives both positive behaviour in ensuring the customer is looked after at all times and if a handover across channel is required (or chosen by the customer), it is managed well.

Fifteen

Management information

15.1 Introduction: strategic, tactical and operational information

Information has some important characteristics.

- ◆ It must be relevant to its purpose. Strategic information about market share should not include information about production costs, for example, as this might distract or even confuse the manager using it.
- ◆ It must be sufficiently timely for its purpose. This means that the manager needs to get the information in time to take some action. There is no point in telling the manager that his or her costs will be over budget after the end of the financial year.
- ◆ It must be sufficiently accurate for its purpose. The accuracy needed varies depending how the information is going to be used. Balance sheets are usually shown in thousands of pounds and this is sufficiently accurate for this purpose. If you are going to calculate rates of return on products, you need much more accurate balances as a small difference in the rate might have a big effect on how the bank or building society markets the product.
- ◆ It must be presented in the right way and to the right person. Information for senior management should generally be presented as charts, perhaps showing trends over time or market share. The lower the level of management receiving the information, the more detail should generally be shown.
- ◆ Information should not cost more to produce than its value to the business.

15.1.1 Some key uses for business intelligence tools in the financial services

◆ Improving customer service – through the creation of single customer views.
◆ Improved customer targeting – through integrating sales, CRM and marketing and product tools to get a rounded picture of customer requirements and methods for improving customer wallet share.
◆ Risk reporting – the integrating of risk reporting across a corporation through the creation of an integrated view of the multiple market, credit and operational risk systems that most large organisations have.
◆ Regulatory reporting – the integrating of operational, risk, sales and financial data into a single reporting framework.
◆ Operational monitoring – use of performance management tools for alters and exceptions reporting.
◆ Sales performance reporting and tracking.
◆ Market performance tracking – through integrating internal sales performance tools with external market data tools.
◆ Resource monitoring – using the integrated reporting environment to study how the firm is using key resources.
◆ Key performance indicator tracking – balanced scorecards aligning strategy with operational goals. Often, this is tracking performance against the requirements of shareholder value programmes.
◆ Key performance indicator building – using analysis tools to look for key indicators of performance that can be used to establish future goals and targets.
◆ Strategy formulation – integrating all of the above capabilities for a true insight into how the firm is performing both internally and in the overall market.

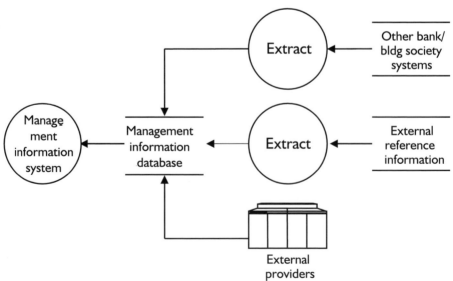

15.2 Management information systems

Management information systems (MISs) are databases which are designed to be used by managers to select and cross-reference data. An MIS consists of a relational database holding the data of interest and a user interface which allows managers to specify the data they want to extract.

Different managerial levels need different types of information. We usually distinguish between:

◆ strategic information, used by senior management;
◆ tactical information, used by middle management;
◆ operational information, used by first line management and supervisors.

The differences between these types of information are summarised below.

	Strategic information	**Tactical information**	**Operational information**
Used by	Senior managers	Middle managers	First line managers
Time horizon	1–10 years	3–18 months	Up to 1 month
Sources of data	External and strategic management information systems	Operational and tactical management information systems	Operational systems
Internal or external	Internal and external	Mainly internal	Entirely internal
Frequency of decision	Infrequent and at irregular intervals	Weekly, monthly, quarterly or yearly	Very frequent during the day
Basis for decisions	Facts, projections and judgements	Facts and projections	Facts
Type of decision	Unprogrammed – each decision is unique	Programmed – follows overall policies and precedents	Prescriptive – follows defined rules and procedures
Presentation	Summaries and trends	Summaries and supporting detail	Usually detailed
Examples	Market share and product profitability	Actual costs and revenues vs budgets	Customer financial histories

MIS will often only provide strategic and tactical management information. Operational management information is often taken from the processing system.

There are usually differences between the information held in an MIS and that held in the corresponding operational database. Reasons for this can include the following.

◆ *Need for history*. Managers need to monitor what is happening over a period of time – for example, monthly sales figures for the past eighteen months. Operational systems usually need data for much shorter periods.

◆ *Operational systems may include physical data related to transactions such as delivery instructions.* This information is usually of little relevance to managers.

◆ *Scope*. Managers often need to compare data from a number of different operational systems and external data sources to get an overall picture.

Because of these differences, MISs are usually built up over time from data extracted from the operational database systems. Much of this data is in summary form.

Data held in an MIS is a copy of data taken from operational systems. This means that it will usually be out of date when the data is accessed. This is rarely important for management information, but it does limit the uses to which it can be put. Data warehouses and datamarts also contain copies of operational data.

The data for an MIS is taken from the operational systems and external sources as shown in the following diagram:

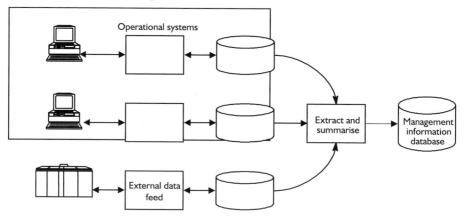

The features of an MIS include:

◆ Either a query language or a number of standard queries into which the manager can enter parameters.

'Canned queries' are a feature of older MISs whose query language capabilities were often limited. A series of basic queries was set up into which managers could enter parameters such as date ranges, market segments and minimum and maximum amounts.

Modern query languages are easier to use and include functions such as 'query by example'. This allows managers to show the system what information they require and allows the query language to work out how to get it.

◆ Interfaces to electronic office products such as spreadsheets. The simplest way to achieve this is extract data from the MIS into a data file and import this into the electronic office products, and this approach is used in some older MISs. It is also possible to extract data from the MIS in the required form – for example, as a spreadsheet file – or to create a link between the MIS and the electronic office product. Database connectivity, discussed in Chapter Thirteen, can also be used and this allows the electronic office product to request the data directly from the DBMS.

◆ Standard calculations such as cost and profitability calculations. The MIS allows executive management to compare information from across the organisation and standard calculations are needed to make sure the values being compared have the same meaning.

◆ Most MISs hold some data in summary form. An example might be transaction posting data where the amount of data is very large, but the individual postings are not needed as management information and monthly summaries can be used instead.

The ability of managers to enter queries is an example of 'end user computing'. Providing end users with the tools to get the information they need directly, without having to go through the IT function, increases the benefit of IT to the organisation. However, end user computing is less efficient than producing a report to produce the same information and the additional costs must be balanced against the benefits.

We introduced the idea of power users earlier in this text. The problem with end user computing is that it uses computer resources very heavily and often inefficiently. We can improve the efficiency by using a powerful computer language such as SQL, but these are not designed to be used without training. Power users have the training and knowledge to use these languages. This knowledge equips power users to act as a bridge between business users and systems developers as they understand the problems of both sides.

15.3 Executive information systems

Executive information systems (EISs) provide a way of presenting information to senior management. An EIS works in much the same way as an MIS, except that it is usually less powerful at retrieving information, but better at presenting it.

The main features of an EIS are as follows.

◆ It presents information in a way that is very easy to understand. It can highlight figures which are particularly good or bad (green is usually used for above target, yellow for below target and red for well below target). It allows information to be shown as either a chart or table and to be switched between these presentations in a very simple way.

◆ It can 'drill down'. For example, if a region is shown as well below target the manager can see how the area figures contributed to that. If one of the areas is well below target, he or she can go down to the individual branches.

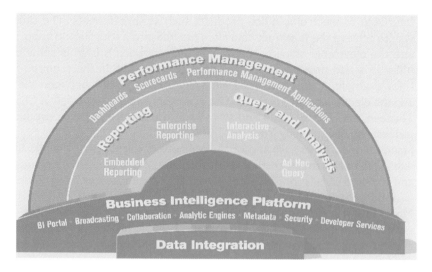

For example, an EIS system and its links to its data sources might look like this.

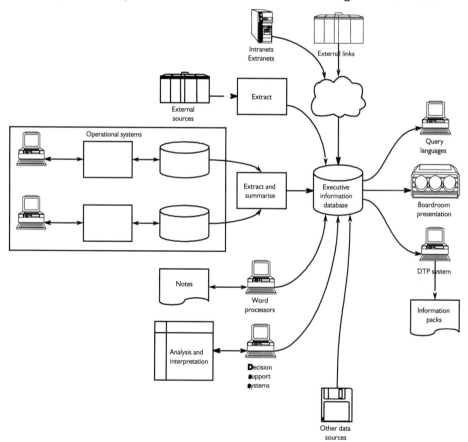

Before being able to decide which software or combination of software would be most beneficial to an organisation, we must look into the usage and the users needs. This means finding out the types of users available at each site and what their needs and expertise would be. The business intelligence community has outlined descriptions of different information users.

User Categories	User Types	Objectives/ Functions	Knowledge	Perspective of World	Usage Pattern
Tourists (Generalists)	Executives, Managers, Casual users	Broad business perspective. Executives, in particular, need basic information to assess the overall health of their companies	Cover a breadth of material quickly, but in little depth. Aware of the data, information and knowledge that the business produces	In terms of business function	Unpredict-able
Operators **(focused)**	Customer Support, Inventory Control, Manufacturing	Use intelligence derived by *explorers/farmers* to improve business. Primary source of feedback into the information process	Provide pressure on information source in terms of availability, data freshness and query performance	In terms of process	Fairly predict-able
Farmers **(Clear)**	Sales Analysts, Financial Analysts, Marketing Campaign Managers, Accounting Analysts	Monitors the effect of decisions on the business by tracking key performance metrics. Provide *explorers* with feedback on effectiveness of predictions	Know what data they want, and how they want it displayed, when they want it and in what media. Understand value of integrated, cleansed data	In terms of dimensions (time, product, geography) and metrics (usage, revenue, counts, costs)	Fairly predict-able
Explorers (Innovative)	Marketing Analyst, Actuaries, Process Control Engineers	Endeavour to understand what makes the business work by looking for hidden meaning in the data. Strive to predict the future based on past events	Very knowledgeable about content of data within and outside of business. Have little or no idea of what to expect prior to query execution.	In terms of data and data relationships	Unpredict-able

User Categories	User Types	Objectives/ Functions	Knowledge	Perspective of World	Usage Pattern
Miners (Thorough)	Statisticians, Expert Marketers, Risk Controllers, Logistics Specialists	Scan large amounts of detailed data to confirm hypothesis or suspected patterns	Good idea of what to expect prior to query execution	Operate on a base of very flat, highly de-normalised data that has been pre-conditioned for analysis	Reasonably predict-able

Source: Gartner Group, Bill Inmon

Once the users have been designated as belonging to one of the above categories, a simple analysis can be performed. This analysis is two part, ie what quantity of users are there in each category and from this which software should be implemented to acquire the biggest return (with respect to number of users and action ability). In short, the software required will be based on the business user data needs and the sophistication of these users.

The easiest way in assessing the software needs is to look within your user community and identify the number of 'data' or information users and the categories that these users fall within. As an example, if there were 20 users that are all branch managers and/or executives, this would suggest all the users are 'tourists'. The tourists' 'needs' can be met with an EIS or Online Analytical Processing (OLAP) tool.

If, however, there are 20 users and 15 are marketing experts and analysts and the remaining five are executives, it will be more appropriate to forego the EIS and concentrate on OLAP, statistical tools and a campaign management tool. The statistical tools will allow the users to group the customer into similar segments, while the campaign management tool would be key in an environment where there are numerous campaigns. This tool would be used to co-ordinate multiple campaigns from multiple customer touch points.

The user types and categories are important in deciding the appropriate software to meet the users' needs.

User Categories	User Types	EIS (Executive Information System)	OLAP (Query/ reporting)	Statistical Language or Decision Support	Campaign Manage- ment	Data Mining
Tourists (Generalists)	Executives, Managers, Casual users	X	X			
Operators (Focused)	Customer Support, Inventory Control, Manufacturing		X			
Farmers (Clear)	Sales Analysts, Financial Analysts, Marketing Campaign Managers, Accounting Analysts		X	X	X	
Explorers (Innovative)	Marketing Analyst, Actuaries, Process Control Engineers		X	X	X	
Miners (Thorough)	Statisticians, Expert Marketers, Risk Controllers, Logistics Specialists		-	X	X	X

15.4 Tactical and operational management information systems

15.4.1 Examples of business intelligence tools

For example, IBM provides a suite of products called the IBM 'Data Information Factory', which consist of three products, all of which can be linked to form a seamless reporting environment.

Ad hoc query and reporting

IBM has partnered with Business Objects to provide this function. Business Objects products provide non-technical business users with access to information stored in data warehouses, datamarts and packaged business applications. Business Objects provides a complete suite of decision support tools offering ad hoc query and reporting capabilities, as well as integrated analysis functionality, for both client/server and Internet environments.

OLAP–DB2 OLAP server

An enterprise-scale, online analytical processing system for a wide range of multi-dimensional reporting, analysis, modelling and planning applications. DB2 OLAP Server is based on Hyperion's Essbase OLAP Server.

DB2 OLAP Server can be used for a wide range of applications:

- management and reporting;
- planning and modelling;
- sales analysis;
- profitability;
- market share;
- supplier analysis;
- EIS;
- financial consolidations;
- budgeting;
- forecasting.

15.4.2   Expert systems

The most common are knowledge-based systems. An expert in a particular field describes the process he or she goes through to assess something. The steps are coded as 'rules' and entered into a 'knowledge base'. Someone with less expertise can consult the system, which will ask a series of questions. Depending on the responses to those questions, the expert system's 'inference engine' will use the information in the knowledge base to decide the most likely answer to the question. Some systems have a self-learning capability – they can adjust the rules depending on the results of their decisions.

We can show a knowledge-based system as a diagram.

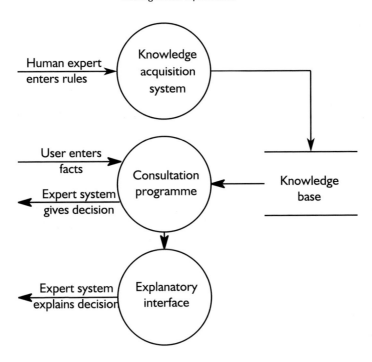

A typical approach to building an expert system might be as follows.

- ◆ A human expert would define a set of rules, working with an IT expert systems specialist or possibly directly with the computer. These would be entered into the system's knowledge base.
- ◆ The system would be tested and the rules adjusted depending on the results. This process would be automatic if a neural network or self-learning program were used.
- ◆ A user would be able to consult the system by answering questions or by supplying data. The inferencing engine will compare the information against the rules in the knowledge base and reach a conclusion. This may be a single statement or it may be a range of possibilities, each with a percentage probability (expert systems used for medical diagnosis often work this way).
- ◆ If the user does not understand or does not agree with the conclusion, he or she can ask the explanatory interface how it has been reached. This will show which rules were applied and how the conclusion was reached.

Limitations of expert systems

There is nothing magical about expert systems. They are only as effective as the rules entered into them. They are used for fraud detection for credit cards and for some loan assessment and portfolio management systems.

Knowledge-based systems, without a self-learning capability, are the most common form of expert system used in financial services organisations. Their main advantage is that they give consistent answers, unlike the other systems where the answer will be affected by what the system has learnt from recent experience.

The disadvantage of knowledge-based systems is that they assume that the rules stay the same. Although this is generally true in retail finance it is not the case for the wholesale markets and neural networks and genetic algorithms are widely used in, for example, securities trading. Neural networks and genetic algorithms are also used in fraud detection.

Case-based reasoning is used to some extent in the credit assessment of small business customers. It allows customers to be ranked against other firms in the same line of business. This is more common in the United States where information about industry segments is available through the bankers' trade association.

15.4.3 Neural networks

Neural networks are becoming increasingly important. These learn in much the same way as the human brain. They contain a large network of inter-connected processors. Information fed into this chooses its own path through the network, based on rules which have been entered and on past experience. If a particular path has been successful under a set of circumstances, it is more likely that the same path will be chosen if the circumstances are similar. By running a large number of cases through the neural network, it learns and improves its rate of success.

15.4.4 Genetic alogorithms

Another relatively new approach is the genetic algorithm. These 'evolve', with the less successful in each generation becoming extinct, while the more successful go through forced mutation to form the next generation. As with neural networks, feeding a large number of cases through the genetic algorithm allows it to learn and improve its rate of success. An important difference between neural networks and genetic algorithms is that the latter only require software and can be run on a standard PC.

15.4.5 Case-based reasoning

Case-based reasoning is a different approach. This relies on a large library of similar cases with known results. Every problem that is presented is compared with the cases in the library and the most similar cases are identified. The result of the new case can be predicted on the basis of the results of similar past cases.

Expert systems can take 'decisions' based on rules and experience. There are three main types of expert system.

The most common are knowledge-based systems. An expert in a particular field describes the process he or she goes through to assess something. The steps are coded as 'rules' and entered into a 'knowledge base'. Someone with less expertise can consult the system, which will ask a series of questions. Depending on the responses to those questions, the expert system's 'inference engine' will use the rules in the knowledge base to decide the most likely answer to the question. Some systems have a learning capability – they can adjust the rules depending on the results of their decisions.

15.4.6   Credit scoring systems

Credit scoring systems attempt to predict how likely a borrower is to repay a loan from a combination of demographic information (age, occupation, residential status, etc) and past account behaviour. They carry out the functions of expert systems, although they are not generally developed using expert systems technology.

How credit scoring systems work	Loan applicants are given a 'score' depending on their answers to the questions on the application form. For example, a residential status of owner occupier might be worth 20 points, whereas a status of tenant might only be worth 5. Credit scoring systems also include policy rules. These are conditions under which the loan will automatically be refused. The scores for all the questions are added up and compared against a cut-off. If the total score is below this, the loan will be refused. If the score is above the cut-off and all the policy rules are satisfied, the loan will be granted.
Credit reference agencies	Credit scoring systems often include links to external credit reference agencies. These match applicants against records such as the electoral roll, county court judgements and information drawn from applicants' credit history. This may include both 'black' (late or missed repayments) and 'white' (good credit record) information, although not all credit providers look at white information.
Advantages	Credit scoring systems have three main advantages for the banks and building societies.

- ♦ They ensure that customers are treated in the same way throughout the branch network. By automating the system, they avoid situations where the same loan application would be treated differently by different managers.

◆ They allow lending decisions to be made by less experienced (and therefore cheaper) staff.

◆ The bank or building society can adjust the cut-off score and policy rules depending on its overall strategy. If the organisation is trying to build market share, it can lower the cut-off score, accepting more business. If it is trying to cut loan losses, it can raise the cut-off score. This is much easier than changing the lending behaviour of hundreds of individual managers.

Demographic scorecards give loan applicants a 'score' depending on their answers to the questions on the application form. For example, a residential status of owner occupier might be worth 20 points, whereas a status of tenant might only be worth 5.

Behavioural scorecards work in the same way, but use account history information. For example, if the customer has not gone over limit at all in the last 18 months, this might be worth 20 points, one or two limit excesses might be worth 5 points and three or more limit excesses might be worth –10 points.

Credit scoring systems also include policy rules. These are conditions under which the loan will automatically be refused, for example, if there are county court judgements outstanding against the applicant.

The scores for all the questions are added up and compared against a cut-off. If the total score is below this, the loan will be refused. If the score is above the cut-off and all the policy rules are satisfied, the loan will be granted.

15.5   Workgroup computing

Workgroup computing allows people to work together in groups, even if they are in different physical locations. It uses computer systems and telecommunications networks to allow people to communicate and co-ordinate their work.

An example of a workgroup computing system is Lotus Notes. This is a text database and differs from relational databases in that the information in the database is held as large blocks of text rather than in fields. Lotus Notes does have fields, but these are used mainly for keys.

The features available in workgroup computing systems include the following.

◆ File, navigation and editing features similar to those available in word processors.
◆ Database features. The ability to define keys which can be used to present the information in the database as a series of 'views' allowing users to see the data in the order most relevant to their needs. The ability to produce forms to enter data.

◆ Audit trail features. The ability to record who has proposed changes to documents and what has happened to them. An approach taken in products such as Lotus Notes is to record proposed changes as 'responses' to the original document and comments on these proposals as 'responses to responses'.

◆ Knowledge management features such as search engines. The ability of the workgroup computer system to act as a 'corporate memory' recording management experience.

◆ Replication. The ability to change copies of the database held on different computers and to reconcile these changes at a later stage. This allows workgroup computing systems to be used on portable computers and any changes to be added to a central database when the portable computer is next linked to a telecommunications network.

Some features have also been incorporated into word processors, for example, the ability to collect comments from different reviewers and to combine them with the original document.

15.5.1   The intranet

Intranets use Internet technology over an internal wide area network. Web browsers are used to access the intranet. The following diagram shows an intranet.

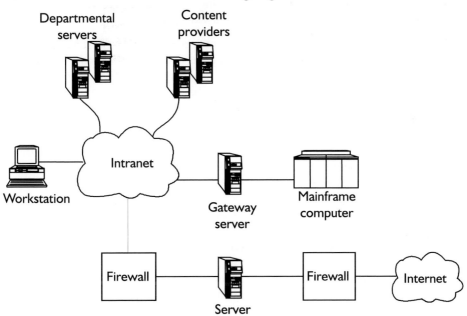

Intranets can be used for a number of purposes. They are widely used to distribute information. Procedures manuals, internal telephone directories and training material are examples of information commonly distributed over the intranet. Intranets can be used to replace the organisation's wide area network by distributing application software.

The intranet can also be used for knowledge sharing and knowledge management.

15.5.2   Knowledge management

An organisation's own know how is a valuable resource. Some studies have suggested that 20–30% of an organisation's total costs are the result of solving problems for which the organisation already knows the solution. Knowledge management provides a series of tools and techniques to allow the organisation to exploit this know how.

Knowledge management has been defined as 'codifying the knowledge your company creates and disseminating it to the people who need it – when they need it'. The key words are 'codifying' and 'disseminating'.

- Codifying includes both capturing and categorising information.
- Disseminating includes both accessing information that is relevant and delivering it to the people who need it when they need it.

Categorisation is perhaps the most important and most difficult of these processes. Knowledge is information which can be applied to a valued purpose. We need to categorise all the information we capture in a way that allows us to identify its relevance to the various purposes we may have for information dissemination. Therefore, we first need to develop a system of classification – sometimes called an 'ontology' – which meets the needs of the business.

The categorisation process can be carried out manually, often by attaching keywords to each piece of information. This is time consuming and will need to be reviewed whenever new keywords are added. There are a number of approaches to automatic categorisation.

- The simplest is automatically to search for all occurrences of important words in information. These can then be used to build an index. This can be made slightly more sophisticated by also looking for synonyms – for example, we might want to categorise both 'loan' and 'advance' under loan.
  There are some disadvantages to this. For example, the word 'credit' could refer to a loan or a payment received.
- A variation on this is to look at the 'keyword in context'. The index is based on keywords, but the words immediately surrounding the keyword are also shown. This is useful for identifying how the keyword is used.
- More advanced approaches attempt to identify similar pieces of information based on other words. For example, information containing the word 'credit'

might be categorised differently depending on whether it also includes the word 'card' or the word 'account'. Some search engines use this approach.

Determining what information is relevant depends on our ability to express our needs in a way that matches the way the information is classified. An approach which is attracting an increasing amount of attention is natural language queries, in which the query is expressed as if it were a piece of spoken English and the 'assistants' supplied with the latest versions of office automation products. Some Internet search engines make use of this.

Some of the most important applications of knowledge management techniques are:

- best practice databases;
- summarisation and abstraction;
- knowledge discovery.

Best practice databases record the organisation's experience of the best way to do things. Best practice databases such as Ford's 'Things Gone Right, Things Gone Wrong' act as the organisation's memory and help to avoid the cost of rediscovering knowledge the organisation already possesses.

A new application for knowledge management is in summarisation and abstraction. This allows text information to be automatically summarised without losing any important information. This helps to reduce the amount of information people have to deal with.

Knowledge discovery is the 'non-trivial extraction of implicit, previously unknown and potentially useful information from data'. Data mining is an example of knowledge discovery. Knowledge discovery examines data to look for as follows.

- *Correlations*. These may be events which usually happen together or items of data which are often found together. A trivial example of the latter might be if households that have two cars are more likely to take foreign holidays – this might be useful in suggesting that holiday insurance could be advertised in car magazines.
- *Forecasts*. These are events that form a predictable sequence. An obvious example is that a rise in interest rates precedes a rise in bad debts. Note that the use of data mining to identify forecasts does not require any causal relationship between the events and data mining is perhaps most useful where it identifies relationships which do not have any obvious relationship, but which do seem to be valid.
- *Classifications*. These are different ways of classifying data items. For example, it may be possible to classify groups of customers who will behave in a certain way from data held about them. This can be used for segmentation.

Sixteen

Operational systems design

16.1   Introduction

In this chapter, we discuss some of the factors behind how operational systems are designed.

We briefly discussed the information architecture in Chapter Two. An information architecture describes how an organisation's information systems interrelate. Key components of the architecture are the transaction processing system and the communications infrastructure. All of these are considered in this chapter.

Much of the emphasis of this book has been on information systems and systems to service the customer touch points. This chapter looks at the back office systems that support them.

The chapter finishes with a discussion of training.

16.2   Information architecture

The following diagram is a very high-level schematic representation of the information architecture for a typical financial services organisation.

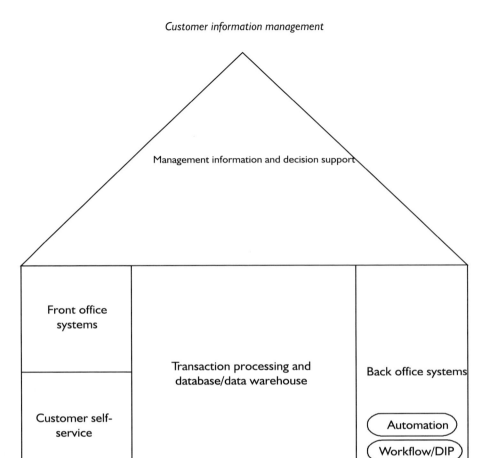

Management information and decision support, front office systems and customer self-service systems have been discussed earlier in the book.

The transaction processing systems and database/data warehouse are central to the architecture and all of the other components are dependent on them. The database and data warehouse have been discussed earlier in this text.

16.3 Transaction processing

We have already described a transaction as a logical piece of work. The way in which transactions are processed has changed as IT has evolved:

◆ batch processing (first generation);

- remote batch processing (second generation);
- online transaction processing (second generation);
- real-time processing (second generation).

16.3.1 Batch processing

In batch processing, transactions are collected into batches of similar items. For example, a batch might contain all cheques presented over the counter. These are entered into the computer and recorded on a transaction file, which is used to update the master files at a later time – often overnight.

The simplest form of batch processing works as follows.

- Forms and documents which need processing are collected during the day.
- At the end of the working day, the forms and documents are sorted by type. Each separate type of form or document will form one or more separate batches. If there are a large number of forms or documents of a specific type, this may be split into a number of batches each containing (typically) between twenty and one hundred forms or documents.
- A batch header slip will be completed. This may contain a batch number (which allows the batch to be identified), a batch type (indicating the type of form or document), a count of the number of items in the batch and a batch total (the total of the amounts on the forms or documents in the batch).
- The batch will be entered into the computer. The batch entry system will also check the batch header information (item count and batch total). The items in the batch will be written to a transaction file, which may also include a batch header record (containing the batch header information) and a batch trailer record to tell the system when it has finished processing a batch.
- The transaction file will be used to update a 'master file'. This may be a sequential file, for example, a file of accounts sorted in account number order, in which event the update process will involve the following steps:
  - the transaction file will be sorted into the same order as the master file;
  - the transaction file will then be matched against the master file, with the changes recorded on the transaction file being applied to the master file record which has the same key;
  - a new copy of the master file will be created, based on the original master file and the changes from the transaction file; and
  - input and error reports will be produced, allowing the results of the update to be checked.

We can show the batch update process as a diagram.

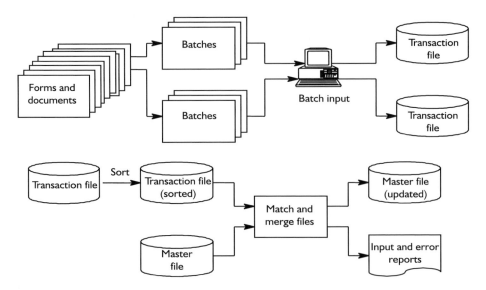

Financial organisations used batch systems for three reasons.

◆ Batch processing uses IT resources very efficiently, especially where very large numbers of transactions are involved and where there is a high 'hit rate' – a high proportion of records on the master file will be changed by the transaction file.

◆ Many financial processes naturally take place outside the normal working day (for example, interest calculation, charges calculation, statements and standing orders) and would not benefit from the higher costs associated with online or real-time processing.

◆ Other financial processes were designed round the use of batch processing. A good example of this is clearing, where the traditional three-day clearing cycle was based on the physical delivery of cheques outside working hours. As a result, financial services organisations have a considerable investment in batch systems to maintain.

This may be inefficient where the hit rate is low. In this event, we could store the master file as a database, allowing us to go directly to the record we want to change. Instead of creating a new master file, we will make the changes directly to the master file we are using. We could enter batches in exactly the same way as described above or we could use remote batch.

16.3.2 Remote batch processing

Remote batch processing differs from the older form of batch processing in that transactions can be entered into the computer immediately they are received. However, when they have been entered, they are still placed on a transaction file and the master files are updated at the end of the day.

Remote batch systems do not include the batch checking (record counts, batch totals) described above and may work as follows:

- forms and documents which need processing are entered when they are received or at any convenient point during the day. There is no batch checking so the data entry system carries out some validation;
- shadow files can be used in remote batch systems to keep critical information such as balances up to date. If a shadow file is used, the transaction code is used to decide what action to take and the key is used to look up the corresponding record. The balance on the shadow file is updated;
- the items are stored on a transaction file during the day;
- the processing is carried out at the end of the day. The master file can be sequential or allow direct access;
- if a shadow file is used, the balances are either ignored or reconciled against the master file after the transactions have been applied. The shadow file is then rebuilt from current balances for the following day's processing.

Many early ATM networks operated in this way, with transactions being recorded at the ATM and sent to the mainframe at night. This minimised telecommunications costs and fitted with the batch processing approach used in the other mainframe systems. This approach has been reintroduced as part of the VisaCash system, with transactions being stored at the merchant's till and sent to the bank's mainframe system at the end of the day.

Another form of remote batch processing processes transactions as a 'background' task during the day when sufficient computer resources are available:

- as transactions are entered into the computer, they are placed on a 'queue'. In effect, this is a temporary transaction file. Records on the queue are processed in the order in which they are received;
- when the transaction reaches the front of the queue and the computer has sufficient spare resources to process it, the record(s) to be changed will be read and updated. Note that remote batch processing as a background task is only effective where the master file records can be accessed directly – usually through a database.

Again, a shadow file can be used to ensure balances are completely up-to-date.

16.3.3   Online transaction processing

Online transaction processing also involves transactions being entered into the computer when they are received. However, the transaction immediately updates the master file.

Online processing works as follows.

- As forms and documents are completed, they are entered into the system.
- Each item entered will have a transaction code. The system will use this to decide which program will need to process it.

◆ The program will validate and process the item and update the master file, which must be stored as a database.

16.3.4 Real-time processing

Real-time processing applications are a special type of online processing application. The important difference is that an application only involves real-time processing if the event which causes the transaction is almost simultaneous with its being entered into the computer and the database being updated.

Consider a dealing system as an example. If the dealer enters the details into the system while carrying out the deal and the payment instructions and account updates are produced immediately, this is a real-time system. If the dealer completes a dealing slip and the details are entered by the back office, this is either an online transaction processing system (if payment instructions and account updates are produced immediately) or a remote batch system (if account updates are processed later – for example, overnight).

Real-time systems work in much the same way as online systems. As the originating event is taking place at the same time as the real-time transaction, it is important that the system performance is acceptable and that the user is not kept waiting for a response. This requires a database.

If forms are used, they will be completed on the computer screen. Some real-time transactions, such as ATM withdrawals, do not require forms.

In practice, there is often little difference between online transaction processing systems and real-time systems. Even though the data is not updated simultaneously with the event causing the transaction, the update usually happens seconds or minutes later. This is sometimes called 'pseudo-real-time' or 'near time'.

16.3.5 Straight through processing

We use the term 'straight through processing' to describe an environment in which transactions are processed without any manual intervention by financial services organisation staff. Examples of straight through processing include ATM withdrawals and EFTPOS transactions.

The increase in direct banking and the use of service centres has contributed to the increased interest in straight through processing. Direct banking channels such as the Internet are ideal for straight through processing – as the customer enters the information, no manual intervention is needed provided the computer systems can process the transaction.

Other technologies that support straight through processing include interactive voice response, intelligent speech recognition and optical character recognition. We will discuss optical character recognition below, under document image processing.

Interactive voice response and intelligent speech recognition can be used in call centres to filter incoming calls. Automatic recognition of access codes and PINs allows the identification and verification step to be completed without manual intervention. Simple transactions such as balance enquiries, which account for a high proportion of calls, can also be dealt with completely automatically.

The issue with straight through processing is how to balance the cost savings due to automated processing with the cost, risk and inconvenience of providing it.

- ◆ *Cost*. The cost of developing a system to support straight through processing depends largely on the complexity of the transaction. Simple transactions such as balance enquiries can be developed at low cost. One particular problem with straight through processing is what to do about errors – if we want to avoid manual intervention, we may not be able to refer the problem to a member of staff to sort out.
- ◆ *Risk*. There is a risk that the transaction may be fraudulent or that an error may have been made – for example, the customer asking to make a payment of £5,000 instead of £50.00. Straight through processing systems need effective controls.
- ◆ *Inconvenience*. The term 'voice mail jail' is sometimes used for interactive voice response systems that lock the customer into a long series of questions and answers to carry out a transaction. These are particularly irritating if they do not give the customer an opportunity to correct mistakes. As we attempt to process more transactions on a straight through basis, we need to ask the customer more questions to identify which transaction is required.

16.4   Communications

16.4.1   Local area networks

Local area networks (LANs) were originally introduced to allow computer resources such as storage devices and printers to be shared, usually within a single department.

A LAN usually includes the following:

- ◆ a file server which stores files and computer programs for the LAN;
- ◆ a print server, attached to one or more printers;
- ◆ a number of microcomputer workstations;
- ◆ often, a gateway which connects the LAN to a WAN;
- ◆ sometimes, repeaters to extend the length of the LAN;
- ◆ sometimes, bridges and routers which connect the LAN to other LANs.

We discuss gateways later in the chapter.

File servers store the software that runs on the LAN, including the network operating system that controls the LAN. Software designed for use on a LAN is sold on the basis that only a certain number of users can use it at the same time, and the software usually has controls to count the number of users and ensure these limits are met.

File servers can also be used to store data created or used by users of the LAN. Data that needs to be shared – accessed by different LAN users – should always be stored on the file server. Some storage devices, called 'network attached storage', can be attached directly to the network to provide additional storage capacity at a lower cost.

Software and data stored on the file server can be more tightly controlled than software and data held on workstations. Physical access to the file server is usually controlled (for example, by placing the file server in a locked room). Software upgrading – updating software whenever a new version comes out – is easier if it is stored on the LAN as the upgrade only needs to be made in one place. Back-ups – copying software and data to another storage medium in case of fire or other damage – are easier if the software and data are stored on the LAN, again because this only needs to be done in one place.

Print servers are usually workstations attached to one or more printers. Data for printing is 'spooled' – copied to disk – and a print request is sent to the print server. This schedules the printing with requests received from other workstations and prints it when a printer is available. The order in which print requests will be dealt with may be changed or print requests may be removed from the schedule. Printers can also be attached directly to the LAN.

Microcomputer workstations allow users to access the LAN. They can themselves store software and data, and they can even be connected directly to a printer (this is useful where one LAN user needs to use an unusual type of printer – for example, a plotter).

A repeater amplifies a digital signal. It allows the length of a LAN to be extended by amplifying a signal to overcome the loss of signal strength as the LAN gets longer.

Bridges and routers are used to connect different networks. A bridge is usually used to connect networks of the same type – for example, each building an organisation uses may have a separate LAN, but these may be connected together with bridges. Routers can be used to connect networks of different types. Routers are central to the operation of the Internet.

A LAN can be arranged in different ways (or topologies), of which the three most important are the 'bus LAN', the 'star LAN' or the 'ring LAN'.

Bus LANs

A bus LAN uses a continuous communications cable to which the servers and workstations are attached. This type of LAN is sometimes called an Ethernet LAN (after one of the most important early suppliers) or a Carrier Sense Multiple Access with Collision Detect (after the way in which the LAN works) LAN.

Each device 'listens' to the LAN at all times (this is 'carrier sense'). If a device wants to send a message, it will wait until the LAN is quiet and then try to send its message. If another device wants to send a message at the same time ('multiple access'), the device will identify this ('collision detect') and *both* messages will be ignored (this stops them getting mixed up).

Instead, the two servers or workstations will wait for a short period and try again. A system of random numbers determines how long the devices wait (this is to stop them trying to send at the same time again) and they will listen to the LAN to make sure it is quiet before trying again.

Bus LANs are cheap to set up and repeaters can be used, allowing very large LANs. Their main disadvantage is that their performance deteriorates badly when the LAN gets busy – more messages mean more collisions.

A bus LAN looks like this.

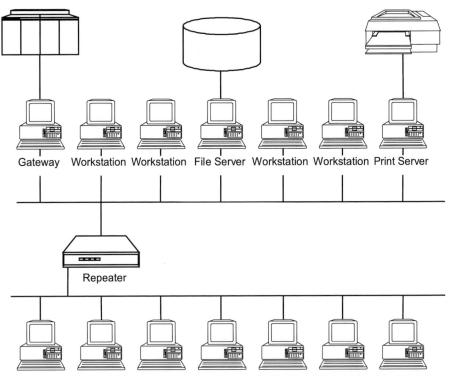

Star LANS

A star LAN works in much the same way as a WAN. The file server is at the centre of the star, with all the workstations connected to it. Workstations can send messages to each other, but only through the file server.

The file server polls each workstation in turn, sending a message to it to check if the workstation wants to send or is due to receive any messages.

The advantage of a star LAN is that it gives a consistent level of performance, not greatly affected by any increase in the number of messages sent.

A star LAN looks like this.

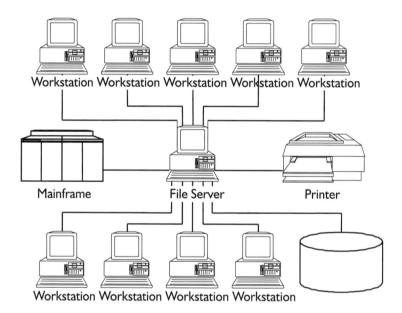

Ring LANs

In a ring LAN, the servers and workstations are arranged as a continuous ring. They are usually attached through a multi-station access unit (MAU). The main purpose of the MAU is to prevent the ring from being broken in the event that the workstation or server is not switched on or does not work – if a MAU is not used and this happens, the LAN will not work.

Another purpose of the MAU is that additional devices can be attached to it. In effect, the MAU can act as the hub of a star LAN containing up to seven devices, all attached at a single point on the ring LAN.

The most common form of ring LAN is the token ring. A special message called the 'token' is passed round the ring. When a server or workstation receives the token, it must first check whether the token is marked as 'busy'. If not, the device can send a message (by marking the token as busy and attaching the address and message). If the token is busy, the device cannot send a message, but must check to see if the message the token is carrying is addressed to it.

The token will then pass round the ring until it reaches the destination device, which will take the message. The token will still be marked as busy and will pass round the ring until it returns to the server or workstation which sent the message. Only then will the device remove the address and message, and mark the token as free.

The performance of a ring LAN depends on the number of messages sent. Unlike the bus LAN, the deterioration in performance is proportional to the increase in the number of messages. The main limitation of ring LANs is the maximum distance between workstations (100 metres) which makes the topology unsuitable for large LANs.

A ring LAN looks like this.

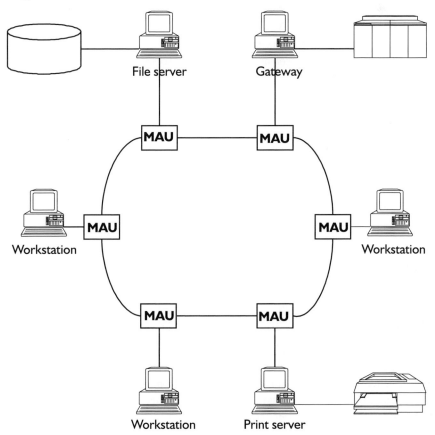

16.4.2 Wide area networks (WANs)

Simple WANs

The simplest way to design a wide area network (WAN) is to have a central mainframe computer with a number of terminal computers (or 'terminals') attached directly to it. The terminals do not need to do any processing (this is carried out on the mainframe) so they are made up of little more than a computer screen and a keyboard. The terminals are usually linked to the mainframe over ordinary telephone lines. These may be leased from the telecommunications provider or they may be 'dial up' lines connected through the normal exchange network.

We do need one extra piece of equipment and this is called a 'modem' (short for 'modulator-demodulator'). This converts (or 'modulates') a digital signal from a computer into an analogue signal, which can be sent over a telephone line. At the other end, a second modem demodulates the analogue signal back into digital form for the computer.

Some telephone lines can carry signals digitally. The two main technologies are Asynchronous Digital Subscriber Line (ADSL) and Integrated Services Digital Network (ISDN). These have a number of advantages, including:

- the lines can carry more information;
- messages can be corrected automatically and so are more likely to be received correctly.

So our simple WAN will consist of terminals, each of which is attached to a modem. These modulate the digital signal from the terminal into an analogue signal, which is then transmitted over the telephone line to another modem. This modem demodulates the analogue signal into a digital signal, which goes to the mainframe computer.

Multiplexed WANs

This very simple type of WAN requires a very powerful mainframe computer just to handle the number of separate terminal connections. Also, the cost of having a separate telephone line for each terminal is very high. One way to improve this is to use a multiplexor.

A multiplexor allows several terminals to share the same telephone line. We could, for example, connect five terminals to the multiplexor. The multiplexor would then be connected to one modem and messages from all five terminals would be sent over a single telephone line. Again, there would be one modem at the other end and the messages would go to another multiplexor. This would separate ('demultiplex') the messages into five sets of messages – one from each terminal – for processing by the mainframe computer. Using a multiplexor allows us to reduce the number of telephone lines we need, but the mainframe computer still needs to be able to handle one connection for each terminal.

There are two types of multiplexor, frequency division multiplexors and time division multiplexors.

Frequency division is the oldest type of multiplexing. This works by splitting the 'bandwidth' of the telephone line into 'logical channels'. The bandwidth is the range of frequencies that the telephone line can carry without distortion. A typical voice grade telephone line has a bandwidth of 96,000 hertz.

A frequency division multiplexor will split this into 24 logical channels. Each channel will have a bandwidth of 3,000 hertz for the signal with another 500 hertz on each side being left free to make sure signals do not overlap – in effect, each channel has a total bandwidth of 4,000 hertz.

The disadvantage of frequency division multiplexing is that signals sometimes interfere with each other, despite the gap between the logical channels. It has now largely been replaced by time division multiplexing.

Time division multiplexing works by allocating separate time slots to each signal. Before describing the methods used, we need to consider the difference between synchronous data transmission and asynchronous data transmission.

Using synchronous data transmission, data is sent in blocks and is accompanied by timing information – two or more 'synchronisation characters' at the start of the message. These are of a standard format known to the receiving modem, which will measure how long it takes to receive them. From this, the receiving modem knows how long it will take to receive any other characters and can demodulate the message correctly.

Using asynchronous transmission, data is sent a character at a time. Each character has a 'start bit' attached to the front and one or two 'stop bits' at the end. The start bit tells the receiving modem that it is going to receive some data and also tells it how long it will take to receive each individual bit of that data.

Synchronous data transmission is more efficient when large amounts of data need to be sent. The signal is also less likely to contain errors. Asynchronous data transmission is better for small amounts of data and is usually used by microcomputers.

Three methods of time division multiplexing can be used for synchronous transmission.

- ◆ Polling, where the multiplexor sends a message to each device in turn. We discussed this under local area networks (star networks) above.
- ◆ Clocking, where each device has a fixed schedule for sending or receiving messages. The multiplexor and the devices attached to it synchronise their clocks to ensure that messages are sent when expected by the receiving device.
- ◆ A system by which a device with a message to send can reserve a time slot. This prevents time slots being wasted by polling or clocking devices which do not have messages to send.

Time division multiplexing for asynchronous transmission usually relies on Carrier Sense Multiple Access/Collision Detect which we discussed under local area networks (bus networks) above.

Packet switched networks

Packet switching breaks messages down into 'packets' of information. It is used for the Internet, where a 'connectionless' approach is used by which each package may be sent by a different route. An alternative is to set up a 'virtual circuit' between the sending computer and the receiving computer that will stay open until the last packet has been sent.

Messages first need to be sent to a 'Packet Assembler/Disassembler' (PAD). The PAD will add header information (for example, the address to which the message is being sent), break the message down into packets of standard size and add a tail which contains additional information allowing the message to be checked.

From the PAD, the message goes to the 'Packet Switching Exchange' (PSE). The PSE sets up the virtual circuit through other PSEs to the final destination.

At the final PSE, the message is passed to another PAD that rebuilds and checks it before passing it to the receiving device.

Some devices are described as supporting the 'X.25 interface'. This is the standard for packet switching networks and these devices can be directly connected to a PSE without requiring a PAD.

Gateways

Another approach is to use microcomputer workstations instead of terminals. The microcomputer workstations can be arranged as a LAN and a 'gateway' can be used to connect the LAN through the WAN to the mainframe computer.

The advantages include the following.

- Only a single telephone line is needed and the mainframe computer only needs to be able to handle one connection for each LAN irrespective of the number of workstations attached to the LAN.
- An additional microcomputer workstation can be added to the LAN without making any changes to the mainframe computer – this makes it faster and cheaper to add new workstations.
- Microcomputers not being used to process transactions over the WAN can be used for other purposes, for example, word processing or spreadsheets.
- The microcomputer workstation can carry out a certain amount of processing itself. This can save work for the mainframe computer and reduce the number of messages sent over the telecommunications links, resulting in some cost savings.

16.4.3 Complex networks

We have discussed the various types and components of networks and the use of gateways to link these together. How a financial services organisation uses these in practice defines its 'network architecture'.

A number of factors affect this architecture. Workstations in a large branch network will not be linked directly to the organisation's main computers. Modems and analogue telecommunications will not be used where large amounts of data need to be transmitted. Contingency arrangements will exist in case of hardware or telecommunications failure.

The network architecture for a financial organisation may be along the lines of the following.

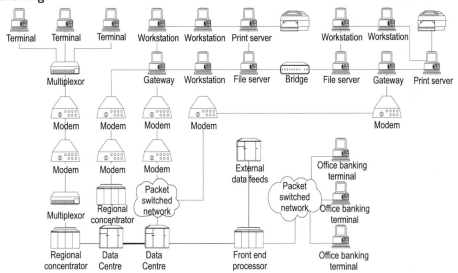

There will usually be a minimum of two data centres. High-speed links will allow the rapid transfer of data between them and there will be sufficient spare processing capacity to allow the network to continue operating even if one data centre fails (although there may be a reduced level of service).

The branch network will be linked to the data centres through regional concentrators. There may be several levels of regional concentrator between the branch and the data centre. Regional concentrators collect messages sent from a number of branches and send them to the data centre over high-speed links.

The advantage of this is that cheap, low-speed telecommunications links can be used for the branches. The regional concentrator allows the most efficient use to be made of expensive, high-speed links into the data centre. In a sense, the regional concentrator is being used as a multiplexor, but with the added ability to store messages when the links are busy and send them when they are quiet.

The branches will usually be connected to the regional concentrator through a gateway on the branch LAN. Some branches may be linked; bridges or routers being used to connect their LANs through a single gateway. Some branches may not have LANs, in which case a multiplexor may be used.

Connections between data centres and from regional concentrators to data centres will be digital. Large branches will also have digital links, but very small branches may use modems and analogue links. Digital or analogue, the main network will use telephone lines leased from the telecommunications supplier.

Contingency arrangements should allow every branch at least two routes into two different data centres. These will often use dial up lines, by which the branch simply dials into the public switched telephone network (PSTN) using a modem and low-speed analogue line to connect to the packet switched network. The data centres, regional concentrators and possibly some branches may have direct X.25 links to the packet switched network.

Customers (office banking), external information services and external networks (for example, ATM networks, EFTPOS and EDI) will be connected to the data centres. A front-end processor will usually be used to handle any differences in standards and, especially for office banking, to provide additional security features such as authentication and encryption. 'Firewalls' may also be used to prevent hacking.

16.4.4   Client server

Client server allows a distribution of work where a 'client' can request a 'server' to carry out a task on its behalf. The client and server are usually computers – for example, a terminal or workstation as a client requesting information from a mainframe computer as the server. The client and server can also be software – for example, an application program requesting data from a database management system.

If we go back to the idea of the client and server as computers we can identify four forms of work sharing illustrated in the diagram opposite:

We would not usually regard distributed presentation as client server in any real sense. Almost all of the work is carried out by the server with the client taking only a minor role. The other three forms of work sharing are forms of client server.

- ◆ Co-operative processing splits the application processing between the client and server. This makes use of the client's processing power without risking the integrity of data due to the weaker data protection offered by a workstation. This approach was very common in the early stages of the third generation.
- ◆ Remote data management uses the server purely as a source of data with all processing carried out on the client. This approach is similar to the use of data warehouses, datamarts or the Internet as sources of reference information.

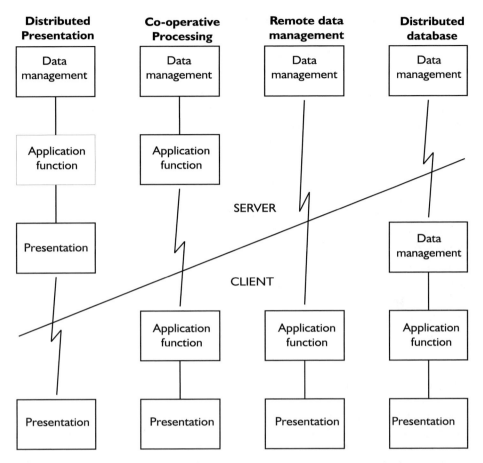

- Distributed database shares management of the data between the client and the server. To achieve a distributed data environment, we must be able to manage a database spread across different computers. The main concerns with this approach are data protection and data integrity.

  If the data held about customers is not carefully controlled, this may give rise to problems with the Data Protection Act. Data integrity problems can occur if the data held on the clients is inconsistent with that held on the server and a technology called 'replication' should be used to ensure consistency.

Financial services organisations invested heavily in client server technology during the third generation. Telecommunications costs were high, but server and workstation processing power was cheap, so it made sense to move from the centralised approach of the second generation to the use of client server – generally co-operative processing.

Using this approach, application processing was split between the mainframe and the workstations. The applications themselves were stored on the file server and loaded onto the workstations when needed. Some data was stored on the server to save telecommunications costs, but this was a copy of data from the mainframe, so this was not a true distributed database. The data stored locally was usually either data specific to the local environment – for example, security information about the users on the local network – or 'high usage low volatility' data such as currency codes and country names.

We can show how this type of network operated as follows.

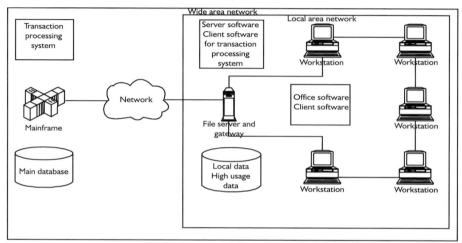

16.5   Back office systems

16.5.1   Introduction

Financial services organisations have increasingly moved 'back office' processing away from branches. Where has this work gone?

Much work has moved into service centres – for example, the HSBC district service centres. These are large 'factory' environments carrying out work for several hundred branches (often based offshore in lower labour cost countries). Service centres may also carry out work for direct channels, but a preferred method is automated fulfilment or 'straight through processing'.

16.5.2   Straight through processing

We use the term 'straight through processing' to describe an environment in which transactions are processed without any manual intervention by financial services organisation staff. Examples of straight through processing include ATM withdrawals and EFTPOS transactions.

The increase in direct banking and the use of service centres has contributed to the increased interest in straight through processing. Direct banking channels such as the Internet are ideal for straight through processing – as the customer enters the information, no manual intervention is needed provided the computer systems can process the transaction.

Other technologies which support straight through processing include interactive voice response, intelligent speech recognition and optical character recognition. We will discuss optical character recognition below, under document image processing.

Interactive voice response and intelligent speech recognition can be used in call centres to filter incoming calls. A high proportion of calls are simple balance enquiries which can be dealt with automatically.

The issue with straight through processing is how to balance the cost savings due to automated processing with the cost, risk and inconvenience of providing it.

◆ *Cost.* The cost of developing a system to support straight through processing depends largely on the complexity of the transaction. Simple transactions such as balance enquiries can be developed at low cost. One particular problem with straight through processing is what to do about errors – if we want to avoid manual intervention, we may not be able to refer the problem to a member of staff to sort out.

◆ *Risk.* There is a risk that the transaction may be fraudulent or that an error may have been made – for example, the customer asking to make a payment of £5,000 instead of £50.00. Straight through processing systems need effective controls.

◆ *Inconvenience.* The term 'voice mail jail' is sometimes used for interactive voice response systems that lock the customer into a long series of questions and answers to carry out a transaction. These are particularly irritating if they do not give the customer an opportunity to correct mistakes. As we attempt to process more transactions on a straight through basis, we need to ask the customer more questions to identify which transaction is required.

If we cannot process a transaction on a straight through basis, we want to minimise the amount of manual involvement. In a call centre environment, we can achieve this by ensuring our agents can carry out as wide a range of transactions as possible without needing to refer to other people.

Again, there is a cost issue. To provide agents with the training and IT systems to support our entire product range is expensive. Therefore, we concentrate our effort on the simpler and more common transactions. The agent will refer more complex transactions to a supervisor or a specialist advisor.

16.5.3 Automation

We discussed business process automation in Chapter Six. The clearing system provides an example of the automation of a back office function.

Before automation, the clearing system worked as follows.

◆ The customer paid cheques in at a branch of the collecting bank.
◆ The collecting branch forwarded the cheque to the collecting bank's clearing centre.
◆ The cheques were hand sorted by sort code at the collecting bank's clearing centre.
◆ The cheques were forwarded to the central clearing house for exchange.
◆ The cheques were collected and taken to the paying bank's clearing centre.
◆ The cheques were distributed to the paying branches, where technical checks were made.

The first stage of automation, which occurred during the first generation of IT, was the introduction of magnetic ink character recognition (MICR technology). Each cheque was printed with a codeline that included the paying branch sort code, the customer's account number and a transaction code. The branch added the amount, also in magnetic ink, to the codeline when the cheque was paid in.

The magnetic ink could be magnetised and read using a reader sorter. This allowed the cheques to be sorted automatically, instead of being hand sorted. It also allowed the total value of cheques collected by paying banks to be calculated, making inter-bank settlement easier.

The second stage of automation was inter-bank data exchange (IBDE). The collecting bank stored all of the codeline information from the reader sorters on a file and sent this, with the cheques, to the paying bank. Cheque clearing was now a supported activity – the paying bank would receive codeline data as well as the cheques and would match the two. Inter-bank settlement was based on the IBDE file, with differences being adjusted later, which speeded up the process.

The amount encoding of cheques received at the branch also stopped. The teller still typed in the amount, but this was put on the IBDE file rather than the cheque. This reduced costs as branches no longer needed encoders.

The next stage is cheque imaging. The cheque is scanned, as discussed under 'document image processing' below. This can be used to speed up the handling of enquiries, as the image can be used with no need to retrieve the item itself.

A further stage is to exchange the images rather than the cheques themselves. This has happened in the US as a result of the Check 21 Act. This will allow cheques to be held at the collecting bank – this is called 'collecting bank truncation' – and will reduce costs and the time required.

16.5.4 Document image processing

Document image processing (DIP) uses a scanner to record the image of documents coming into the system. Instead of physically moving the document between different processes, its electronic image is transmitted over the computer network.

The features available on DIP systems include:

- ◆ Data storage and retrieval features. Documents are usually stored on a database held on an optical disk 'jukebox' attached to a mainframe computer. The document must be indexed to identify the customer, the date received and the type of document. Bar codes are sometimes used to identify the document type. The ability to retrieve any document rapidly using information such as customer, document type and date is required.
- ◆ Concurrent working. As the document is held as an image, several different people can work on it at the same time.

A DIP system might be as shown in the following diagram.

One advantage of DIP is that documents can be scanned and stored in one location and processed in another. This can save valuable office space and reduce costs.

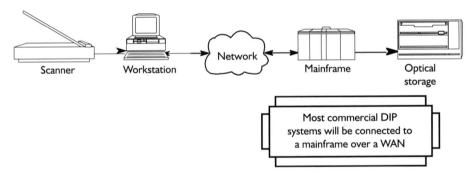

DIP can be used on its own or with an optical character recognition (OCR) or optical mark recognition (OMR) system. OCR allows typed or printed characters to be interpreted. Some OCR systems can interpret handwriting, especially block capitals and numbers. OMR can be used to recognise ticked boxes on forms and also to identify whether the form contains information such as notes or signatures.

OCR and OMR can be used to support straight through processing in service centres. The document is scanned and OCR and OMR technology are used to interpret it. Tolerances can be set to allow the document to be rejected if there is any doubt about the interpretation of a field – different tolerances can be set to allow stricter checks to be made on fields such as amounts and account numbers, as opposed to fields such as names. If a document is referred, it will go to an operator who will confirm or correct the interpretation as described under 'workflow' below.

DIP can also be used as part of a workflow automation system.

16.5.5 Workflow automation

Most computer systems are designed to automate a single process ((for example, opening an account). The overall workflow of the organisation – how the application is received, what checks are carried out and where documentation is filed – remains largely manual.

Workflow automation systems automate everything from the initial receipt of the document through to final archiving or disposal. Instead of the operator deciding what to do and using the computer to support individual processes, the computer controls the sequence of events.

Telemarketing and telephone banking systems also make use of workflow automation. They rely on scripting to tell the agent exactly what action to take during the call. They also use the statistics produced by the system to monitor the agents' work. These systems are described in Chapter Sixteen.

The features available in workflow automation systems include:

- identification and routing features. The ability to identify the type of document and to send (route) it to an operator with the appropriate skills;
- queue management features. The ability to monitor the number of items of each type in a 'queue' waiting to be processed. This allows work to be switched to different operators to ensure that priority items are completed and to avoid large backlogs of one type of work. Problems and errors are also handled using queues – if an operator is uncertain what to do or makes an error, the work item is routed to a supervisor for resolution;
- modelling features. The ability to describe the transaction in terms of a process model. Some workflow automation systems allow the flow of work through the process model to be simulated, which allows inefficiencies and bottlenecks to be identified. These models are used in business process re-engineering, as we discussed in Chapter Six.

Workflow automation is often used in conjunction with DIP. Processing will typically go through the following stages:

- scanning;
- indexing;
- routing;
- processing;
- checking;
- filing.

Documents are scanned as near as possible to the point at which they are received. Scanning stations may be adjacent to or even in the post room. We discussed scanning above.

Indexing identifies the type of work and sometimes the customer.

In some cases, the type of work may be identified from the form type. Forms may be marked with some form of identifier. This could be a bar code, similar to those used to identify goods in supermarkets, optical character recognition could be used or the system could be designed to recognise a part of the form. When the document is scanned, the identifier is used to identify the document type.

It is not always possible to index the document automatically. It may not be possible to identify the work type, for example, if the same form is used for more than one work type. The form may also include notes that will need to be read before it can be processed.

Indexing may also identify the customer. It is rarely possible to automate this, although optical character recognition can sometimes be used to recognise a customer or account number. Customers are sometimes sent pre-printed forms that already contain their details, and the customer can be automatically identified on these forms.

Indexing is very important, as documents that are wrongly indexed will not be routed correctly. The need to re-index and re-route such documents will increase cost and time.

Workflow is used to route the document to an operator who has the appropriate skills to process the work type. This is called 'skills-based routing'. Each operator has an individual work queue. The workflow system has a profile for each operator identifying the work types for which the operator is trained. It decides to which queue it will add the work item depending on the length of the work queues, the work type and the operator profiles.

The operator will process the document. OCR and OMR are used to recognise as much of the information on the document as possible. This minimises the amount of keying required of the operator.

The operator will enter information that has not been recognised automatically. Workflow systems often use a split screen showing an image of the document on one half of the screen and a partially completed input form on the other. The operator can read from the image and type the information into the input form.

Some documents may contain more than one work type. For example, a form might include written instructions to carry out a different type of transaction. The instruction may be processed by the same operator, but will often be routed to a different operator who is currently dealing with this work type.

Operators in service centres will typically be trained to deal with up to six work types. If we compare this with the many different types of work back office staff would have been traditionally expected to process, we can see that service centre operators have the opportunity to develop a very high level of skills.

Many workflow systems operate as remote batch systems. The processed documents are placed in a queue and sent to the mainframe computer by software 'robots'. There are two reasons for this:

◆ processing on the mainframe computer can cause a delay while the operator waits for a response (this is called the 'response time'). Workflow is used to maximise throughput – the number of items that can be processed – and such delays are unwelcome;

◆ dealing with errors breaks the operator's working rhythm and there are some errors that the operator may be unable to resolve. It is often better to present errors as a fresh work item.

The input is then checked. The mainframe computer system provides one level of validation. If it detects errors, the item is sent back and may be added to the original operator's work queue or may go to a separate error queue to be dealt with by a supervisor. The approach to be adopted may depend on the type of error – simple data input errors will often go back to the original operator, whereas more complex errors might go to an error queue.

Depending on the work type, a proportion of items may need verification. The work item is routed to a second operator who will only enter the most important fields – (for example, account numbers and amounts. Workflow systems can apply complex rules for verification – for example, to verify all payments in excess of £200, 50% of payments between £100 and £200 and 10% of payments below £100. These rules can also take account of the operator, allowing a higher proportion of items to be verified for less experienced operators.

Verification is mainly a risk management technique, but sampling combines risk management and performance measurement. A proportion – usually between 1% and 5%, but up to 100% for trainee operators – of an operator's work is sampled and routed to a supervisor's queue for checking. This is a purely visual check – data is not normally re-keyed – but any errors may be marked and routed back to the operator's work queue for correction.

Both the original document and image must be filed. Ideally, the document should be filed immediately after it is scanned. Some form of document reference number is allocated to each document and attached to the image, allowing the original document to be retrieved if necessary.

Another option is to destroy the original documents and rely on the Civil Evidence Act 1995. If the original has been destroyed, the image becomes 'best evidence' and is admissible in legal proceedings provided the scanning process complies with the British Standard. This approach leads to significant cost savings for the organisation, but tends to be used for only a limited range of documents.

The most expensive option for the organisation is to file the document with other customer documentation. The documents will need to be held until they are indexed. The indexer will identify the customer and the document can then be filed.

The image will be filed on a database. The work type and customer number should be stored with the image. Images need a lot of storage and are usually stored on optical disk 'jukeboxes'. Tiered storage systems are sometimes used, with the most recent images stored on magnetic disk, optical disk used for older images and magnetic tape used for long-term storage.

Performance measurement is a critical feature of service centre environments. Possible measurements include the number of items processed, the number of errors and the amount of time the operator is working. Workflow automation systems can record this information automatically.

Another feature of service centres is an emphasis on continuous improvement. Because operators deal with a relatively small number of work types, they are in a good position to identify how to improve the processes. Continuous improvement techniques such as quality circles can be very effective in a service centre environment.

A system combining workflow with DIP might be as shown in the following diagram.

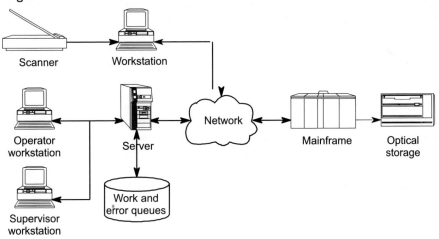

16.5.6   Outsourcing

We discussed outsourcing as applied to the development process and the management of computer systems (facilities management) in Chapter Eight. Business processes can also be outsourced.

The problem with outsourcing is that the organisation loses control over the process. Therefore, financial services organisations originally only used outsourcing for non-financial activities such as catering.

Outsourcing was gradually extended to non-core financial activities. In some cases, joint ventures made this a necessity. The Joint Credit Card Company was set up by Lloyds bank, Midland bank and National Westminster bank to launch the Access credit card. The Joint Credit Card Company is now part of First Data International (FDI), which continues to provide outsourced credit card processing to financial services organisations.

A similar example is Mondex International, a joint venture between National Westminster bank, Midland bank and BT to launch the Mondex card.

Outsourcing extended to activities that would traditionally be regarded as core financial services activities. The clearing system is an example, with many UK financial services organisations now using either EDS or IPSL to process clearings.

IPSL – Intelligent Processing Solutions Limited – was a joint venture between Unisys, Barclays and Lloyds TSB. Other financial services organisations, including HSBC and HBOS, have subsequently outsourced their clearing activities to IPSL.

Cheques collected at the branch are still sent to a process centre, but the process centre is owned and operated by IPSL rather than the banks. IPSL may have access to account balance and limited information, but will not refer cheques – items that would take the account over-limit are referred back to the bank for a decision.

A team drawn from both organisations is responsible for monitoring the performance of the outsourcer and the financial services organisation – for example, whether items are delivered to the centre in a timely fashion. This team is also responsible for query and dispute resolution. The outsourcer also provides the financial services organisation with management information, for example, the number of items processed, and quality information such as error rates.

The outsourcer will often take over some of the staff, premises and equipment from the financial services organisation's existing paper clearing operations. Staff terms and conditions of employment will be protected, with the financial services organisation being responsible for re-deploying any staff not taken by the outsourcer. The outsourcer will usually continue to run the financial services organisation's existing systems for a period while gradually introducing its own methods and systems.

The advantages of outsourcing are as follows.

- ◆ The organisation is able to focus on customer and product management rather than processing activities. This should result in a clearer vision and a more effective organisation.
- ◆ The outsourcer specialises in running process centres and should be able to operate them more efficiently. The outsourcer may also be able to benefit from economies of scale, operating larger centres and benefiting from better purchasing terms.
- ◆ The outsourcer is responsible for equipment upgrades. This frees the organisation from budget conflicts and from the need to monitor technology developments.
- ◆ It can change the basis on which transactions are charged from being largely fixed (because the organisation has a high level of fixed costs that must be paid regardless of the number of transactions) to largely variable (although a minimum number of transactions each year may be specified in the contract).
- ◆ The contract may allow the organisation to share the benefit of any process improvements introduced by the outsourcer.

- Charges may be fixed for a period or for the duration of the contract, insulating the organisation from price changes.
- The outsourcer is under a contractual obligation to meet agreed levels of performance. If the outsourcer fails to meet these levels, the organisation may be able to levy service penalties.

The disadvantages of outsourcing are as follows.

- The organisation loses control of the process and may lose control of the information collected. This can result in organisations having to buy information about their own customers back from the outsourcer.
- The organisation is dependent on the outsourcer for an essential service. If the outsourcer gets into trouble, it may be difficult or disruptive to find an alternative source in the short term.
- Outsourcing is most effective for simple, standard operations. It may be expensive to change the process or if the organisation has unusual requirements.
- The organisation's reputation may be damaged if the outsourcer fails to provide the levels of performance expected by the organisation's customers.
- The outsourcer may find it cheaper to pay service penalties occasionally than to make the level of investment necessary to meet service levels fully.
- The organisation loses know how about how the process works. This can, for example, make it difficult to appreciate opportunities offered by new technology.

16.5.7   Offshoring

Offshoring takes advantage of the lower labour costs overseas to move processing to another country, usually China or India. The financial services organisation may set up its own offshore centre, it may set up a joint venture or it may outsource the process to a local business services company.

Offshoring was first used on a large scale for call centres. All contact is over the telephone and there is no physical paper movement, both of which make call centres suitable for offshoring.

Many organisations continue to offshore their call centres, which allows them to benefit from highly-qualified staff (Indian call centre staff will usually all be university graduates) while paying wages at a fraction of UK levels. However, there has been a recent trend for some organisations to bring call centres back onshore. There are a number of reasons for this including:

- customers may find it difficult to talk to offshore agents. They may find their accents difficult to understand and the agents lack knowledge of the local UK environment;
- call centres are highly visible to customers and customers may disapprove of UK jobs being outsourced to other countries.

DIP has allowed process centres to be offshored. The usual approach is to scan and index the documents in the UK and then send them offshore for processing.

Offshore process centres are mainly used for routine work such as maintaining customer information and setting up standing orders. They can also be used for higher-value work. For example, one UK financial services organisation operates a will writing service in India, using highly-qualified graduates trained in UK law.

16.6   Training

Training is very important if we are to realise the benefits IT offers. Staff need training to understand how to use and get the best out of the systems available to them. Training is also important as a motivator. It increases employees' skills and represents a real and obvious investment by the employer in the employee. This has become more important as career expectations have changed. The traditional 'job for life' expected by financial organisations' employees has been replaced by greater uncertainty.

Training is:

> '... a planned process to modify attitude, knowledge or skill behaviour through learning experience to achieve effective performance in an activity or range of activities. Its purpose, in the work situation, is to develop the abilities of the individual and to satisfy the current and future manpower needs of the organisation'.

> *Manpower Services Commission (1981)*

We can view training as a six-stage process [Kenney and Reid (1988)]:

- identify the learning requirement;
- set learning objectives;
- determine training strategy;
- design and plan the training;
- implement the training;
- evaluate the training.

16.6.1   Identify the learning requirement

One way to identify training needs is to look at the 'skills gap'. This is the gap between what the employee can do and the needs of the job. We should not only consider what the job is now, but also how the job is going to change (for example, through the introduction of new technology) and the employee's next job.

An alternative approach is to look at 'competencies'. These are underlying characteristics which affect an employee's ability to do the job. An example of a competency might be written and verbal communication. Assessment of competencies is often used for identifying long-term career development needs.

16.6.2 Set learning objectives

We need to set training objectives which will meet the training requirement. We cannot always do this directly – there are some needs which cannot be fully met by training. Lending is an example of this – we can teach the basic techniques, but the character judgement which is a key part of it needs to be developed by experience.

Training objectives need to be 'SMART' – specific, measurable, achievable, relevant and timebound.

16.6.3 Determine Training Strategy

The training strategy is the overall approach – in particular, the mix of on-the-job training, off-the-job training and planned experience. The decision is based on the learning objectives, effectiveness, resources and factors specific to the trainee such as learning style.

Training methods are discussed later in the chapter.

16.6.4 Design and plan the training

Scheduling training is very important. In general, training should be given shortly before the new skills are needed, perhaps with refresher training a few weeks or months later. If training is given too early, the trainee will forget important parts before he or she gets the chance to use them. If training is given too late, the trainee will not have time fully to understand the training.

In addition, training materials must be developed and the trainers must be briefed.

16.6.5 Implement the training

Trainees can now have online access to training material over the Internet or intranet (e-learning) or access to material in an easily-distributed form such as a CD-ROM. This makes it practical to deliver training directly to the trainee's own desk to an extent that has not previously been possible.

Blended learning uses a mix of training methods and mixes training with planned experience. E-learning is usually an important component of blended learning.

16.6.6   Evaluate the training

Evaluation includes two processes – validation and evaluation.

Validating the training means checking that it has worked – after completing the training programme, can the trainee meet all the training objectives? Note that the training can only be validated if SMART objectives were set initially.

Evaluating the training means checking that it is value for money. Is the value to the organisation of meeting the training objectives greater than the cost of the training programme? This is not usually a problem for IT training as people need to know how to use the system in order to take advantage of the facilities it offers them. Evaluating training is also useful for comparing different training methods – is it worth using a cheaper method that gives slightly less thorough training?

16.6.7   Training for information technology

Training has always been important, but the increase in the use of IT has had a major impact on the demand for training. Reasons for this include the following.

♦ As we discussed in Chapter Two, IT is a major investment. Financial services organisations can only maximise their return on this investment by ensuring that employees have sufficient training to use IT as effectively as possible.
♦ As we discussed in Chapter Five, the rate of change of technology is very high. This creates a demand for constant changes and improvements to IT systems, creating a corresponding demand for training.
♦ As we discussed in Chapter Four, the use of IT creates a demand for the development of new, IT-related skills.
♦ More generally, IT acts as an enabler to support changes in the nature of work. This creates a constant demand for employees to learn new skills and for retraining for employees whose skills are in declining demand.

16.7   Training methods

Training methods describe how we deliver the training. Various training methods can be used. We can split these into on-the-job methods, where training is carried out in the work environment, and off-the-job methods.

16.7.1   On-the-job training

On-the-job training is delivered in the workplace, either at scheduled times during the working day or during less busy periods. Some of the methods can be used either on-the-job or off-the-job. The main on-the-job training methods are:

◆ coaching;
◆ computer based training;
◆ videos;
◆ training database;
◆ books and manuals;
◆ circulars.

On-the-job training methods are generally seen as cheap, because employees do not have to be taken away from the workplace. However, there are often hidden costs, as the trainees call on other employees for advice and support and these reduce the cost advantage of these methods.

Coaching

Coaching involves an experienced member of staff sitting next to the trainee and showing them what to do.

The advantages are that this method is cheap, as it does not require specially produced training material and it makes good use of staff knowledge.

The disadvantages are that the trainee may learn bad habits, that the training may not cover all situations and that it disrupts the work of the experienced staff member.

Computer based training

Computer based training (CBT) uses a computer program which takes the trainee through the training material, with exercises to assess progress.

The advantages are that this method is cheap to deliver and that the CBT can cover all situations.

The disadvantages are that CBT is expensive to develop and update with changes and that it may not be seen as relevant to work.

Videos

Training material may be distributed on video. This may also include exercises. Videos are often used with a workbook.

The advantages are that this method is cheap to develop and deliver and can cover all situations (especially when used with a workbook).

The disadvantages are that the communication is one way – the trainee does not receive feedback – and that the trainee may get bored.

Training database

A training database is a separate database used only for training. This allows trainees to try out computer system facilities without affecting the 'real' database.

The advantages are that this method is cheap to develop and deliver and is usually cheap to update.

The disadvantage is that this does not give the trainee any guidance or feedback, unless it is supplemented with CBT.

Books and manuals

Books and manuals are published training material, written by a teacher or 'technical writer'.

The advantages are that this method is cheap to deliver, it covers everything and it can also be used for reference.

The disadvantages are that the trainee may get bored and books and manuals have poor visual impact.

Circulars

Circulars are information circulated by the employer containing updating information.

The advantages are that this method is very cheap to deliver and is quick to produce, ensuring it can be up to date.

The disadvantage is that it is not good for large amounts of information.

16.7.2   Off-the-job training

Off-the-job training cannot be delivered in the workplace. The main off-the-job training methods are:

- ◆ lectures;
- ◆ briefings.

Lectures

Lectures are also called 'talk and chalk' and are delivered by a lecturer standing up in front of a class and talking.

The advantages are that this method is good for large amounts of information and that the lecture notes provide reference material.

The disadvantages are that trainees may get bored, the lecturer cannot easily adjust the pace to meet individual needs and the quality of feedback depends on the lecturer's knowledge.

Briefings

Briefings are similar to lectures, but are less formal – they usually present only a summary of the material.

The advantage is that this method is good for updates on very recent material.

The disadvantages are that briefings lack depth and may be incomplete or biased.

16.7.3   Comparison of methods

Generally, on-the-job methods are cheaper than off-the-job methods. Not only are the methods themselves often cheaper, staff do not have to be taken away from work (which increases costs as these absences need to be covered). On-the-job methods can also be scheduled to fit in with the normal working day – using CBT during quiet periods, for example.

Against this, on-the-job methods can often be disruptive – trainees asking questions, for example. On-the-job methods such as coaching can result in the trainee picking up bad habits from the coach. Off-the-job methods are much better for training complicated skills because there are no distractions and because the trainer can be an expert in the subject. Off-the-job methods are also often better for new skills, where there is no one in the workplace who could answer questions and the trainee might feel lost if on-the-job methods are used.

References

Kenney J and Reid M (1988) *Training Interventions* Institute of Personnel Management.

Manpower Services Commission (1981) *Glossary of Training Terms.*

Seventeen

Delivery channels

17.1   Introduction

A hundred years ago, there were only two ways in which a customer could interact with a financial services organisation: by physically visiting a branch to talk to someone or by using the postal service. The mass adoption of the telephone created the first remote delivery channel where a customer could interact with a banker without them both being physically in the same location.

Banks initially embraced the telephone slowly, with concerns over identification and confidentiality diminishing the power of this channel. However, the development and integration of telecommunication and information technology over recent years has led to an explosion of delivery channels, culminating in the Internet and the capability to creating a virtual bank with no physical branches.

Each new channel has its own characteristics and, like the atomic bomb, they cannot be dis-invented or ignored.

Financial services organisations, therefore, are compelled to examine and embrace each one through choice, customer demand or competitive pressure. It is often claimed that many of these new channels offer the dream of reducing costs, whilst increasing customer access, satisfaction and sales. In this chapter, we will examine the channels and their contribution to the distribution capability of the organisation.

17.2   Distribution strategy

Modern financial services organisations interact with their customers across multiple channels.

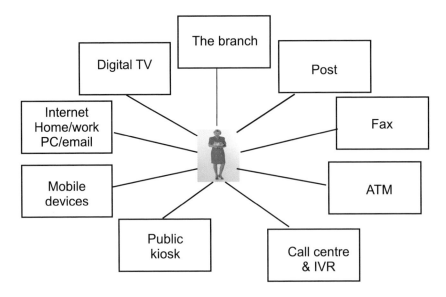

With all these channels available, an organisation is faced with a number of strategic questions.

- How do our customers wish to access our services and buy our products?
- How is customer behaviour and channel usage mix likely to change over time?
- Can we afford to offer a universal (all channel) service and if so to all customers?
- How do we provide an integrated back office to support multiple channels?
- How do we ensure a consistent brand and customer experience across all channels?
- How do we compete with the mono-channel and mono-product providers?

17.3 Physical branch network

Despite all of the predictions of the rapid demise of branch networks, customer behaviour still indicates they have an important role to play in both service and sales. However, the design and functions carried out by the branch are changing. The branch is no longer at the centre of the customer relationship for all customers and this implies that information can no longer reside in the branch alone, but must be held electronically and available, as appropriate, to all channels.

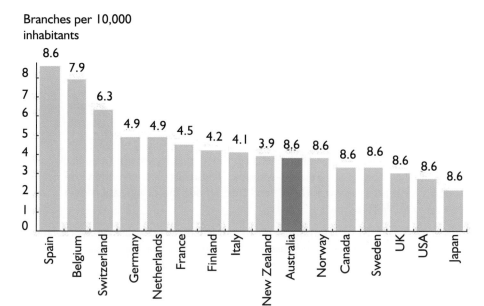

Branches per 10,000 inhabitants

The UK, USA and Australia retain a very high density of branches.

Bank Name	2004
Lloyds TSB	1,845
Barclays	1,681
National Westminster	1,634
HSBC	1,587
HBOS	1,105
Abbey	753
Royal Bank of Scotland	643
Woolwich	389
Alliance & Leicester	310
Yorkshire	238
Clydesdale	236
Cheltenham & Gloucester	207
Bradford & Bingley	204
Lloyds TSB Scotland	186
Co-operative	102
Northern Rock	56
Total	11,176

The functions of a full service branch normally consist of:

- transaction capability: pay-in/pay-out;
- sale of products: (for example, accounts, insurance or investments);
- customer needs analysis (for example, financial planning);
- servicing (for example, problem resolution);
- sanctioning and control of lending (although this may be physically managed at a central site);
- relationship management for a portfolio of customers.

The technology used in a branch includes the counter systems, the back office systems and customer self-service systems. These are linked within the branch through a local area network (LAN) and throughout the organisation over a wide area network (WAN).

Counter systems use a counter terminal (which is a multi-tasking workstation) attached to a cheque reader and card reader. Some financial services organisations have passbook accounts and may also have a passbook reader/printer attached.

Application software is stored on the branch server and can be accessed through the counter terminal. It includes product opening systems, transaction processing systems and a CRM system. The CRM system provides the teller with a single customer view and sales prompts, as well as allowing contact information to be kept up to date. The teller can also access the branch intranet to get access to information and procedures.

There may be other workstations distributed around the branch, in open areas or interview rooms. These will not usually have any transaction processing capability (for security reasons), but they will allow product opening and they may have customer needs systems, for example, financial planning systems. They may have financial information systems, for example, share prices and exchange rates. These can be used by staff to support interviews with customers.

Most back office operations are now carried out in process centres, but there will usually be some workstations with file maintenance capabilities.

Branches usually include a number of customer self-service devices, including ATMs, customer activated terminals, multimedia terminals and sometimes Internet banking terminals.

The application of technology together with the removal of back office processing to central sites or automated systems has enabled the branch to be re-engineered, freeing up space for customer service.

17.4 Tailored service branch

By understanding the customer profile and potential of an area, many banks are now tailoring their physical proposition to match. For example, if the demographics indicate a high population of students (for example, a branch near a campus), then design components may emphasise Internet access and automated equipment with little demand for a traditional counter. In a retirement area with low commercial traffic, the branch could include easy access to stock market information to encourage investments and dealing. Indeed, some branches are being designed exclusively for the use of a high-value customer segment (for example, HSBC Premier and Barclays Premier). These branches can be either 'attended' (with staff present some or all of the time) or unattended relying on automation with perhaps the support of a telephone, Internet or video link.

17.5 Mobile salesforce

Many customers prefer home visits and therefore many banks now have mobile salesforces that have evolved from their insurance and investment sales teams. Typically, the mobile salesforce undertakes the following functions:

◆ relationship management;
◆ investment management/financial advice.

The manager's role is increasingly mobile, particularly for commercial customers where visiting the offices and factories to discuss needs is a key customer requirement.

This also extends to high-value individuals to reflect the growth in high net worth individuals through the expansion in 'private banking'. For many customers, financial planning is considered complex and their preference is to discuss their requirements with a specialist at home or place of work.

The technology used by the mobile salesforce has been briefly discussed earlier under mobile working. Sellers are usually equipped with laptop computers or personal digital assistants (PDAs). Data from these can be transferred to the organisation's main computers through a wireless network or by bringing the laptop/PDA into an office and transferring it over an internal network.

The laptop/PDA will have Internet access, intranet access, CRM, a customer needs system with 'what if' modelling, portfolio management and risk assessment software installed. It may be pre-loaded with the details of the customers that the seller is planning to visit. The laptop/PDA is also likely to have administrative software (for example, to record expenses) and office applications such as word processor, spreadsheet and presentation software.

Security is very important and the laptop/PDA will be set up so that the hard disk is encrypted and can only be accessed with a power-on password. Data communications will also be protected.

323

17.6 Automated teller machines

ATMs are widely used for basic banking services. Customer activated terminals (CATs) are similar to ATMs, but provide additional facilities. All of the major banks and building societies use ATMs to offer cash withdrawal, balance enquiries, transfers between accounts and facilities such as ordering statements and cheque books.

Number of cash dispensers and ATMs

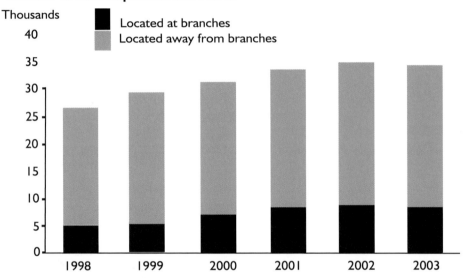

Barclays bank introduced the Barclaycash cash dispenser in 1967. Although this worked off-line and had no functions other than dispensing cash, its competitors soon introduced similar machines. Barclays was again the innovator when it introduced the first true ATM – with cash dispensing, balance enquiry and statement ordering – in 1975. This was also off-line, but online ATMs were introduced from the late 1970s.

The first account designed around the ATM rather than the branch – the Cardcash account – was developed by the Halifax Building Society in 1983. This allowed access to a wide range of services through the ATM, including cash withdrawal, paying in (cash or cheques), ordering statements, mini-statements, balance enquiries, transfer between accounts and personal identification number (PIN) selection. Bill payments were added in 1985.

Although financial services organisations have their own ATM networks, these are now connected together through the Link network, which allows bank and building society customers to use the ATMs of other organisations in the network. The banks and building societies monitor withdrawals made by their partners' customers and make 'reciprocity charges' if more use is made of their machines by their partners' customers than the other way round.

To date the banks generally have not passed these charges on to their customers, although Link permits this. Recent consumer and media pressure forced the banks into removing direct usage charges from their own ATMs, although non-bank organisations run their own ATM networks for which charges apply.

Most financial organisations' ATMs are also linked to either the Visa or Mastercard network, providing an international ATM network. Other international networks include Cirrus and Europay. ATMs are also linked within the HSBC group providing a global network.

However, recent years have seen the growth in 'private label' convenience cash machines which, while accounting for only a small number of total transactions, make a charge and represent 20% + of the total ATM network.

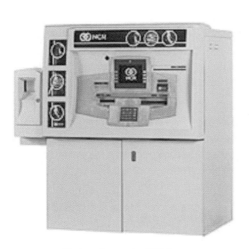

Drive through ATM   Internal ATM

An ATM includes a reader for a magnetic strip card/smart card, a computer screen and keypad which the customer can use to give instructions to the ATM. The ATM is connected to the financial services organisation through telecommunications links.

When a customer wants to use an ATM to withdraw cash, he or she will put a card in the reader. The computer in the ATM will check that the card is valid and will ask the customer to enter a PIN to prove that it is his or her card. The computer will check the PIN against information held on the card and against information held on the financial services organisation's computer. It will also check the account balance and any withdrawals made the same day. If everything is in order, the ATM will issue the cash and will update both the magnetic strip on the card and the financial services organisation's computer.

325

Most bank ATMs are now online. The transaction is recorded on the bank's mainframe computer, but the account balance is not updated until the end of the day. Many financial services organisations have real-time systems, where the account balance is updated immediately. Remote batch systems – where the ATM carries out its checking against the information held on the magnetic strip and stores transactions itself to load to the mainframe computer at the end of the day – are no longer used in the UK because of the risk of fraud.

One innovative application of technology to ATMs is its use to image cheques. The cheque image is printed on the receipt to provide proof of deposit. This has been developed by the Citizens Federal Bank of Dayton in the US.

17.7   Making self-service smart with customer insight

Bryan Foss, Global Customer Insight Solutions Executive, IBM banking industry, Financial Services Sector, writes:

> 'While the bank branch remains a primary channel for customer management, the smart bank will exploit every contact opportunity for integrated sales and service gaining revenue development, while providing exceptional customer experience in a multi-channel environment.
>
> Banking customers increasingly use not only the ATM, but also new self-service channels including the web, kiosks, digital TV and even mobile cell-phone access, but research and experience suggests that adding self-service channels to meet competitive pressures simply adds more transactions and expense. New channels have rarely removed the more expensive full-service transactions, but, instead, have encouraged even more customer interactions with added costs.
>
> Web transaction rates continue to rise, potentially lowering the cost per transaction and providing more insights into consumer behaviour and additional opportunities to make smart propositions that pay back.
>
> However, while ATM transaction numbers are relatively high, the substantial fixed cost base creates a high cost per ATM transaction for a commodity service which makes very little (if any) revenue for the bank.
>
> While competitive pressures are often the reason for adding new channels, the recognition of actual costs is forcing banks to consider the real value of these additional channel interactions and to determine whether they can be made worthwhile. Today there is little interaction between most of these channels, for example, the ATM may be physically in or near a bank branch, but there is rarely mutual support

in providing a more effective and profitable approach to customer management.

So how can the smart bank make their self-service smarter too? Through focusing on the effective use of the multi-channel experience, rather than optimising operations by channel! Understanding the relative channel costs and effectiveness for acquisition, cross-selling, retention and servicing can be an early step towards deciding on channel integration priorities for short-term ROI.

Banks are now starting to pilot and adopt combinations of serviced and self-service operations – some already used successfully in other industries. For example, self-service airline check-in kiosks are supported by roaming assistants and integrated with "fast baggage drop" facilities. In the same way, some banks are trialling smart teller operations that work with and manage perhaps three self-service machines that can initiate or complete a transaction in conjunction with the teller – all part of a single integrated process!

Early measurements suggest enormous productivity improvements are possible, reducing typical teller transaction times and releasing time for additional transaction handling or for lead generation and customer servicing activities. Some banks choose to gain throughput and efficiency improvements, while others direct free time towards smart revenue generation activities (such as cross-selling).

Higher function, in-branch "web kiosks" can enable branch staff to introduce online services to their customers, providing consistency of user interface and self-service applications at every touch point. For some banks or customer groups, smart self-service will be about selling simple products, for others, it will include access to more complex needs analysis, real-time decision making and persuasive explanations that match the products and services proposed.

Seamless and smart processes for cross-selling and effective servicing require consumer insights, including access to a single view of the customer with all planned and previous contacts across key (if not all) channels.

Knowing which channels are most cost-effective for each customer management operation can enable the smart bank to plan a series of cost and efficiency improvements, enabling outstanding channel flexibility in a multi-channel world. Smart banks will combine both serviced and self-service capabilities for optimal revenue development and an outstanding (and consistent) customer experience.'

17.8 Kiosks

ATMs can offer a broad range of services, with some offering a kiosk-type environment with interactive video links to call centres. The linking to the Internet and provision of browser-based applications further enhances their capabilities for providing financial information (for example, stock prices) and product sales (for example, travel insurance).

For example, Lloyds TSB use kiosks with touchscreens and video links to provide customers with an easy and effective way to buy insurance. The kiosk also provides offline information about the insurance products.

The potential of the kiosk lies in its ability to put the customer in direct touch with an expert at the touch of a, button. This is important for Lloyds TSB as the largest distributor of personal lines insurance in the UK with 4.5m policies.

Kiosks are also used by National Westminster bank/Royal Bank of Scotland and the Nationwide Building Society. The National Westminster bank/Royal Bank of Scotland kiosks offer loan quotes, travel facilities (currency and insurance) and information about savings products. The Nationwide Building Society was something of a pioneer in introducing kiosks and has also used biometrics (iris recognition) as a method of customer identification in this environment.

The kiosk can operate in standalone mode for some insurance types and uses an ISDN video conferencing link for others. The link allows a customer/client to contact a 'remote expert', an insurance sales consultant located in a call centre.

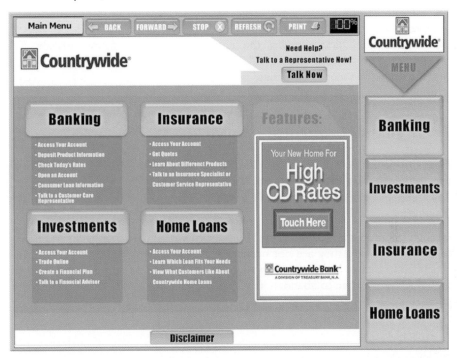

For products that can be purchased with the kiosk in off-line mode, the customer enters personal data (name, address and bank details) on the touchscreen to allow the kiosk to print out a personalised insurance quotation and application forms.

For products requiring the remote expert, the customer requests a quote and the kiosk establishes a video link with the call centre. Any data that is required is entered by the remote expert, who will also display data at the kiosk end for inspection/approval by the customer.

The customer accepts a quotation simply by signing the application form (a direct debit mandate) and posting it back into the kiosk with immediate cover being provided there and then.

The technology required for kiosks includes local area and wide area networks, secure communication lines, satellite links for remote access ATMs and video links to a call centre, usually using Integrated Services Digital Network (ISDN) lines.

The applications loaded in a kiosk include the Internet, intranet, CRM system, customer needs systems (financial planning and advice), 'what if' modelling and product opening.

A kiosk will typically include the following:

♦ a multi-media presentation using video, sound and image to demonstrate the organisation's products;
♦ a touch screen allowing the customer to request more information about products;
♦ a videophone link allowing the customer to speak to an advisor. The organisation can also use the videophone to monitor what is happening near the kiosk for security purposes.

17.9   Virtual branches

Kiosks can be used with ATMs to provide an unmanned 'virtual branch' offering most of the services of a full branch. Many financial services organisations offer a small number of virtual branches and bank lobbies often function as virtual branches outside banking hours.

Although customers welcome a small number of virtual branches as an addition to the branch network, they are not prepared to accept the large-scale replacement of manned branches by virtual branches. The only bank to attempt this is Lloyds TSB, which was forced to abandon its trial in the Reading area because of customer opposition.

17.10   Telephone banking – the growth of the call centre

The most popular form of direct banking remains telephone banking. Most banks and some building societies now offer telephone banking via call centres for personal customers. An effective telephone banking system relies heavily on the use of IT to get customer information as quickly as possible – delays which may be acceptable when the customer is standing at a branch counter are not acceptable on the telephone.

The two main approaches are to use human agents or 'automated agents'. Calls to human agents are routed to the next free agent using automated call distributors (ACDs). Automated agents use technology such as interactive voice response (IVR), which recognises the tones from a telephone keypad.

Telephone banking can offer a very wide range of services, especially if human operators are used. This includes balance enquiries, transfers between accounts, standing order maintenance, bill payments and applications for products.

The first stage of any telephone call is to establish the caller's identity and to verify it (identification and verification or 'ID&V').

The most important methods use passwords or PINs. Customers are issued with passwords or PINs that they can give when they telephone the call centre. PINs have the advantage that they can be checked by the IVR filter, completing the ID&V process before the caller speaks to a human agent. If passwords are used, the agent usually only asks for certain characters, which ensures the full password remains confidential. Customers may also be asked for secondary verification information such as their date of birth, mother's maiden name or the name of a significant place. Account activity may also be used to confirm a caller's identity.

Voice recognition, discussed in Chapter Four, is an alternative. Do not confuse voice recognition with IVR.

17.10.1   Inbound call centres

When a telephone call arrives at a call centre, it is received by an ACD system . The ACD controls a 'queue' for each agent and decides to which queue to route the call depending on the following.

- ◆ Whether the agent has the skills to handle the call (skills-based routing). Call centres can be set up to allow the customer to dial a different telephone number or to choose a different option on an IVR (discussed below) menu depending on the service required. The ACD can identify the number dialled or the option chosen to identify which agents are suitable to handle the call.
- ◆ Whether the agent is free or likely to become free in the next few seconds. The ACD can identify whether each agent is available to take a call. If all agents are busy, the ACD can identify how long each call has taken and will choose the queue for the agent expected to be available first.
  The number of calls waiting and the length of time for the longest wait are shown on electronic 'wallboards' in the call centre. Call centre supervisors are also aware of calls waiting and may re-allocate calls to different queues or may take waiting calls themselves.

Automated agents can be used as well as, or instead of, human agents. These include IVR systems and speech recognition or intelligent speech recognition (ISR) systems.

IVR systems recognise telephone 'tones' – the sounds made by pressing a number on a touch-tone telephone. IVR systems are often used as filters. The customer's call is only routed to a human agent if the query cannot be answered by the automated agent. An IVR system can also be used to provide a telephone banking service.

An alternative is to use speech recognition, allowing the customer to give instructions directly to the computer. This is more complicated than an IVR system because the computer needs to recognise words spoken by people who may have colds or strong accents.

Early speech recognition systems recognised a limited number of words and phrases. These had to be spoken 'discontinuously' – with the speaker pausing between words. This type of system was good for handling a relatively small number of standard transactions and enquiries. These have developed into ISR systems that can recognise continuous speech and a much larger number of words and phrases. These are usually used to provide a telephone banking service, rather than as a filter.

Computer telephony integration (CTI) is used to link an ACD to a computer system. When a telephone call is transferred to another agent, the details on the screen are transferred as well. This saves time when transfers are made and also allows 'blind transfers' where a call can be transferred to an agent who is unaware of the caller's identity – this is useful for taking password changes over the telephone as the agent handling the change does not know the caller to whom it relates. The call can also be transferred to an automated agent.

We can show this as a diagram.

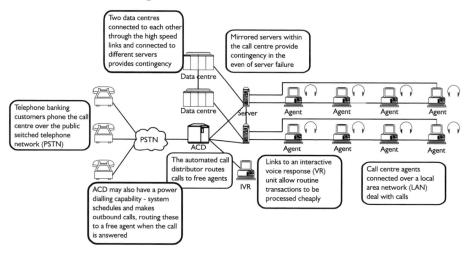

Caller line identification (CLI – also called 'dialler line identification' or DLI) is used occasionally. CLI recognises the caller's telephone number and tries to match it against customers' telephone numbers. CLI cannot be used for identification because it identifies the telephone rather than the caller and another method must be used to establish the caller's identity before giving out any information. However, organisations such as Capital One have used CLI to speed up the identification process.

Call centres use 'scripting' to ensure that the agent complies with any legal requirements and to deliver a consistent message to customers. Calls may be recorded to provide further legal protection in the event of a dispute.

The agent may also need to carry out 'wrap up' when the call has completed. This may include activities such as completing forms and handing work off to another person. The agent is not available to take calls during wrap up and call centres try to minimise the time needed by doing as much as possible online during the call.

Call centres are very efficient and the number of agents needed in a call centre can be determined from the number of calls received, average call time and desired service levels. All of this information is available from the ACD. Call centre managers can break the number of agents needed down to half-hour periods, allowing them to arrange shift patterns to ensure cover for daily peaks. The disadvantage of this is that agents who do not turn up for work can have a very serious effect on performance levels.

Statistics are very important in call centres and are used for monitoring performance.

♦ The performance of the call centre as a whole is monitored against service levels and abandonment rates. Service levels are usually expressed as (for example) '80 PCA 15'. This means that 80% of calls must be answered within 15 seconds. Abandonment rates are the number of customers abandoning a call (hanging up the telephone) before it is answered.

♦ The performance of individual agents is monitored against average call times and telephone technique. Telephone technique can be monitored by supervisors listening in to calls and by supervisors calling customers back to ask whether they are happy with the call. Telephone calls can also be recorded, either so supervisors can listen to the call later or so computer software can be used to analyse the call for the use of courtesy terms such as 'please' and 'thank you'.

The ACD collects the statistics needed to calculate service levels, abandonment rates and average call lengths.

A call centre dealing with inbound calls takes telephone calls away from the branch environment. This can directly improve productivity by removing work interruptions and agents may handle calls more efficiently because they are specialists in telephone interaction who have been selected on the basis of their skills and have received appropriate training.

Call centres may result in the identification of additional demand. In the branch environment, calls may be left unanswered at busy times or the delay in answering may be so long that the caller hangs up. This is less likely to happen in call centres, which improves customer service, but may result in the call centre processing additional work. Anticipated cost benefits may not be achieved, but there may be quality benefits instead.

The market leader in telephone banking is the HSBC subsidiary, FirstDirect. FirstDirect has chosen to use human operators instead of voice response or speech recognition. This is slightly more expensive, but it makes the customer feel more comfortable and allows First Direct to use the telephone contact to try to sell extra services to the customer. A similar approach can be used to sell other financial products such as insurance (for example, Direct Line) and mortgages.

Some financial services organisations segment their telephone banking offerings. For example, they may offer a basic service using automated agent technology aimed mainly at lower-value customers. The majority of customers may have access to human agents through an IVR filter. Wealthier, 'mass affluent' customers may have direct access to human agents, with the wealthiest customers having direct personal access to their relationship managers. All of these can be located in the same call centre, with the number dialled being used to route the call to the right service.

First Direct is also one of the first banks to see its customer base migrate to using the Internet to such a degree that call volumes are dropping and it is now more appropriate to call it an Internet rather than telephone bank!

17.10.2   Outbound call centres

So far, the discussion has focused on inbound call centres – call centres set up to deal with incoming calls from customers. However, outbound call centres are also set up to make outgoing calls to customers. The most important examples of these are telemarketing centres and collections centres. Although ACDs can be used to place outbound calls, call centres usually use predictive diallers.

The agent needs to identify the customer, although the ID&V process is not as comprehensive as that used for inbound calls. Agents follow a script.

Such call centres usually set very aggressive targets for average call length and produce substantial cost savings. However, customers are often unhappy with these calls and the agents' need to manage call lengths can make them seem impolite. Agents may also be targeted on sales (telemarketing centres) or recoveries (collections centres).

A call centre dealing with outbound calls also takes calls away from the branch environment, taking staff out of branches. This saves branch costs, but results in the loss of a 'pair of hands', reducing branches' flexibility in coping with busy times.

These call centres are able to operate much longer hours than a branch and will be able to contact customers who cannot be telephoned during the normal working day.

Outbound call centres can also use ACDs to place outgoing calls. However, they usually use predictive diallers.

A predictive dialler uses CTI to read information from the organisation's systems and place calls to customers. It can predict when agents are expected to become free (based on average call time) and only places calls when an agent will be free to take it. When the telephone call is answered, the predictive dialler routes the call to a free agent's queue.

Predictive diallers have a number of powerful features. They can use information about the customer to schedule telephone calls – for example, to schedule calls to an area for an evening when the local football team will be on television. They can also schedule a further call to the customer at a time when he or she will be available.

An alternative to the predictive dialler is the powerdialler. Powerdiallers have many of the same features, but they do not predict when an agent will be free. This means that a customer may answer the telephone when there is no agent available and the powerdialler must either hang up or put the customer on hold. This would be considered a nuisance telephone call in the UK.

17.10.3   Call centres as a working environment

Call centres have been described as the battery farms of the electronic age and they can be high pressure environments. During quiet periods, staff may be expected to process infill work on behalf of process centres and social interaction may be limited. Call centre staff also deal with a higher proportion of complaints than branch staff and tend to see the worst of the organisation.

Call centres are often associated with high staff turnover, but this depends greatly on local labour markets. The tendency for clusters of call centres to open in the same area increases staff turnover and salary levels, although it does allow organisations to benefit from recruiting more experienced staff.

The growth in the number of people employed in call centres was one of the most obvious features of the UK economy in the 1990s. This has been reversed in recent years as more and more call centres have been offshored, with India a particularly favoured location.

17.11   Banking on the mobile telephone

Financial services providers have embraced the Internet and PC banking as channels to market, but it is the mobile phone with its benefits of ubiquity, reach and convenience which looks set to become one of the most powerful distribution devices in the 21st century.

At present, the main function of GSM is to provide a telephony service, but it can also be used to send and receive data. It also offers a practical service known as SMS (short message service) for the delivery of short text messages and this has formed the backbone of today's mobile phone banking services.

However, this technology is now taking giant steps forward with the emergence of new, advanced mobile phone standards.

17.11.1　Wireless applications protocol (WAP)

WAP allows the complete integration of equally powerful voice and data transmission capabilities in one device.

Effectively, WAP brings a whole host of HTML type functions to the mobile phone, turning it into an all-round communications medium which allows users to access the Internet, send e-mails and even create web pages, as well as make telephone calls. However, the data transmission rates of the first generation of WAP phones is slow (typically 9600 Baud) making their use cumbersome and unreliable. Adoption in the UK is slow, with customers feeling the marketing message of 'surf the net with your phone' as being over hyped.

17.11.2　3G (third generation devices)

3G is a short term for 'third-generation wireless', and refers to the latest personal and business wireless technology, especially mobile communications.

The third generation, as its name suggests, follows the first generation (1G) and second generation (2G) in wireless communications. The 1G period began in the late 1970s and lasted through the 1980s. These systems featured the first true mobile phone systems, known at first as 'cellular mobile radio telephone.' These networks used analogue voice signalling and were little more sophisticated than repeater networks used by amateur radio operators. The 2G phase began in the 1990s, and much of this technology is still in use. The 2G cell phone features digital voice encoding. Examples include global system for mobiles (GSM). Since its inception, 2G technology has steadily improved, with increased bandwidth, packet routing, and the introduction of multimedia. The present state of mobile wireless communications is often called 2.5G.

3G include capabilities and features such as:

- ◆ enhanced multimedia (voice, data, video and remote control);
- ◆ usability on all popular modes (cellular telephone, e-mail, paging, fax, video conferencing and web browsing);
- ◆ broad bandwidth and high speed (upwards of 2 Mbps);
- ◆ routing flexibility (repeater, satellite and LAN);
- ◆ operation at approximately 2 GHz transmit and receive frequencies;
- ◆ roaming capability throughout Europe, Japan and North America.

While 3G is generally considered applicable mainly to mobile wireless, it is also relevant to fixed wireless and portable wireless. The ultimate 3G system might be operational from any location on, or over, the earth's surface, including use in homes, businesses, government offices, medical establishments, the military, personal and commercial land vehicles, private and commercial water craft and marine craft, private and commercial aircraft (except where passenger use restrictions apply), by pedestrians (hikers, cyclists and campers) and space stations and space craft.

Proponents of 3G technology promise that it will 'keep people connected at all times and in all places.' Researchers, engineers and marketeers are faced with the challenge of accurately predicting how much technology consumers will actually be willing to pay for. (Recent trends suggest that people sometimes prefer to be disconnected, especially when on holiday.) Another concern involves privacy and security issues. As technology becomes more sophisticated and bandwidth increases, systems become increasingly vulnerable to attack by malicious hackers (known as 'crackers') unless countermeasures are implemented to protect against such activity.

UMTS (Universal Mobile Telecommunications Service) is a 3G broadband, packet-based transmission of text, digitised voice, video and multimedia at data rates up to 2 Mbps that offers a consistent set of services to mobile computer and phone users no matter where they are located in the world. Based on the GSM communication standard, UMTS, endorsed by major standards bodies and manufacturers, is the planned standard for mobile users around the world and is at present still being made available. Once UMTS is fully available geographically, computer and phone users can be constantly attached to the Internet as they travel and, as they roam, have the same set of capabilities no matter where they travel to. Users will have access through a combination of terrestrial wireless and satellite transmissions. Until UMTS is fully implemented, users can have multi-mode devices that switch to the currently available technology (such as GSM 900 and 1800) where UMTS is not yet available.

Today's cellular telephone systems are mainly circuit-switched, with connections always dependent on circuit availability. A packet-switched connection, using the Internet protocol, means that a virtual connection is always available to any other end point in the network. It will also make it possible to provide new services, such as alternative billing methods (pay-per-bit, pay-per-session, flat rate, asymmetric bandwidth and others). The higher bandwidth of UMTS also promises new services, such as video conferencing. UMTS promises to realise the virtual home environment in which a roaming user can have the same services to which the user is accustomed when at home or in the office, through a combination of transparent terrestrial and satellite connections.

17.11.3 Mobile phone = 'A credit/debit card with an aerial'

The mobile phone, with its SIM card, offers the capability of an integrated payment mechanism and this is already a reality in some of the Nordic countries. Coca Cola have developed a prototype drinks dispenser which is activated by a phone call, the cost of the drink appearing on your phone bill.

The mobile phone's potential as a convenient distribution channel for bank statements, bank balance information, credit card information and other financial details is already being well exploited outside the UK.

In Hungary, for example, Interbank Europa has been offering mobile phone banking services since 1995. Features of its service include account balance details and day-end closing balances, as well as receipt of transfers.

In France, three leading banks have established their own mobile phone banking services that enable customers to choose the banking information they would like to receive via their mobile phones and when they receive it.

Interested customers can subscribe to any mobile phone operator and use any handset as long as it is SMS (short message service) compatible.

Finally, in Holland, ABN AMRO is testing the benefits of this medium by offering free mobile phone banking to 5,000 established, active customers.

The potential of the mobile phone as a delivery channel may have been vastly under-estimated by retail financial services providers. Mori research has revealed that the largest proportional uptake of mobile phones would be in the 16–24 age bracket (34%) and in the DE social class bracket (22%). The availability of new payment options, such as pre-payment and pay as you go, has clearly made mobile phones more affordable to a greater segment of the population.

In the UK, three financial providers have already experienced significant success with mobile phone banking.

FirstDirect responded to its customers' demands for mobile phone banking. It developed a service in conjunction with ICL, which enables customers to receive mini statements detailing the last five bank transactions they made and also informing them of their balance on two of three types of account – savings, cheque or Visa via SMS messaging.

FirstDirect extended the service's functionality by allowing customers to personalise it to receive alert messages. This effectively means that customers can program their mobile phones to inform them of specific events such as when their salary is paid or when they are within £100 of their overdraft limit.

Barclays bank also offers mobile phone banking services in the UK. It offers an integrated mobile phone and smart card package that allows for the future possibility of downloading electronic cash via a mobile phone. Customers can use this service to access Barclaycard and Barclays bank accounts and the features available include mini statements, credit card limit enquiries, balance enquiries and payment due enquiries.

From a banking perspective, ultimately, the mobile phone could evolve into the 'ubiquitous device', the portal used by consumers to manage their access to financial information, not only to receive transactional information, but also to make online purchases. There are estimated to be more mobile phones in the UK than the population!

17.12 Internet

The growth in use and access to the Internet has created the framework for a whole new delivery channel for financial services organisations. (Operation and use of the Internet is covered in depth earlier.)

17.12.1 Internet access

In the fourth quarter of 2004, 52% of households in the UK (12.6 million) could access the Internet from home, compared with just 9% (2.2 million) in the same quarter of 1998.

Percentages

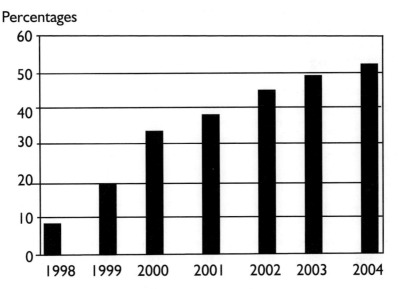

In February 2005, 59% of adults in Great Britain had used the Internet in the three months prior to interview. 56% of these adults had bought or ordered goods, tickets or services. A higher proportion of men (60%) than women (52%) had used it for purchases.

Of those adults who had used the Internet for personal or private use in the 12 months prior to interview, the most common purchases were travel, accommodation or holidays (55%), videos or DVDs (43%), music or CDs (37%) and tickets for events (36%).

In February 2005, 35% of adults had never used the Internet. Of these, 44% stated that they did not want to use, or had no need for, or no interest, in the Internet; 42% had no Internet connection and 37% felt they lacked the knowledge or confidence to use it. These adults were also asked which of four statements best described what they thought about using the Internet. 53% of non-users chose the statement

'I have not really considered using the Internet before and I am not likely to in the future'. This core group of non-Internet users represented 19% of all adults in Britain.

Development of the Internet can be broken down into four generations.

17.12.2 First generation

First generation Internet sites offered little more than information on the organisation and their products. In most cases, you could at best order a brochure on line or identify a telephone number. Access was through slow (typically 28k) modems and relatively expensive. There were few ISPs.

17.12.3 Second generation

Second generation sites offer access to bank accounts for balances and some limited transactions. Typically, some limited quotations can be requested prior to brochure ordering. Higher speed modems and more reliable connection, typically 56k. Computer viruses exploit 'holes' in operating systems and security starts to become a big issue.

17.12.4 Third generation

Third generation sites offer true interaction with the ability to open accounts and products, buy and sell shares, etc. The sites were offering very similar services to a traditional service branch. The mass availability of broadband access (typically 1mb) revolutionises the online experience increasing usage and confidence in purchase. Security remains a major concern, but ISPs provide firewalls and access to anti-virus and anti-spyware software. Identity fraud and phishing become new concerns.

17.12.5 Fourth generation

Fourth generation sites offer full customer customisation where CRM tools enable the system to respond in an seemingly intelligent way to the individual customer's needs and preferences. This can range from simple screen organisation (always show me the value of my portfolio and favourite share prices) to undertaking share deals automatically based on my attitude to risk and preferred investment strategies.

The world's first Internet bank was the Security First Network Bank (SFNB), set up in 1995 in the US. SFNB carries the virtual banking concept to its limit – it does not have any branches and it does not itself provide financial services. SFNB acts as a delivery channel and the financial services it sells are provided by other financial services organisations. SFNB's unique method of operation gives it a very low cost base.

Royal Bank of Scotland was the first UK bank to offer full service Internet banking. It was followed by the Nationwide Building Society and the TSB. Most major UK financial services organisations now have websites and allow direct banking through the Internet. Internet banking offers services including:

- balance and statement enquiries;
- ability to transfer funds between accounts;
- ability to set up standing orders;
- ability to make bill payments;
- ability to make product applications (for example, cards and savings accounts).

Bill payment is the only service developed specifically for direct banking – originally for telephone banking and now for Internet banking. This allows the customer to set up a bill payment arrangement and to make payment (either on demand or on a specified date) through the BACS system. Unlike the electronic cheques (e-cheques) offered by US banks such as Bank Boston and NationsBank, a bill payment arrangement must be set up before a payment can be made.

Financial services organisations have tended to use their websites as an advertising medium. Therefore they have offered other services – both financial and non-financial – to attract visitors. These include:

- branch and ATM locators;
- mortgage repayment calculators;
- links to personal financial management software;
- links to virtual shopping malls;
- sporting and other non-financial information.

One of the most important non-banking financial services to be delivered over the Internet is share dealing. The possibilities of this have been demonstrated by the success of Charles Schwab in the US and its entry into the UK.

Security is paramount. The system provides customers (or anyone with a PC) with access to the organisation's main computer systems. The protection of data, systems and messages is essential. There must also be certainty – if the customer loses the connection to the organisation's systems in the middle of a transaction, has it taken place or not?

Internet banking works as follows.

- Customers will need to prove their identity in order to register. This is sometimes possible through other direct banking services such as telephone banking. They will be sent security information allowing them to use the service.

- Customers can access the financial services organisation's websites through the Internet. A small amount of information may be stored on the PC, but this will not include any computer programs.
- When the financial services organisation changes its website, all customers will automatically see the latest version. There is no need for the customer to install any software.

We can show this as a diagram.

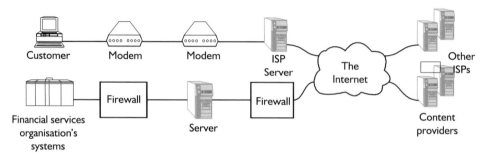

Some financial services organisations are becoming ISPs – the Nationwide Building Society pioneered this and Barclays bank is also adopting this approach – and it is possible to foresee organisations such as these positioning their sites as portals providing access to a range of financial services.

17.12.6   Account aggregation

'Account aggregation is a new breed of online service that will offer customers a single aggregated view of all their financial information, across multiple financial services vendors – all on one screen'.

This definition is taken from the special report on account aggregation in the *Financial World* of September 2001. The customer connects to the account aggregator's website and the aggregator connects to the financial services organisations with which the customer has a relationship. This allows the customer to see his or her total financial position on one screen.

Account aggregation has a number of advantages for the customer.

- Customers only need one ID and password.
- Customers can bring all their financial information together, allowing them to understand their total financial position.
- Customers can see all their financial information in a consistent format, making it easier to understand.
- Customers may have more control over how they see their financial information.

Account aggregation services can be offered by organisations other than traditional financial services organisations, for example, Yahoo!

Advantages for the account aggregator include the following.

◆ Account aggregation is an additional service that financial services organisations can offer to customers. It is believed that aggregation will be most highly valued by the wealthier customers, for example, the mass affluent and high net worth customer segments, and the market for these segments is particularly competitive.

◆ The aggregator has access to better information about the customer's overall financial position. This has been used to justify the provision of account aggregation services in the United States, but organisations would need to be careful not to breach data privacy legislation in the UK.

◆ The aggregation service acts as a financial portal.

Aggregation can work in two ways:

◆ screen scraping;
◆ direct exchange of data.

Using the screen scraping approach, the aggregator connects to the financial services organisation's website using the customer's ID and password, as if it were the customer. It interprets the financial services organisation's response, 'scraping' balance and transaction information from the screen image. It then adds this information to its own screens and presents this to the customer. Note that the financial services organisation does not need to agree to provide the aggregator with access to the customer's financial information and may not be aware that this is taking place.

The direct exchange approach can only be used if the financial services organisation agrees to provide the aggregator with the customer's financial information. The information is provided in an agreed format and the aggregator adds this to its screens and presents it to the customer.

Screen scraping is currently the most important approach, but there are issues with it.

◆ It compromises the confidentiality of the customer's ID and password.
◆ It assumes that the aggregator can identify the customer's information on the website.

Customers release their IDs and passwords to the aggregator to allow access to their financial details. There is a risk of this information being misused and releasing IDs and passwords may breach the terms and conditions of their financial services provider. Even if there is no breach of terms and conditions, the customer may suffer from lower levels of protection (for example, limits on customer liability may be increased). As account aggregation is a new service, the legal position is unclear.

343

If the financial services organisation changes the design of its website, the customer's financial information may not be in the same place. Therefore, the account aggregator may pick up incorrect or meaningless information.

The direct exchange approach avoids these problems, but relies on the financial services organisations to collaborate with the aggregators, who are likely to be actual or potential competitors. There are as yet no agreed standards for the exchange of data, although extensible mark-up language (XML) would be a possibility.

XML is the basis for the Interactive Financial Exchange (IFX) standard for account aggregation, which is being developed by the US banking industry. This would also merge two proprietary standards – Open Financial Exchange (OFX) and Gold. OFX was developed by a consortium including Microsoft, Intuit and Checkfree. Gold was developed by a consortium including IBM and Integrion.

17.12.7　Intelligent agents

Intelligent agents are software programs which gather customer information for financial providers.

Such agents are hosted by distribution channels – the Internet, ATMs, kiosks and even the TV – and can be used to advise customers on their finances. At the same time, they gather information about individual customers which can then be used to build profiles and offer customers appropriate products and services.

The current agent set includes: life planning agents, retirement planning agents, pension product finders, house moving agents, authentication and general insurance product renewal agents.

For example, Epicenter's TIA (trusted Internet advisor) provides human-like interaction with the user by personalising the online experience and assisting in locating the user's requests, as well as providing intimate information about products and services to introduce additional sales.

TIA can address users by their first name and remember the user's name in subsequent visits. TIA's intelligent deduction engine can 'learn' from each visit by a user and make recommendations to the user based on previous patterns and past history. For example, TIA can greet the user, assist the user in browsing and recommend sale or promotional items of interest to the user.

TIA can also recommend product upgrades. For example, if a user is browsing a toy grouping such as Star Wars action figures Darth Maul, Obi-Wan Kinobi and Qui-Gon Jinn, TIA can recognise the user's interest and recommend that those figures also come in a play set featuring the Battle at Naboo Hangar. TIA may also suggest that the play set is currently on special offer and, if purchased now, postage is free.

TIA can carry on a conversation with the user, much as if TIA were a real person. Additionally, TIA is fully integrated with the natural language search interface and the 3D Navigator. Currently, TIA is a human-like, high resolution animated female.

TIA personalises the user's online experience and actually serves as an online sales representative or helpful shop assistant.

17.12.8   Advice agents

Advice agent technology focuses on the use of animated characters to give financial advice and information to consumers via a range of channels, including TV, the Internet, kiosks and even compact discs.

Effectively, advice agents are expert systems which take in the knowledge of human financial advisers and then use this to give advice via an image or animation to the financial consumer. The use of natural language processing enables the consumer to converse with the animation and ask it questions, either by speaking directly to it or by typing into a keyboard.

Advice agents will become a very cost-effective way of offering advice on personal pensions and other financial products in the future.

An example of an advice agent is the ICL Virtual Adviser, a 3D financial adviser, which exploits opportunities to deliver financial services to consumers in the home.

This technology takes consumers for a 'car journey' down the 'road of life' – an arcade game style interface – and presents them with information and key-event scenarios such as marriage and moving house. During this period, the consumers reveal their aspirations and the adviser helps them to plan for them.

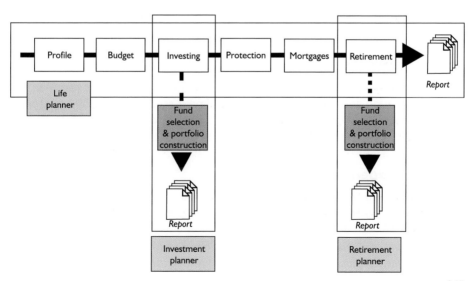

17.12.9 Internet investment adviser

Similarly, an investment advisor is an Internet-based system which offers advice on the purchase and sale of a wide range of investments and can handle the entire transaction process.

For example, the system monitors the performance of stockmarket shares and advises on which ones to buy, with criteria ranging from best performance to lowest risk. It also offers consumers advice on a range of investments which include ISAs and even derivatives.

When allocated a sum of money and criteria to follow, an Internet investment adviser can handle the entire portfolio management process for the customer, including the purchase and sale of investments.

17.12.10 Interactive digital TV: technology fails to 'catch on'

Digital terrestrial and digital satellite television can not only carry signals from the broadcaster to the subscriber's television, but can also be linked (typically by a phone line) to carry signals back again. This connection can be used to make telephone calls and also makes interactive services such as home shopping and banking.

With the help of a set-top box with a phone line connected to the TV, we can overlay TV programmes, such as financial programmes, with financial advice or information derived from the Internet. The strength of this approach is that consumers can actually order information or even buy financial products, while watching a TV programme.

The development of this type of service was pioneered by OPEN in the UK, part of the Sky broadcasting service.

Primarily, OPEN provides three types of interactive service.

17.12.11 Link to TV advert/programme

The customer selects an interactive icon during a TV advert and this launches the OPEN application and takes the user to a fulfilment screen where they can select the product or service. At this point, the user will go online with the set-top box making a connection to the OPEN mainframe via the user's telephone line.

17.12.12 Open 'shop'

The customer selects an 'interactive' button on the remote control and this launches the OPEN application allowing customers to select from information already downloaded into the set-top box or sent in 'cycles' (similar to teletext) with the television signal. Basic calculations, quotations and ordering can all be done off line. However, to place the order or undertake functions, the user will log on to the appropriate service through OPEN. For example, HSBC's shop enables you to obtain quotes for a personal loan off-line and then to go online to apply for the loan.

17.12.13   OPEN 'banking'

Banks such as the Woolwich, Abbey National and HSBC all offered access to customers' banking accounts through the OPEN service. The customer selected the 'interactive', button on the remote control and then selected the appropriate banking service. Connection was made via the phone line and the customer taken through security and given access to their accounts. HSBC currently offer the broadest range of services enabling bill payment, transfers, product ordering and statements.

However, usage and adoption levels did not live up to the predictions. Two primary reasons appear to explain the failure. Firstly, the TV is seen as a 'group' device, whereas undertaking your financial affairs is seen as more of an 'individual' activity. Secondly, the technology was seen as both slow and difficult to use based principally on the TV remote control. As a result, HSBC and others have closed or downgraded their services.

Digital televisions have the electronics built into the television set. Analogue television sets can be equipped with a set-top box to interpret the digital television signal and to connect to the telephone line (note that this would usually be analogue – IDTV does not require a digital telephone line). The digital television or set-top box can interpret additional information sent with the television signal called 'cycles' (this is similar to teletext) and can store information received over the telephone line.

IDTV can be provided through cable television, which can carry signals from the broadcaster to the subscriber's television and can also carry signals back again. Alternatively, a combination of digital terrestrial or satellite television and a telephone link can be used.

We can show this as a diagram:

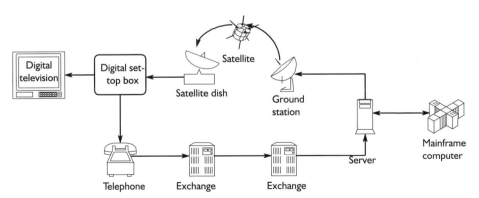

347

17.13   Card-based delivery

17.13.1   Electronic funds transfer at point of sale (EFTPOS)

EFTPOS systems use magnetic strip cards or smart cards and both debit cards and credit cards can be processed. Electronic cash systems such as Mondex 'electronic wallet' work in a slightly different way and are considered later in this chapter.

Up to six different parties may be involved in an EFTPOS transaction – the customer, the customer's bank, the card issuer, the retailer, the merchant acquirer (who processes the transaction for the retailer) and the network which links these together.

If payment is made by credit card, the retailer gets paid immediately. Debit card transactions were originally settled three days later (the same as a cheque), but they are now often settled earlier – next day settlement is usual for very large retailers. Settlement is made between the retailer's bank and the customer's bank or building society using the Bankers Automated Clearing System (BACS), which credits the retailer's account and debits the customer's account.

The national roll out of Chip and PIN is replacing the magnetic strip cards formerly used for EFTPOS with smart cards. These are not electronic cash (e-cash) cards and they do not store value on the card itself. Instead, the chip is used to provide improved security.

The retailer needs a smart card reader attached to a point of sale terminal. When the customer offers his or her card for payment, it is placed in the reader to read the information recorded on the chip. The computer in the point of sale terminal first checks that the card is valid. The customer will type his or her PIN on the keypad attached to the reader.

The retailer will have a 'floor limit' and transactions up to that limit do not need further authorisation. If the transaction is above that limit, the point of sale terminal will send a message to the computer controlling the network. This will check that the card is not recorded on the industry hot file (which is updated as cards are reported lost or stolen) and will send a message to the card issuer to check the balance or limit.

The card issuer may be the customer's bank or building society or an organisation such as MasterCard or Visa. If the transaction is in order, the card issuer will 'earmark' the amount of the transaction to prevent the customer drawing out funds which would make him or her overdrawn or overlimit and will send an authorisation message back through the network to the retailer. If the computer controlling the network or the card issuer's computer rejects the transaction, a rejection message will be sent instead.

17.13.2   Electronic cash ... still failing to catch on

Electronic cash (e-cash) systems store 'cash' as value on a smart card. The two main e-cash systems that have been tested in the UK are Mondex and Visacash. E-cash cards are stored value cards and need to be loaded with money before they can be used.

E-cash is issued by loading 'bullion' cards held by the card-issuing banks. The bullion cards are loaded under the supervision of the monetary authority – the Bank of England in the UK.

The customer loads the card through an ATM or over the telephone – a modified payphone or an adapted home phone. When the customer loads the card, value is transferred from the bullion card to the customer's card, debiting the customer's account.

The card can be linked to a specific account. If it is, the card is always loaded by a transfer from that account. If the card is not linked, loading it from an ATM involves:

- inserting the e-cash card into the ATM to request it to be loaded;
- inserting a debit card for the account from which the funds are to be taken into the ATM;
- re-inserting the e-cash card to complete the loading.

The Mondex card is multi-currency in that it can store values in up to five currencies. Each currency will have a separate issuer and they can only be exchanged through a bank account. This is different from the position with credit or debit cards where the customer can pay a bill in (say) US dollars, with his or her account being debited in (say) sterling.

The Mondex card is non-accounted. This means that there is no central record of transactions made. The only record is on the card where the customer can look at the last ten transactions carried out. Visacash is an accounted system. Accounted cards store the transactions on the merchant terminals and transfer them to the issuer's computer system when they bank their takings at the end of the day.

Cardholders can load electronic cash onto their cards through a variety of Mondex devices including cash machines, telephones and Mondex Service Points. They can also receive Mondex direct from other cardholders. This 'cash' can then be spent in Mondex accepting retailers and service providers or in a variety of specially adapted unattended points of sale.

An e-cash card can only transfer value to another e-cash card. When the customer pays for goods, value is transferred from the customer's card to the retailer's card. The value on the customer's card is immediately reduced and the value on the retailer's card is increased. The retailer 'banks' the takings by transferring value from the retailer card to the bullion card, crediting the retailer's account.

We can show this as a diagram:

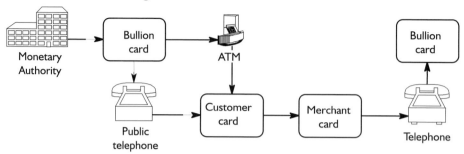

The entire process is built on the ability of one Mondex chip to recognise and communicate with another to complete Mondex value transfers between them in a secure fashion. Mondex enables payments between individuals or organisations to be made through a variety of telecommunication channels, including fixed and mobile telephones, the Internet and set-top boxes used in conjunction with your television at home.

The chip-to-chip communication to enable value transfer is a highly-secure process that is claimed to be resistant to attack, hacking and emulation. It also provides an environment in which the cost of a transaction is virtually zero, allowing retailers to receive low value payments cost effectively.

Mondex security takes three forms.

- *Handshaking*. The two Mondex cards will 'talk' to each other to ensure that they are both valid Mondex cards before any value is transferred.
- *Encryption*. All messages to load cards or bank takings are encrypted to ensure that they cannot be read or altered during transmission.
- *PIN*. Each Mondex card has a PIN which can be used to lock it – preventing it being used for payment.

The Mondex card, unlike the rival Visacash card, is 'non-accounted'. This means that there is no central record of transactions made. The only record is on the card where the customer can look at the last ten transactions carried out. This makes security very important as there would be no way of identifying whether e-cash on a Mondex card were forged.

Mondex allows customers to transfer money to another individual's Mondex card using an electronic wallet. Accounted systems do not allow this.

E-cash cards are integrated smart cards containing a processor and three different types of memory – random access memory (RAM), read only memory (ROM) and electronically erasable programmable read only memory (EEPROM). ROM cannot be changed and holds the card's operating system. EEPROM can be changed and is used for storage of variable information, including security information such as the PIN, electronic money and the programs which provide the e-cash service. The operating system and any other programs must be loaded into RAM before they can run.

The Mondex card is an integrated circuit card (ICC), a 'smart' card – a normal plastic card with a small microcomputer chip embedded in it. The card takes the form of an ISO 7816 integrated circuit card – the international standard for ICC cards.

This microcomputer has been programmed to function as an 'electronic purse'. The electronic purse can be loaded with value, where it is stored until it is used as payment for goods or services at retailers or service outlets or transferred to another Mondex card by inserting the card into a card reader.

The electronic purse can also be locked using a personal code so that only the card's owner can access the value on it. Mondex chips have been designed to withstand normal extremes of cold and heat, damp, X-rays or electrical interference.

The key components of a Mondex chip are:

- the contact plate, which provides electronic access to the chip itself;
- the chip, connected to the contact plate by interconnect wires, has an 8 bit CPU, a 16K ROM, 512 bytes of RAM (and 8K EEPROM for data storage).

Compared to a PC, which typically can run at above 500Mhz, the Mondex chip has a clock speed of up to 10Mhz and is less than 20mm square.

The packaging material is an epoxy based resin to bind the chip, contact plate and interconnections together. The card body is made of PVC or similar plastic material and holds all of these components.

The first of the product development specifications for Mondex was issued in April 1994 – with updates appearing in June 1995 and May 1996 following close consultation with manufacturers involved in developing products. Currently, more than 450 companies in over 40 countries are working with these specifications.

The specifications are designed to enable manufacturers to develop Mondex-compatible products such as point-of-sale terminal equipment for retailers and bank cash machines.

The specifications also allow the more general production of other Mondex devices such as the Mondex electronic wallet and the Mondex personal balance reader – or their integration with manufacturers' existing products.

MasterCard, Visa and Europay have developed a standard for e-cash cards, the Europay MasterCard Visa (or EMV) system. This is an accounted system, in which there is a central record of transactions. MasterCard's involvement in this consortium preceded its takeover of Mondex, but Mondex partly complies with the EMV standard.

E-cash cards have been less successful than many commentators expected. Mondex was trialled by National Westminster bank, Midland bank and British Telecom in

Swindon, in 1995, but the trial did not result in a large-scale national launch. There was another trial involving both Mondex and Visacash in New York in 1997.

It is interesting to contrast the (relative) lack of success of these trials with the success of small-scale trials such as that conducted by Barclaycard at the Dallington Country Club in the 1980s and the Jerseycard trial. One notable difference was that these trials involved multi-function cards, which offered other services in addition to e-cash.

Internationally, one of the most successful e-cash schemes is the Belgian Proton card. This was launched in 1995 and had more than one million card users by 1999. As well as its e-cash capability, Proton is a multi-function card and can be used for telephone calls, vending machines, ticketing, transport, etc.

Another e-cash scheme is the Oyster card. This is an international card – it is used in Hong Kong, for example, – that has been introduced to pay for transport in London. However, it can also be used as an e-cash card and Transport for London are actively promoting its wider use.

17.13.3   What is MULTOS?

MULTOS is a high-security, multi-application operating system for smartcards. It enables a number of different applications or products to be held on the same smart card, separately and securely. This means that applications such as electronic cash, credit, debit, loyalty, travel tickets, etc, which previously needed separate cards, can be carried on a single card.

MULTOS was originally developed by Mondex International. An independent consortium, called MAOSCO, has been created from a group of the world's leading players in the smart card industry to develop MULTOS as an open industry standard. Consortium members are: Mondex International, American Express, Dai Nippon Printing, Discover/Novus, Europay, Fujitsu/ICL/Amdahl, Giesecke & Devrient, Hitachi, Keycorp, MasterCard and Siemens.

MULTOS's open approach means that anyone (individual or company) can take an application development licence and develop applications.

MULTOS ensures the security and integrity of each business service on the card through the use of firewalls between applications. It also allows the controlled addition or removal of applications via a PC, the Internet, telephone or network while the card is still in the hands of the consumer.

MULTOS was developed as the operating system for Mondex, but is now being marketed as an independent product.

17.14 Bank statements

Even the humble bank statement is being developed as a customised delivery channel. It is being used to provide consolidated financial information bringing together all of the accounts and products held by the customer. It is also being used to provide individualised statement messages offering tailored messages and advice together with financial diary reminders, for example, house insurance due for renewal, tax-free savings allowances not used yet.

17.15 Paper mail

Increasingly, paper mail is being redirected to central processing sites either physically or through imaging and workflow technology. Some organisations, such as HSBC, Standard Chartered and American Express, are using imaging technology to transport work beyond country borders to processing centres in other countries where labour costs are less.

17.16 E-mail

One of the major challenges facing financial services organisations is how to deal with e-mail. Customers will wish to send 'free format' messages and expect a quick response (faster than paper mail). Handling the likely volumes and complexity of requests is a huge logistics problem. Two types of solution are emerging: the first is to use automatic e-mail responders. The second is to introduce structured e-mail templates to enable automatic routing of requests to the appropriate processing function.

17.16.1 E-mail responders

This is designed to take away the labour-intensive task of reading and replying to the many different types of e-mail which a financial organisation may receive. It reads incoming e-mails, segregates the type of message, auto-responds to those which it can and, where it cannot respond to an e-mail, passes it on to a human operator.

E-mail responders claim to respond to about 75% of the e-mails which a financial organisation receives automatically and can easily take away simple tasks, such as requests for information and forms, freeing up staff to deal with the complex value generating requests.

Eighteen

Channel integration

18.1   Introduction

In the last chapter we discussed the main channels, or touch points, used by customers and the issues raised by having so many channels. In this chapter, we explore the technology behind these and consider the technical challenge of how we integrate them.

> 'For most people, banks are an awkward stop on the way to the ship, in a street where parking is impossible.'
>
> *Distribution Management Briefing, April 1999*

Financial services organisations want to offer their customers a range of delivery channels. One way of doing this would be to develop a different system for each channel but this would be very expensive and it would be difficult for the organisations to ensure that each system behaved in the same way.

The preferred alternative is to have a single 'back end' system to process the transactions and one 'front end' system for each delivery channel. These systems are linked using 'middleware'. We can show this as a diagram.

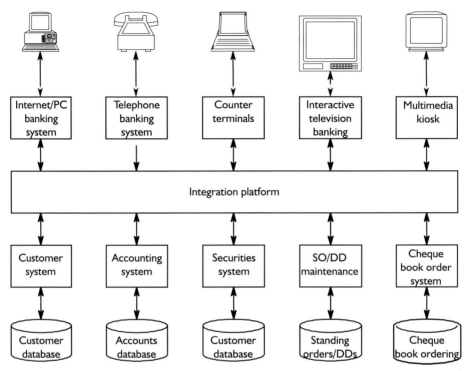

This involves bringing together different technologies. A single back end system must be able to meet the very different requirements of a PC banking system, a telephone banking system and a branch counter terminal system. We can use middleware to translate messages between the various formats required and route them to the appropriate back end system.

18.2   Channels: anytime, anyhow, anywhere

'Banking is useful, banks are not … they are dinosaurs' – Bill Gates' statement publicly threw down a challenge to banks and questioned the traditions that have underpinned banking for many years. The emergence of new delivery channels is stretching the ability of banks to adapt even further, bringing greater competition and threats to survival.

It is the customer's experience of delivery channels; this will be the critical battle ground for all players. This chapter covers:

- ◆ the experience customers will want in the future and the challenges this poses for financial organisations;
- ◆ what successful practitioners will be doing to meet this;
- ◆ the establishment of some basic principles upon which banking differentiation and competitive advantage can be based.

Major changes in the provision of retail financial services in the UK have left the traditional retail banking fraternity with little room for complacency. The proliferation of methods of distribution (or delivery channels) requires the development of an integrated channel management strategy supported by a sophisticated CRM system.

Retail banks today are having to come to grips with the fact that they must rethink how they manage their business and look carefully at the proposition which they put before their customers. This means that they must escape from the confines of legacy systems and be prepared to harness and exploit a growing range of new ways to interact with customers.

The drive for change in the retail banking sector stems from three main factors. In the first instance, banks are coming under greater pressure to increase their profits and improve shareholder value. This is against a backdrop of the removal of the traditional barriers to entry such as a physical network and increased margin pressure from the new 'virtual' network players. The result has called for a focus on cost reduction through improved efficiency in the way they manage their business and, consequently, the way in which they use the technologies available.

At the same time, banks are becoming increasingly aware of the importance of customer loyalty. While new customer acquisition continues to be seen as a means of increasing business and enhancing profits, banks are becoming more wary of the need to retain existing customers and maximise their profitability by understanding (and predicting) their customers financial needs.

18.3 Customer demand for accessibility

Consumers themselves are also becoming much more sophisticated and exacting in terms of the products and services they expect from their financial provider. Changes in lifestyles – more women working, longer commuting hours and longer working hours – have led them to expect a higher quality of service and they are looking much more closely at what they are getting for their money. Indeed, one of the key trends identified by a recent ICL/MORI survey is that customers today want more availability and choice when handling their financial affairs. They are no longer content to wait until branch opening times to pay bills or withdraw and deposit cash, and are looking for providers who can guarantee them an 'anytime, anyhow, anywhere' service.

Historic loyalties are consequently becoming threatened. As the research revealed, 28% of consumers would be happy to switch providers if there were a more convenient way of handling their finances.

18.4 Competition

With this in mind, it is hardly surprising that the third main change-inducing factor is the increasing competition in the financial services marketplace as a whole. Recent years have not only witnessed greater rivalry for custom among traditional players, but a wave of new entrants to the sector, as well as a surge in interest from foreign banks, all of which are staking their claim to a slice of the action.

The new entrants, led by well-known names such as Virgin, Tesco and Sainsbury's, or new brands from traditional players such a FirstDirect (HSBC), Egg (Prudential) or IF (Halifax) pose a particular threat with aggressive marketing and advertising campaigns, grasp of new technologies, innovation and commitment to meeting customer needs.

Such innovation and responsiveness has also been witnessed among foreign banks, such as Citibank, which offers a telephone and Internet banking service geared exclusively at the needs of AB business people who are busy and on the move. The consumer orientation of these players, at a time when financial customers are becoming all the more demanding, clearly means they are ready to mount a major challenge to traditional providers. In fact, the situation can be, perhaps, best summarised by a comment in a recent conference speech by KPMG: 'Banks are no longer able to exist in the way they do now. If they don't address their customers – the retailers will take them away'.

18.5 Channel integration

So what solutions should traditional providers of retail banking now be pursuing to ensure their futures? On the one hand, they need to react to customers' requirements for an 'anytime, anyhow, anywhere' service and work towards offering products through a wider range of distribution channels – ATMs, kiosks, call centres, the Internet, interactive TV, mobile phones and personal digital assistants.

... where everything is connected...

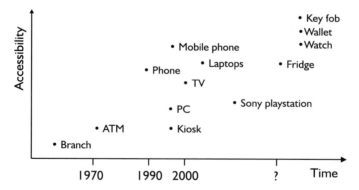

The proliferation of new delivery channels is shown in the above diagram; indeed, NCR at their research and development labs have connected microwave cookers and fridges to the Internet !

Financial organisations are looking towards embracing one-to-one marketing techniques and target individual customers with appropriate products at the right time.

This can only be achieved through an integrated approach to channel management with CRM providing the 'corporate glue' to hold the customer relationship together across channels.

Multiple delivery channels may create opportunities, but also present drawbacks. Each investment in new channels is akin to putting a new animal in a zoo – it requires its own specialists to look after it, its own technical environment and creates its own customer experience, together with an ongoing lust for resources.

Channels akin to animals in a zoo!

◆ More animals in the zoo **COMPLEXITY**
◆ They all need to be fed   **COST**
◆ No animals are becoming extinct **COST**
◆ People move between animals at will **COMPLEXITY**
◆ Integrate or die **COST**

Just creating channels in a 'me too' environment without understanding how they integrate to provide the right customer experience can be, at the very least, expensive and reputationally damaging and, at the worst, organisational death.

An organisation's reputation and brand will be created by the customer experience in the weakest of their channels.

Additionally, at a time of pressure for profits, new channels to market represent a major cost implication, a cost which must be weighed up against the effectiveness of each channel in terms of usage and the profitability of customers attracted to it. The key to success will be determined by the ability of organisations to integrate these channels to reflect how customers want to buy and receive service.

A third key concern is how to embrace one-to-one marketing techniques when servicing customers. Traditional 'product led' distribution model through a variety of distribution channels. A greater number of channels means that the customer data used for analysis has to be captured at a variety of locations; it then has to be collated together, stored and made sense of in order to be used to full advantage.

359

Traditional 'product led' distribution model

The traditional 'Bricks' Bank

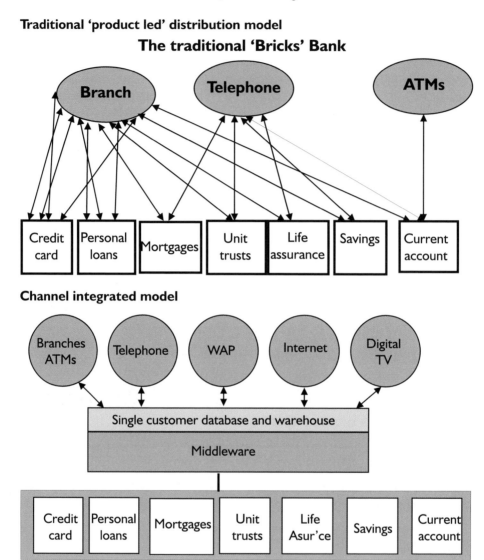

Channel integrated model

Source: Woolwich

18.6 Branches: a costly anachronism?

Once, their physical presence was a pre-requisite to garner deposits or lend. They offered reassurance of those more intangible elements of trust, permanence and fidelity. News of the death of branches is very premature for most personal and business customers. Yet they, or newer channels, no longer offer such re-assurance of future success and profitability.

This shift in attitudes in recent years has been accentuated by the massive influx of new players following de-regulation to an already congested, but clearly an attractive, market place. Society has changed as well, with new forms of relationships, working patterns, jobs and attitudes to lifestyles. New competitors see a gap in what the market offers or how it is offered and they have an interest in drawing attention to it. This has helped lead to:

◆ emergence of new brands and competition;
◆ faster market entry for new services;
◆ erosion of margins and price commoditisation;
◆ enhanced consumer choice;
◆ much greater complexity and confusion;
◆ rising customer power and demands for value, individualism and equality.

Paradoxically, the older UK banks in recent years have achieved some of the best returns on capital, increases in profitability and share values ever. Are the new entrants wrong, or has the market changed so much that looking backwards is not a good approach to walking forwards?

In the future, it is clear that consumers, be they personal or business, will insist on using *their* money and select *their* banking services on *their* terms. They are becoming more aware, banking is becoming demystified and choice abounds. The explosion in new channels of delivery has highlighted the opportunities and threats facing banks. The range is endless. PC, TV, the Internet, microwave, watches, palm tops and telephone. Everyone is peddling their delivery channel with the claim that this is *the* virtual high street of the future in which bankers must reside if they are to survive.

18.7 Customer experience: understanding how the customer feels

Yet with all this rapid change and technology complexity, how does the consumer feel?

◆ 'You have given me more ways to talk': originally the branch, then an ATM, then on the telephone, now a PC and right now TV.
◆ 'You have made it easier': most banking is now 24 hours a day, with bank holidays soon to become a misnomer.
◆ 'You are great for transactions': automated balances, enquiries, payments and credit cards are all available.

But

◆ 'You have put distance between us': 40% now do not go into their branch (or any branch).

- 'Your competitors have also made it easier': there are now more entrants entering through new delivery channels obviating the need for a visit to the high street.
- 'You have not invested in our relationship': customers do not believe that banks act in the customer's interest, banks are self-serving and do not understand what customers want.
- 'You are not interested in me': research consistently shows that customers want to be treated more as individuals, whereas banks are perceived as only offering services they want to sell, how they want to, when they want to.

Are these new automated 'cold' delivery channels in danger of increasing the utility feel of financial services?

Alan Hughes, ex CEO, FirstDirect, summed up the problem:

> 'So having increased accessibility for transactions (rational services) and therefore increased cost bases, traditional banks have reduced their accessibility for relationships (emotional services). Are traditional banks playing into the hands of the new entrant and making it less likely that we will be able to broaden and deepen relationships with customers just when they need to?'

What does the consumer really want from their bank? Financial services, yes, but more than that. Buying financial services is a chore, it is only a means to an end. Most customers want reassurance and simplicity. Bank branches knew that once. When it comes to it, the requirements are simple:

- recognise my value to you;
- know me and treat me as an individual;
- provide expertise I can get at;
- be on my side;
- leave me in control;
- be my trusted advisor (editor of choice).

Yet financial organisations have made it harder to provide these basic needs consistently across an expanding confusion of delivery channels.

How then do banks reproduce those essential elements of a relationship when they are no longer face-to-face and handling that whole customer's banking arrangements? How do they create and establish a new multi-channel banking experience?

Only by providing a better and more consistently rewarding banking experience, based on meeting these needs. It is recognising that technology alone is not sufficient – it is the fusion of many elements including systems, culture, brand and staff behaviour. Building a better experience will be the cornerstone of sustainable competitive advantage. Knowing this is one thing, achieving it is quite another.

18.8   The challenges

Where do we start from in this challenge?

First, unlike many industries, banks are still vertically integrated. They research, design, manufacture, promote, distribute and service most of their key products and services. It was upon this paradigm that IBM operated until the advent of PCs radically upset the computer industry. The major food manufacturers likewise dominated the food industry until retailers realised that they commanded the essential element of the chain – the link with the consumer. The advent of new channels is challenging the banking model in the same way. Prudential's 'Egg' aims to become the consumer's trusted advisor and first point of contact for financial services on the Internet. They source their services across a range of companies, not just in-house. It is a brand and organisation designed for that purpose.

Secondly, there are organisational schisms with overlapping channel and product silo mentalities. The customer wants a consistent experience no matter where they touch the organisation. The internal barriers created in separate product areas hamper achievement of this. Customers want to be treated holistically for their overall relationship with their bank and have their value respected in dealings wherever they be.

Thirdly, legacy systems, separate company IT purchases decisions, skill shortages and increasingly sophisticated technology that allow an almost immediate leap frog of competitors. Compare this with the competitive lead that new financial service providers have entering the market. They own new flexible systems that are designed for multi-channel access and managing customer contact.

Finally, the proliferation of channels. This has led to increased infrastructure costs (what channel has ever closed?), higher opportunities for customer promiscuity through choice and easier access for new players, without the need for traditional outlets. Moreover, just building new channels does not solve the problem.

18.9   If you build it, they will come: M25 effect of channels

Experience from FirstDirect illustrates this. It had 75% (2004) customers using Internet banking. It is interesting to see how they use it. Customers have substituted their basic transactional calls with online enquiries – self-service, in effect. Yet requests for advice have remained constant. It shows that customers will tailor their use of these new services according to their needs and the capability of the channel – they will channel hop and expect the bank to know, anticipate and deliver that consistency of contact and understanding across all channels, any time, anywhere.

To say customers are more demanding in their expectations of banks is a cliché, but, like most clichés, it is also true and often overlooked. Banking requires a high level of consideration and online efficiency, more than any other service. This reflects the complexity of the service, but also the importance placed by customers on having reassurance, from trusted advice, from brand and from their experience. Any successful online service needs to give the customer the ability to communicate with experienced advisors. Without this, customers will purchase on basic criteria such as price. Remember: a brand is only as good as the experience the customer had the last time they interacted with it.

18.10 Issues with more channels

Providing more channels poses issues for banks and their shareholders.

- More channels mean increased management complexity and greater need to integrate into existing delivery media.
- Set up costs are high with lengthy paybacks and uncertain attribution of income (are they retaining, winning or just substituting income?).
- Channels rarely fade away neatly to allow costs to be reduced.
- Customers move between channels at will with consequential requirements for consistency, immediacy of knowledge and value: they are demanding integrated channel management.
- Some new channels (telephone) may be a transitional phase (why call someone else to look at a screen you can be in control of on your own TV?); how much should banks continue to invest now?
- New players do not have the same cost overheads or issues over pricing discrimination between channels that existing players face.
- Customers will consume more information before coming to a purchase decision and will be more knowledgeable: there will be more pressure on margins and greater expectations of service.

Overall, customers will want to see more value in return for their banking relationship.

18.11 Role models – cyber heroes

What can we learn of role models in the new channels? There are some key messages and lessons to be learnt already of how to win in the new high street.

Individualisation   Dell computers allow people to customise their buying experience, choosing the best for them (www.dell.com).

Intermediation	Expedia, operating in the travel business, acts as an online search agent linking customers directly to their holidays Disintermediating the airline and the customer (www.expedia.com).
Relationship marketing	Amazon.com develops a profile of each customer, their likes and dislikes, build trust and then broadens their offering accordingly.
Trusted adviser	Autobytel, operating in the car purchase sector, offers their expertise to negotiate on your behalf or just let you make comparisons and self select. The customer again chooses and can access expertise as they need it (www.autobytel.co.uk).
Integration	Tesco are now building their online services as part of their total proposition, leveraging the high street traffic and brand halo (www.tesco.com).
New capability	Ebay and Pay Pal use Internet capabilities to create new ways of doing business and disintermediating banks and retailers (www.ebay.com; www.paypal.com).

All these players are exploiting technology, plus a brand name, to give consumers both the value and confidence they require, while at the same time, in some cases, integrating the new channels into existing ones. They are also re-defining the way customers can purchase and setting principles others will have to follow.

18.12   Lessons of new channels

Bill Gates is correct, banks have no right to survive unchanged if new options better meet customers' practical and emotional needs. Every aspect of banking will be transformed by the digital economy; the big question is what comes next.

In 1996, many people said the Internet was irrelevant, would not have a significant effect on client behaviour and was not worth investing in.

In 1999, many of the same people decided they were late: the Internet was very important and they should spend huge sums of money to catch up.

In 2001, the same people changed their minds again. The Internet was significant, but not central, and as little should be spent on it as possible.

In 2005, the Internet continues its exponential growth in transaction volumes, value of financial services conducted, the breadth of financial products trades and in the depth of relationships conducted using digital channels.

There seem to be several important lessons.

18.12.1   The customer is in charge

> 'If you have an unhappy customer on the Internet, he doesn't tell his six friends, he tells 6,000 friends.'
>
> *Jeff Bezos, CEO, Amazon.com*

Online service means outsourcing to the customer – they become more confident, more demanding, more value conscious and potentially more promiscuous. Customers expect better treatment and understanding: a segment of one, that in a retail environment is hard to attain, suddenly becomes possible. Worse, customers will demand it and penalise you if they do not receive it. The development of new brands and services is fast – look at the growth of Amazon. To achieve adoption, customers need to see tangible benefits compared to their existing physical world experiences. Amazon did this based on a combination of benefits not least choice, speed and reliability of delivery and advice as well as the early taster of price…and it does not matter if these 'dot.coms' survive or not, they have changed the rules of customer engagement.

18.12.2   Grow your customer

Develop and foster customer relationships that are profitable. Tomorrow's portals will be price sensitive agents and intermediaries. As a result, brand alone will not be enough unless the customer feels they derive benefit from the relationship – the equivalent of mutuality. As recruitment costs decline, but attrition rises, increased emphasis will focus on retaining the profitable relationships and the post purchase experience.

18.12.3   Contact your customer

By 2001 it has been estimated that 25% of all customer contact will originate through e-mail and web-based forms. Can our structures cope with this new form of communication? Where does it sit – in the branch or a central site? Who handles it? How do we use the information to respond to the customer's needs? How do we encourage customers to purchase our services? Information on the customer must be harnessed quickly and deployed to enable staff to take action. Our contact strategies must allow customer choice and preference to influence our approach: costs and price will play a part, but ultimately the customer will win. More interaction can be good or bad. More staff must be able to handle more contacts with confidence, authority and discretion in a consistent way. A real challenge for a command and control hierarchy. How the customer felt about the last contact will be at least as important as what it achieved.

18.12.4 Don't fragment: integrate

Customers will expect the new channels to talk to one another. A common brand across channels may help, but equally can be damaged if there is not consistency and integration. Fragmentation will increase costs and inefficiency. Worse, it will lower customer satisfaction as internal messages get garbled or go unactioned. The key is to behave like the consumer – sample your services and see where a hand over works or does not.

Customers will search on one channel and buy on another. Every new channel adds an order of magnitude to organisational complexity. A mortgage service is available simultaneously in the branch, on the telephone, on the PC and on the TV. Yet most customers elect to take quotes remotely and then sign up with an advisor. It combines their need for information when they want it with access to a trusted advisor. The customer decides.

18.12.5 Stay flexible

To succeed, banks need open data platforms that allow rapid deployment to meet new emerging channels. A consistent picture of the customer is required wherever and whenever they touch the organisation. Equally, the level of service the customer experiences must be consistent across channels and commensurate with their value. The power of networks means that the web platform is growing faster than all others are. As technology platforms converge, integrated customer service becomes attainable. However, so does the risk of over servicing less profitable customers at the expense of other more profitable, but more traditional, users. Knowledge of the customer will become more key to avoid inappropriate channel and customer investment. Ask any chief information officer of a major financial institution how long it takes to roll out a completely new system onto every desk of every executive and you get roughly the same answers: at least a year to get the system in place and usually at least a further year before it works well and everyone is using it. If you ask how long it takes for the board to make a decision about which system to go for, the answer can range from six months to a year, from being an 'any other business' item at the end of a board agenda to final decisions. That means the cycle of innovation can be at least three years long.

The problem is that an individual can make a similar jump in less than three hours by going to the nearest computer store and buying the latest laptop with, for example, the latest video/e-mail system.

So the reality is that large institutions can be three years behind. That means they have to start planning and building today the systems that will be needed in three years' time: systems that are unwanted today look foolish right now, that meet no consumer demand, fit no market research profile and all using technology which is currently almost science fiction.

Smaller institutions win every time when it comes to packaging creative new products. Take, for example, Virgin, which started as an airline and went on to become a bank. Bank of Scotland is a traditional large bank crippled by old legacy systems like all its major competitors. Along comes Virgin with a bright idea and a request for some wholesale finance. Their idea was simple and brilliant: start a new retail bank which combines all current, deposit, loan, mortgage and credit card accounts into one big account, secured on property.

All money in the account is then used to reduce the mortgage on a daily basis. If mortgage rates are – say – 6%, then the amount saved is equivalent to a gross interest rate on the deposit of 10% before tax and how can you get such a rate on short-term cash any other way? Any extra short-term loans – overdraft, credit card, car loan or other debts – are also serviced at only 6% – a saving of up to 12% on current loan rates. Every month, account holders get a single statement showing all income, outgoing and total net worth.

The fact is that although the idea took off, many traditional banks did not have the technology to make such accounts work. Their systems could not even begin to produce the right kind of statement calculations. In this case, Bank of Scotland became a wholesaler of finance, while all the real banking work was done by Virgin.

18.12.6   Protect your brand

Customers, faced with a multitude of choices and criteria, will, in time, look for trusted and familiar names. Yet the brand does not equate to the size of the advertising budget – it is effected most of all by the customer's experience, feelings and satisfaction. New channels not only add to costs, but allow new players to build their brands at much lower cost. Customers will judge brands not only by attractiveness on the web, but also on the phone, downtime at ATMs, length of the queue in their nearby branch and perhaps most by the tone of voice and initiative or 'humanity' shown by the last person they spoke to. It is the total experience that counts.

Today, it is possible for even the largest most profitable global companies to be brought to their knees by a single story that damages their reputation. Organisations must be prepared for the unexpected, what was legal in the past being illegal in the future as consumer power and corporate social responsibility examine ever more closely the values of the business.

18.13   What will customers do next?

As customers become more familiar and confident with the new channels, their knowledge and therefore their expectations will increase. Customers will:

- search, become informed and channel hop at will;
- buy from people they trust and who gave a good experience last time;
- want speed and ease as prime hygiene factors: make it hard for them and they will go elsewhere;
- expect their needs and preferences anticipated (and then met);
- want to enjoy the experience.

18.14   Evolve or die

Over the last decade, we have had a golden age of banking where customers bought what the banks chose to sell them. Increasingly, customers will expect banks to tailor their products to their individual needs. In the future, use of these new channels and intelligent search engines will enable customers to dictate to banks what they wish to buy, how they wish to buy it and when they want it. Evolution will be driven by customer expectation, government intervention (for example, *The Cruickshank Report, The OFT investigation into Business Banking and Social Exclusion*) and competition.

In the future, worry about three things.

1. Channel integration.
2. Customer management.
3. Brand – the customer's experience.

In effect: 'it is how you make me feel'.

The mantra of retailing has been location, location, and location. As banks have just begun to understand those implications, it has changed again. In the future it will be experience, experience and experience. Customers want the same things today as they did in the past: trust confidence and good value. Marble pillars may have been replaced, but the feeling must be the same. It can be or customers will go elsewhere.

Index

C